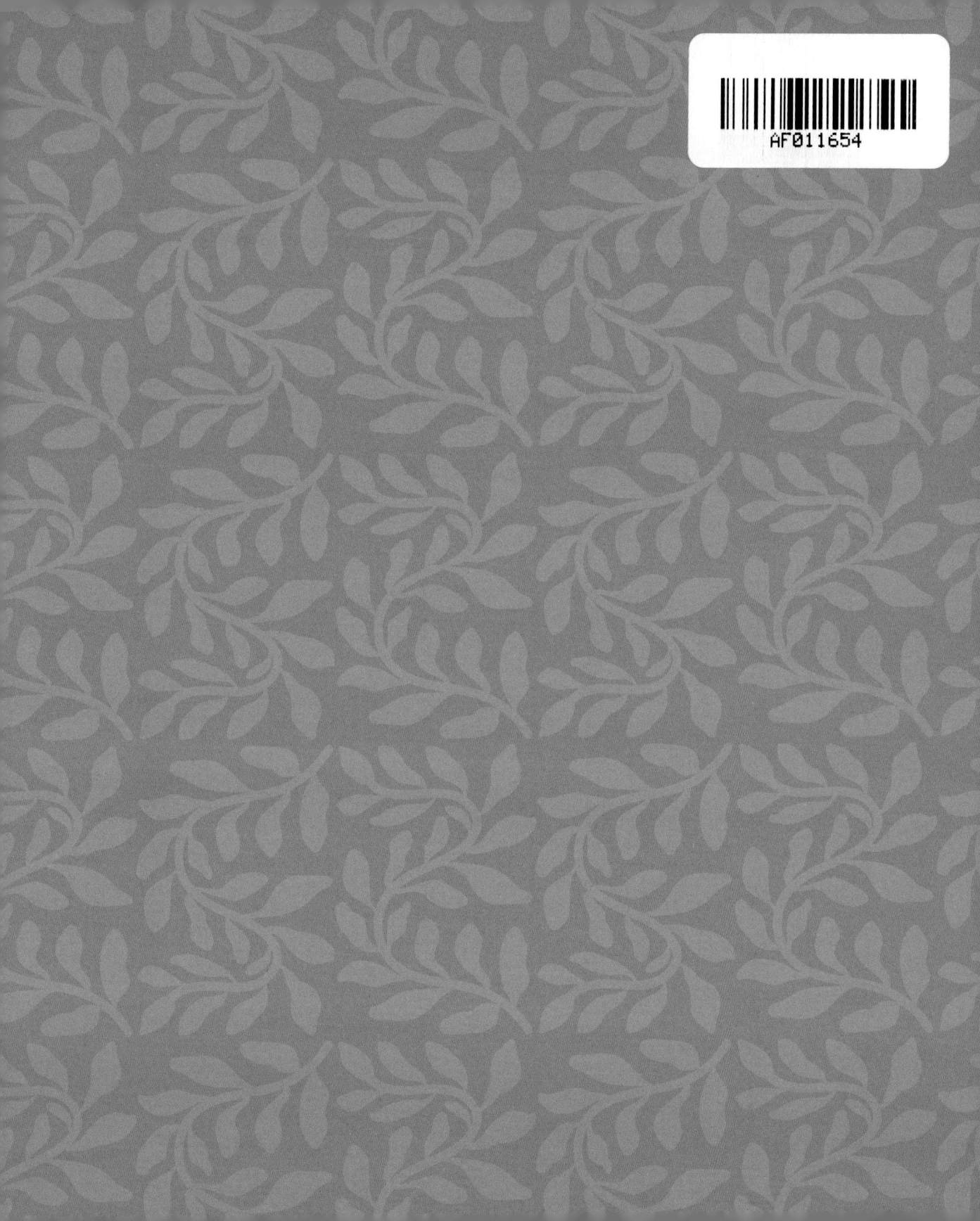

FOR THE LOVE OF HOUSE PLANTS

FOR THE LOVE ❦ OF ❦ HOUSE PLANTS

Caring for & Keeping Plants with Confidence

TANNER MITCHELL

with **LAUREN SALKELD**
Photography by **ASHLEIGH AMOROSO**
Illustrations by **NANCY PAPPAS**

SIMON ELEMENT

NEW YORK   AMSTERDAM/ANTWERP   LONDON   TORONTO   SYDNEY/MELBOURNE   NEW DELHI

SIMON ELEMENT

An Imprint of Simon & Schuster, LLC
1230 Avenue of the Americas
New York, NY 10020

For more than 100 years, Simon & Schuster has championed authors and the stories they create. By respecting the copyright of an author's intellectual property, you enable Simon & Schuster and the author to continue publishing exceptional books for years to come. We thank you for supporting the author's copyright by purchasing an authorized edition of this book.

No amount of this book may be reproduced or stored in any format, nor may it be uploaded to any website, database, language-learning model, or other repository, retrieval, or artificial intelligence system without express permission. All rights reserved. Inquiries may be directed to Simon & Schuster, 1230 Avenue of the Americas, New York, NY 10020 or permissions@simonandschuster.com.

Copyright © 2026 by Tanner Mitchell
Photography Copyright © 2026 by Ashleigh Amoroso
Illustrations Copyright © 2026 by Nancy Pappas

All rights reserved, including the right to reproduce this book or portions thereof in any form whatsoever. For information, address Simon Element Subsidiary Rights Department, 1230 Avenue of the Americas, New York, NY 10020.

First Simon Element hardcover edition April 2026

SIMON ELEMENT is a trademark of Simon & Schuster, LLC

Simon & Schuster strongly believes in freedom of expression and stands against censorship in all its forms. For more information, visit BooksBelong.com.

For information about special discounts for bulk purchases, please contact Simon & Schuster Special Sales at 1-866-506-1949 or business@simonandschuster.com.

The Simon & Schuster Speakers Bureau can bring authors to your live event. For more information or to book an event, contact the Simon & Schuster Speakers Bureau at 1-866-248-3049 or visit our website at www.simonspeakers.com.

Interior design by Farzana Razak

Manufactured in China

1 3 5 7 9 10 8 6 4 2

Library of Congress Control Number: 2025939105

ISBN 978-1-6680-6424-5
ISBN 978-1-6680-6425-2 (ebook)

*To my wife, Erika, whose love shaped me
into someone capable of fulfilling their dreams!*

| Introduction | 9 |

PART ONE: THE BASICS

| "Success" with Houseplants | 20 |

| Why You Can't Keep Your Houseplants Alive | 36 |

| See the Light! | 53 |

| Watering with Confidence | 80 |

| Repot—or Not? | 102 |

| Feeding for Growth | 121 |

| Troubleshooting (It Doesn't Need to Be Troublesome) | 141 |

PART TWO: THE PLANTS

Aglaonema	186	**Monstera**	216
Anthurium	188	**Peace Lily**	218
Bird-of-Paradise	190	**Phalaenopsis Orchid**	220
Bird's-Nest Fern	192	**Philodendron**	222
Bromeliad	194	**Prayer Plant**	224
Cacti	196	**Radiator Plant**	228
Cast-Iron Plant	198	**Rubber Tree**	230
Dragon Tree	200	**Scindapsus**	232
Elephant Ear	202	**Snake Plant**	234
Fiddle-Leaf Fig	204	**Staghorn Fern**	236
Fittonia	206	**String of Pearls**	238
Golden Pothos	208	**Succulents**	240
Holiday Cacti	210	**Tillandsia**	244
Hoya Rope	212	**Venus Flytrap**	246
Kentia Palm	214	**ZZ Plant**	248

Acknowledgments 251
Index 252

CONTENTS

INTRODUCTION

The truth about houseplants is that they aren't meant to be houseplants—they're meant to be outside, growing where they grow best! For all the plants we categorize as houseplants, this usually means somewhere tropical, like Central America, South America, Southeast Asia, or anywhere that has temperatures humans are comfortable in, which is 60°F to 90°F.

I realize that opening a houseplant-care book by telling you plants aren't meant to be inside is an odd way to kick things off, but if you've picked up a book like this, then I have to believe either you're curious about growing some indoor plants and want to dip your toe into what care might look like, or you're trying to find answers to plant questions for the collection you already have. In either case, understanding that keeping houseplants is just as much an act of defiance of nature as it is an act of admiration and respect will help you squeeze every ounce of joy from this hobby, whether you're growing a single plant or a hundred.

When we put plants in our homes, we are taking them out of their natural habitat, which is very warm and often humid, with perfect soil conditions and optimal fertilizing, and then expecting them to thrive inside a tiny pot, in a (comparatively) dry and low-light environment. Cut yourself—and your plant—some slack! If you were plucked from your comfortable home and shipped off to some unfamiliar place, you might have a tough time adjusting, especially if you speak a different language than your caretaker.

There's a certain freedom that comes with letting go of expectations in everything you do, but especially so in the houseplant hobby, and I believe it's the underlying secret to growing plants. While a few dedicated, plant-passionate folks will alter their living conditions to better suit the needs of their plant collection, most of us simply want to enjoy a few nice plants around the home or office without having to worry about them too much. However, when the droopy leaves and brown tips appear, it's all too common for the plant parent's initial joy surrounding their plants to be replaced with dread, and for them to start contemplating what type of person they are because their plants aren't living up to expectations. For some reason, people often look to the health of their plants to affirm or deny that they're a good person. If a plant isn't doing well, it's because it wasn't provided with the conditions for it to do well, but the state of a plant in no way indicates that its owner is less of a person, inadequate, or incapable.

It's also common to blame a plant failure on the plant, with the owner declaring, "This plant just hates me!" I'm sure this statement is said with an air of intended humor rather than being literal, but it passes the buck to the plant, which actually takes the plant parent further from their houseplant goals, not closer. The sooner you can take responsibility for killing a plant, the sooner you'll be on your way to enjoying every aspect of houseplant care! Plants are for everyone, including you.

You must think I'm very bold at this point, declaring that houseplants are for everyone—a cheeky phrase we often tell customers who lack confidence in their plant-rearing capabilities. I get it, especially if you've already tried and failed at keeping one or two alive. You may find it especially bold when you learn that I am probably just like you. I'm not formally educated in horticulture, botany, or anything plant related. I got started simply because I wanted some plants around the house that would look nice and remind me of the lush greenery I grew up with in rural Oregon. But if I've learned anything from growing houseplants, it's that the true joy doesn't come from the satisfaction of keeping them alive; it comes from intentionally participating in the act. This is what I mean when I say that houseplants are for everyone, because whether they live or die under your care doesn't matter. It's enough that you did the thing! I just ask that you keep doing the thing until you find what works for you and your plants. With this book, I hope to help you find a way.

If I had known I would become so romantic about houseplants, I would have started earlier in life, but despite being brought up in a small farming community at the base of the Blue Mountains, eating much of my food from a garden and having almost every relative I can think of growing houseplants, my school-age self was more obsessed with playing sports than growing plants. When I left Oregon for Texas, I had no inkling that one day I'd write a book about plants. In fact, shortly after my wife, Erika, and I opened our plant store, my brother called and said, "Dude, what happened? You were a jock!" I don't recall what I said at the time, but years later I've finally thought of my answer: "Have you ever watched a plant grow?"

I used to love watching Penn and Teller perform magic on television specials back in the '90s. I was as obsessed with how they pulled off these convincing tricks as I was with the idea of true magic. I knew the card tricks, bullet catches, and disappearing elephants were an act, but there was always a part of me that felt like magic should have a seat at the table of reality. People use the word "magic" to describe hiking in the Alps, going on a first date with their future spouse, or what it's like giving birth. We know they don't mean the Alps are covered in unicorns, their date didn't catch a bullet between their teeth mid-conversation, and giving birth does not include a vanishing elephant—though the hospital bill might have you wondering if you somehow missed an elaborate performance in your hospital room. I haven't done most of the things people associate with magic, but it's the most suitable word I've found to describe what it feels like to play a part in growing a plant.

Connecting plants with magic is not how my plant journey started, though. In fact, if you ask Erika, she would describe my early plant obsession as yet another interest, hobby, or just "one more thing." I can't blame her, as I have an intense curiosity about a multitude of subjects. But unlike other pursuits that have come and gone, once I "figured it out," plants were here to stay, and I couldn't stop talking about them. Each new piece of the plant-care puzzle would bring more excitement, and that excitement eventually spilled into my social media.

Prior to my interest in plants, I didn't post on social media regularly. But I was having such a good time growing plants and experimenting with them, while also observing online just how many people were really struggling with them. I thought if I could just show each of these people a little trick I learned or help them with better pot placement, then they would get to experience the same joy and satisfaction as I did. That's why I started posting about plants on social media, and what happened next totally changed the course of my life and the lives of my family forever.

"Does this *have* to be on the counter?" started to be a common question around the house. Erika and the kids were getting increasingly impatient with all the plants, plant experiments, plant projects, and overall disorganization that was coming from my hobby. At that point, I was posting plant-related content several times per week and had gained a few thousand followers interested in my care tips. People were so grateful, and to my surprise, they often asked if they could buy some of my baby plants or pay for my advice. This led me to tell Erika, "I think we need to sell plants!" We already owned a business renting out bounce houses to the local community for birthday par-

ties and celebrations, so entrepreneurship wasn't new to us. We were also small enough that it was mostly a weekend business, which gave me time during the week to devote to this new plant project. At least, that's what I told Erika. But she would soon join me in this planty adventure, as it quickly became more than one person could handle.

I started selling plants by going *live* on social media, showing interested folks what we had and how to care for them. Initially, our customers came to pick up plants at our house, until the online following grew to the point where we needed an option to ship. To avoid live plants sitting in a cold or hot warehouse over the weekend, we found it was best to mail them by Wednesday or Thursday, which meant that for a couple of days following a live sale, our hallways, counter, and dining room table turned into a shipping facility. The boxes of plants lining the walkways waiting for Monday led us to dream about opening a brick-and-mortar store so we could continue to help people enjoy their plants in a bigger way—and regain some of our domestic peace. After many more live sales and dozens of failed attempts at selling plants at farmers' markets, we opened our plant shop, Famous In Oregon, in May 2020. But just days after signing the lease agreement, a strange new virus called COVID-19 forced people all over the world to shelter in their homes to avoid spreading this easily transmissible disease.

People are always shocked when we tell them our store officially opened in the spring of 2020, a time more closely associated with fear and uncertainty than economic success. But boy, did we thrive. With lockdowns forcing more people to be at home, they naturally wanted to enjoy those spaces more, and many people turned to plants, catapulting the industry into a frenzy. Whether folks were finding comfort in the positivity of plants amid the chaos of the present world or simply outfitting their video backgrounds for conference calls, we were just happy a bit of the spotlight was shining on our little slice of heaven.

During all the commotion, my kids encouraged me to share some of my plant tips on TikTok, which was already popular among teens and was starting to be more commonplace for adults to use—once we all realized it wasn't just for silly dance videos. I posted a couple of plant-related videos but soon got distracted by the day-to-day operations of our store. Weeks passed before I opened the app again, so it came as a huge shock when I saw twelve thousand new people following me and an inbox full of notifications. Within a few more weeks, I had surpassed twenty thousand followers, a number I couldn't even comprehend. I remember going to see the Dallas Stars, our local NHL team, and seeing the number in attendance that night flash up on the JumboTron. The arena was filled with 18,300 fans. I looked around at all the people, more than I had ever seen in one place, and was humbled in an unfamiliar way. To this day, I can't think about it without getting teary. I couldn't believe there were this many people in the world who liked plants like I did and who thought what I had to say was valuable enough to want to follow along to see what else I would share.

Years have passed since that experience, and I'm no better equipped to handle the immense gratitude I feel for the now millions of people around the world who are living their own lives in places I've only dreamed of—or perhaps never even heard of—but who follow me. In some way it feels like I'm part of their day, which is immensely special to me.

We still have our store five years after opening, which is a major milestone for entrepreneurs. I won't pretend business acumen is responsible for our making it this far; rather, it's the great fortune of having people around us who are smarter than we are about this type of thing—a necessity for a person like me who has their head buried in plants more often than not! We still do our live sales and love meeting with our audience, and day after day, we are still posting tips about houseplants online.

I didn't have "write a houseplant-care book" on my bingo card of life, but I'm grateful for the opportunity to teach people what I've learned about houseplant care to help bring the joy of plants to as many people as I can. I hope this book is a breakthrough for you in keeping and enjoying houseplants and therefore a breakthrough in our unyielding efforts to help the masses. I dream of a world in which thriving plants in homes are as commonplace as thriving pets. After all, they've been serving man longer than man's best friend!

To do that, I hope you use this book to guide you through the excitement of shopping for your first plant. It's so advantageous if you can choose one that will thrive in the natural conditions of your space. But it's not just about picking the ideal plant. When it's time for watering, repotting, and pruning and you're unsure of the next steps, grab this book and thumb through the pages for the answers. It's easier to find peace when you have a direction to move forward in. When yellow leaves, brown tips, or suspicious spots have your confidence wavering, I hope you pick up this book for help in facing those challenges head-on, arming yourself with certainty in how to handle them and the wisdom of knowing there's joy to be had, regardless of the outcome. And perhaps it's that romantic side of me that hopes you use this book to remind yourself of the small activities that bring you joy in life, to do them often, and to recognize them for the valuable treasure they are.

PART ONE

THE BASICS

CHAPTER ONE

"Success" with Houseplants

Have you ever heard of being "plant blind"? It's a term plant people use to refer to the time before they recognized plants in their daily life. I look back at old pictures from my childhood and always see plants in the background, whether inside or out, and I can't believe that I don't have memories of anyone in my family growing anything, other than my dad and his garden. In contrast, years after my plant blindness went away, I can now tell you about every plant in my house and its specific location.

Something else I've noticed since getting into plants is how many places of business and public common spaces feature them. What I didn't realize before is that not only do plants look nice and provide noise reduction and a sense of calm but research shows they also increase productivity and creativity. I'd say that's a win-win for any business, which is probably why you will—now—notice them everywhere!

While growing houseplants may help create some Zen moments throughout the day, or even spur creativity, those probably aren't the first benefits that come to mind when you think about purchasing them. That is probably reserved for the notion that houseplants purify the air in the rooms they inhabit, an idea popularized by a 1989 study performed by NASA, which showed the top common houseplants for air purification. The truth is that the study was intended for sealed environments and the results didn't apply to regular home settings. Although plants very likely have air purification benefits, I doubt they're as effective as your average air purifier.

There is, however, research that shows that growing plants helps reduce stress and increase mindfulness, which is a worthwhile task at any rate, if you ask me. On that note, I am glad to see a shift in culture these days, with constant hustling being replaced by a yearning for simplicity and peace. I wonder what impact houseplants had on that cultural shift, as their popularity has followed a similar timeline. Regardless, I do believe growing plants contributes to the mindset of seeking simplicity and wanting to live a good life.

One of my favorite benefits of plants is their use in the field of horticultural therapy, which became a formal field of study only in the last hundred years but whose origins date back thousands of years to ancient Egypt, where gardens were used as places of healing and relaxation. More recently, horticultural therapy was used in World Wars I and II to help veterans, and it continues to be used to promote mental health, physical rehabilitation, cognitive development, and social connections. I heard about horticultural therapy only a few years ago and was instantly intrigued. I immediately thought, "What is it about having plants around that provides that sense of positivity?"

SHIFTING YOUR MINDSET ABOUT HOUSEPLANTS

This book is a beginner's guide to growing houseplants, and the pages beyond this chapter are filled with what I'm told is a unique approach to plant care. I don't know how unique the information is—none of my ideas are revolutionary breakthroughs, and I certainly haven't uncovered any new secrets to growing plants. What sets this book apart from other books dedicated to houseplant care is specificity and clarity in explaining care techniques, and this chapter, in which I offer practical advice based on real stories and experiences that plant experts tend to leave out.

I'm not going to tell you to put your plant in bright light and to not overwater. That kind of advice has been written on every plant-care card in existence, and the general public is still no closer to figuring out plants! I'm also not going to grab your hand and dive into the deep end of houseplant science. My goal is to make houseplant care as effortless as feeding the dog, and for you to love it even more. Regardless of why you want to grow houseplants, this book will help you understand the basics of care like you've never understood them before.

But before you jump down the rabbit hole of learning these techniques and the ideas behind them, you need to know that they aren't very important to your enjoyment of houseplant care. Earlier in my own plant journey, I learned that no matter how long you've been growing plants, you'll still kill them from time to time—or more often if you're new to the hobby. The trick to falling in love with plants for the long haul is to give yourself enough time to get to know them. To do that, you'll need to either keep them alive or keep trying until they grow on you—in the beginning, it's most likely the latter. At first, it might seem like one of those relationships you can *feel* is a good thing, even if your logical brain is still raising an eyebrow in doubt.

If knowing the basics of plant care won't guarantee you finding joy in them, what will? How can you enjoy something riddled with failure? The answer is by managing your expectations and preparing yourself to push through when things aren't going the way you want them to. I think author and speaker Mandy Hale said it best: "When you release expectations, you are free to enjoy things for what they are instead of what you think they should be." That doesn't mean I expect you to have a house full of ugly

Why are people so obsessed with plants?

Houseplants are a multibillion-dollar industry, and this is in spite of the fact that most plants die during the cultivation process or while in the care of people like you and me. So, what keeps us coming back?

One could argue that it's simply a matter of decor. I've never seen a space that wasn't improved by a well-placed houseplant, so I think there's some truth to that. But I believe the draw to plants goes even deeper. It may even be part of being human!

Some of our earliest evidence of ancestors eating plants dates back millions of years. Over time, humans began using plants not only for food but also for medicine, tools, clothing, and cultural practices. With so many practical uses, it's not a stretch to assume we became hardwired to gravitate toward plants. Eventually, this connection played a central role in the development of early civilization through the cultivation of crops.

Thousands of years later, the same instinct that would drive our ancestors to pluck a fig from a tree and eat it drives us to the plant shop. I hope that stays in humans forever.

plants and for you to not care and just enjoy them. That would make this a very short book! But I do want you to release any expectations you have, because it's unlikely you'll meet them right off the bat.

I know you bought this book thinking it would be chock-full of technical plant advice delivering all the answers you've been looking for and perhaps even uncovering that one detail of plant care that's the answer to all your problems. We will get to that, but first, let's talk about the mindset you'll need, because the truth is, everyone you know who has a "green thumb" acquired it not by giving up after their first failure, their second, or even their twentieth. They kept trying and failing until they got it right! You thought growing plants was about intuition? Nope! For any activity to become a reliable source of joy in your life, you'll need to be consistent, and consistency takes perseverance, especially in this hobby.

The Trap of Intuition

The biggest deterrent that keeps people from persevering with plants is the idea that they already know how to grow beautiful plants. When I first started working with clients for plant consultations, I was shocked to learn that most of them believed they should be able to tell what a plant wants just by looking at it. If they were meant to keep a plant alive, then they would be able to simply observe it and know that it needed more light or a drink of water. If this sounds like you, then I want you to do yourself and your future plants a favor by dropping that unrealistic standard. While I don't contest that caring for plants can involve intuition, I do think it's a better idea to start—or restart—your plant journey without the expectation that intuition will tell you what to do and instead focus on the logic of plant care.

I focus on teaching the logic of houseplant care instead of intuitive-based plant care because of the gaping disparity in how much training we have in each discipline. I'd be willing to bet there aren't many high school graduates who got their diploma by answering test questions with their intuition. I'd say the same for college graduates and just about any profession as well. People are more skilled at logic than anything else. I'm quite confident when it comes to caring for any houseplant you throw at me, and I'll admit there are times when I do trust my "intuition," but I would describe that as experienced-based intuition rather than the true definition, which is to know something without applying any logic at all. Plus, the moments when I rely on intuition are the exception and not the rule. Even now, with years of plant care under my belt, my plant-care routines are as basic and straightforward as what I share with you in this book.

The idea of intuition being the only guiding principle in houseplant care is a learned idea. When I noticed this trend with my clients, I was curious, because the thought of houseplant care being about intuition never crossed my mind. But I encountered so many people taking this approach that I started to feel like an outsider. Digging deeper with these clients, I found that they all had a family member or someone they knew who could "grow anything," yet all they had to do was look at a plant and it would die, which leads me to another important point about developing the right mindset to care for plants—ignoring the concept of having a green thumb.

The Green Thumb Myth

If I could banish a plant-care idea out of existence, it would be the idea of a green thumb, an idiom that refers to a person who grows plants exceptionally well. The term is not so bad by itself, but it comes with an underlying implication that a green thumb is something you're born with or without, and if you don't have one, you can't possibly grow plants. Of course, this is no truer than the idea that smoking cigarettes is good for your health, which doctors believed to be true until the 1960s. Unfortunately, unlike the fallacy of healthy cigarettes, the green thumb myth persists.

When people talk about having or lacking a green thumb, they often reference a relative—perhaps Mom, Dad, Grandma, or Grandpa—that was blessed with the ability to grow plants. But no one is born with a green thumb; they simply develop one over time and with experience. Consider the fact that the modern world is busier than ever, and previous generations simply had more time to devote to activities like caring for plants. Also, many of our ancestors grew gardens, something that's comparatively less common now. There are many differences between gardening and growing houseplants, but there's certainly some crossover. So, instead of hoping you inherited your grandfather's green thumb, consider the fact that he may just have had the time and experience to know how to care for plants.

Why am I making such a big deal about the green-thumb myth? Science has proven that houseplants can be beneficial to our physical and mental health, but silly ideas like there being a genetic ability to grow plants can cause a barrier to entry that may discourage someone from even trying—or, just as bad, discourage them from being persistent when things initially go wrong, which they often do. Every time you have a perceived failure, that little devil on your shoulder tells you that you're obviously not good at this, so why keep trying? You don't have a green thumb!

The ability to grow plants, or what's known as having a "green thumb," is not an innate talent. It's a skill developed over time and often through trial and error. To get through those small trials and errors, I recommend abandoning any ideas you have about innate talent or natural skills. That's just noise that will get in the way of you learning about and enjoying how to care for plants.

ARE YOU AT THE RIGHT STAGE OF LIFE FOR PLANTS?

Later in this book, we'll discuss more in-depth how your lifestyle fits with caring for a plant and how to match your lifestyle with the needs of different plants, but for now, I want you to ask yourself a larger question: Are you at a place in your life where you can care for plants? That might seem like an odd question, as many people care for plants while also doing all kinds of things, from running a business to raising kids to renovating a home. But let me tell you a story I hope will help you understand the reasoning behind my question.

Shortly after we opened our store, a couple boldly strutted through our doors in the middle of the day. Usually when people enter the store, they do so as "under the radar" as possible, but this couple might as well have busted through the door, with arms raised, exclaiming, "I'M BACK!" even though they had never been there before. We came to learn that they had just dropped their last remaining kid off at college, and they were officially empty nesters. The wife, absolutely brimming with joy, said, "I'm *finally* ready for houseplants!"

She went on to explain how she had always loved growing houseplants in her early adult years, but when she got married and had kids, she found she was too preoccupied with the daily challenges of parenting to care for them. She made the wise decision that, rather than resent plants for taking time away from her kids or resent the kids for taking the joy out of houseplants—not to mention the added challenge of keeping young hands and mouths away from them—she would revisit plants once she had the time to commit to them. Although plants are living, they aren't quite as important to (most of) us as, for example, kids or significant others. Heck, they're usually not even as important as the family pet, which is why taking inventory of where you are in life is so important to consider before trying to grow plants.

Upon hearing this customer's story, I was in awe not only of her awareness of the stage of life she was in and the sacrifices she would have to make as a result but also of her awareness of her own personality. She knew she was the type of person who wouldn't be happy doing both, unlike me and maybe a lot of you reading this book, who try to do everything they want to do, all the time. There are countless people in the world who can juggle several aspects of life at once. They can be an amazing spouse, parent, and friend, while committing to their career and still making time for a hobby they enjoy, but for others, even the thought of keeping up with all that is debilitating.

The fact that this customer made the decision to focus on her priorities early on in her parenting life by sacrificing a hobby she loves shows an uncommon level of maturity that still impresses me, and the joy she expressed on that day, when she finally got to bring plants back as a priority in her life, is proof of the power of plants. The consequence of that decision protected her relationship with plants and her kids. She is now enjoying the life of an empty nester, surrounded by all the houseplants she now has the time to dedicate to.

I don't believe all people, or even most people, need to be this disciplined to enjoy plants. If I had known this customer years prior, I would have suggested she get one that wouldn't take much time away from the kids, like a snake plant or ZZ plant, both of which may only need to be watered about once a month if kept in low light. Everyone has time for that! The stage of life you're in might not be ideal for fulfilling all your plant goals and aspirations, but that doesn't mean you should swear them off until the perfect time arrives. And you can drastically increase the likelihood that your plants will love you (and you'll love them back) if you choose ones that suit your lifestyle. For example, if you're living your life constantly on the go, I recommend buying plants that don't need to be watered often. Make sure to check out my houseplant profiles in part 2 (beginning on page 174), where I cover the needs of thirty of the most popular houseplants, so that you can make an informed decision when it's time to buy your next plant!

THE VALUE OF SETTING GOALS

Setting goals for your houseplants certainly isn't necessary, but for those who have been frustrated in the past and really want to lean in this time, I've found that setting specific goals can help you trudge through when things aren't quite going your way. Are you trying to get an orchid to flower? Maybe you simply want a nice, low-maintenance centerpiece for the dinner table. Some people just want to keep a plant they inherited from a loved one alive. There are no wrong goals when it comes to your houseplants, but when the going gets tough, you can interrupt any spiraling misery by returning to your goal(s) and reminding yourself that any setbacks are just part of the process and the reality of growing plants.

Along the way on your journey of figuring out plants, you'll likely find some tasks you enjoy more than others. Some people hate repotting their plants but can spend hours meticulously dusting their leaves, pruning, and talking to their plants. Other people, like me, love repotting plants but are less concerned with how they look—if you find me dusting a bunch of plants, you'll know it's a rare sighting! When you don't have a goal in mind, it's easy to put those plant chores you don't enjoy as much on the back burner. But having a clear goal will help you stay more purpose driven and motivated to do those less-enjoyable tasks, because you know that by doing them, you'll be contributing to your end goal.

Having goals in mind will also help you stay motivated because you can achieve and celebrate milestones. It's easy to have the wind taken out of your sails when you think about how much time it will take for you to achieve your goal. After all, plants require considerable time to develop, and there's only so much we can do to speed up the process, especially if we're keeping them indoors year-round!

For every new plant you buy, I want you to take a photo of it the day you bring it home. When people come to our store, they love to show me their houseplant collections—and I love to see them! They'll scroll through photos they've taken of the plants they're most proud of and narrate the story of each one. Eventually, their plant photo album (yes, if you stick with this hobby, be prepared to have a camera roll full of plants) will land on a plant they're not so proud of, and the tone of their narration goes from joyful to frustrated.

"This plant just won't grow for me! I've moved it here, moved it there, tried this, and tried that, but it won't grow!" That's my cue to ask, "Do you have a photo from when you first bought the plant?" When they're able to find a photo from that day or near enough to it, I like to wait for the squeals of joy as they realize their plant *has* grown—they just didn't notice it! When you look at something often enough it can be difficult to recognize small changes. All houseplants are either growing or dying; there's no stagnation with living things. Stay ahead of this pitfall by tracking your plants' progress and taking photos throughout your journey. You may be surprised by how much change there actually is!

Once you decide on a goal, I find it best to write it down so you can remind yourself of it as your plant matures. With our busy lifestyles, a handwritten goal can be surprisingly effective at helping you check yourself when things seem to be going off the rails, like when you're dealing with a pest infestation or when you've accidentally overwatered your favorite plant. If you're more digitally minded, you can make note of your goal(s) on your phone, tablet, etc., but studies show that handwritten notes are more effective at inspiring change, so you may want to at least consider pulling out old-fashioned pen and paper.

My initial plant goal was to learn how to make an orchid bloom. While an orchid wasn't the first plant I started growing, setting this goal was the

first time I really focused on achieving a visible and tangible outcome. I wanted to prove to myself that I could successfully cultivate this notoriously challenging plant and witness its ultimate reward—beautiful flowers! Spoiler alert: It's a lot simpler than you think. But that experience of setting a goal, focusing on each aspect, staying the course, and seeing that first bloom spike is one I won't soon forget. It's somewhere around two parts joy, one part relief, and one part disbelief—a recipe that catapulted me into complete fascination with plants and drove my desire to show people that caring for them is quite straightforward.

If I hadn't set the goal to make an orchid flower, I wouldn't have been as motivated to make sure it was getting adequate amounts of light, keep up with watering it, and, especially, remember to fertilize it, which is a task I tend to fall short on. Before we move on, I want to emphasize a very important distinction. I didn't say growing plants was easy, but it *is* simple—just as lifting a heavy weight is a simple action but isn't always easy!

IT'S NOT ABOUT PERFECTION; IT'S ABOUT THE PROCESS

More than any instruction on light, watering, soil, or fertilizer, making a mindset tweak toward your houseplant care is guaranteed to ensure that you derive joy from this hobby. Do you know that feeling you get when you're doing something you really love? Something you could do for hours and be so engaged with that you lose track of time? I've found that in many things, such as exercise, pencil drawing, and, of course, plants. This isn't a requirement for growing houseplants, but if you can make houseplant care something to look forward to, like meditation or a self-care routine, without the burden of expectation, that will carry you through any goals you have for this hobby, not to mention any challenges you face. When you do finally snap out of it and realize how much time has passed, I want you to recognize those moments with gratitude because that's the foundation for widespread success.

When I say "success," I'm not talking about growing a plant larger, longer, or fuller. I'm talking about experiencing joy. If you thought houseplant care was all about getting a tree to live in front of a specific window or getting an orchid to bloom, then you've missed the point entirely. I'm not saying that growing a beautiful tree or getting flowers from your orchid doesn't elicit joy—and I know I just encouraged you to set goals to keep you on track. But whether your plant lives, dies, produces flowers, or grows babies doesn't matter. Achieving plant perfection doesn't matter.

PROTECTING THE HOBBY

It's not enough to simply know that there will be challenges. We're all aware of that to some degree, even if we need reminding from time to time. Whether you deal with overwatering, leaves dropping for seemingly no reason, or pests eating your plant, there will be challenges to overcome. When those challenges arise, your response will strengthen or weaken the relationship with your plants. This is when it's an excellent idea to recenter yourself by going over your goals. When you overcome a challenge in pursuit of your goals, you're committing an act of personal development that will help you in other areas of life that are important to you.

My "what to do when problems arise" protocol is just as important as the protocol that eliminates the problem itself. Spider mites, for example, can be frustrating enough to derail all good intentions and stick a fork in your green-thumb dreams. The first thing I want you to do when issues pop up is to set some time aside. In most cases there's no need to act immediately, so leave it for your next day off, or when you have enough time to be present in addressing the issue, not when you are panicked or rushed. If you're not convinced, let me tell you a story about how not to handle a plant problem.

Early on in my plant journey I got a sizable monstera, my dream plant at

the time. I was incredibly eager to get it out of the pot it was root-bound in and put it in a much larger pot, one that was fit for the giant dream plant it was about to become. But after a few weeks in that new pot, the monstera's soil was still wet—something I knew was a red flag from previous failures. Upon discovering the damp soil and accompanying fungus gnats, a result of watering too often, I panicked and ripped the entire plant out of its new home that very same day.

I chuckle thinking back to myself then. I was distraught and didn't know what to do next. I stood in my living room in the midst of a repotting frenzy with a thin layer of soil beneath my feet that served less as a reminder of a job well done and more as a realization that in my panic I had forgotten the reason I enjoyed growing plants, which was the peace it brings to my mind. At that moment, I realized that I didn't have new soil, and I didn't have a different pot—I didn't even know if I needed a different pot. I also didn't know how to tell if my roots were still healthy or what I was accomplishing by ripping the plant out of its pot in the first place. Was I just making the problem worse?

I went to the garage hoping some pot I had forgotten about would magically reveal itself, but I had to settle on the only thing I could find that could feasibly hold my large plant—a storage bin. I drilled several holes in it for drainage and hurriedly repotted my prized plant in the storage bin, using soil I had salvaged from sweeping up my mess. I hid the plant behind the couch, half to conceal the hideous "pot" and half to hide my shame.

I'm happy to report the plant is now doing tremendously after all these years, climbing a wooden stake and reaching over seven feet tall. However, the stress I put myself through with that plant was nearly enough to make me quit. And all that stress could have been avoided with a calm, collected plan.

In contrast, when a problem pops up now, I give myself some time to react and plan a course of action. If I notice something out of the ordinary happening to a plant in my collection, I'll give it a couple of weeks to solve its own issues. Plants are expert survivalists, and the answer to a newly discovered problem is often to let the plant figure it out on its own without our intervention. After that time, if the plant hasn't shown signs that it's recovering, then I make a plan. I start by going through my troubleshooting checks, then I put the intervention on my calendar and gather all the supplies I'll need in advance. This helps me avoid that sinking feeling I got while standing on a film of old soil and holding my newly uprooted plant, not knowing what to do next and regretting what I had gotten myself into.

Challenges are an inherent part of growing plants in any space, climate, or quantity. When things aren't going your way, I want you to pause, reference this book for guidance, and come up with a plan to help resolve the problem. You will be avoiding not only unnecessary stress but resentment toward the hobby as well. Doing so makes perseverance a breeze.

PLANTS ARE JUST PLANTS

I love to see plant owners find a sense of connection from caring for their collection, but I must warn against taking that feeling too far and losing sight of the fact that your plant is just that—a plant. Problems arise when a plant owner's eagerness to care for their plant leads them to personify it, perhaps even calling it their "plant baby." Yes, this is all somewhat harmless, but consider what happens when challenges arise. All those positive feelings the plant parent had toward the plant, and toward their ability to care for it, can turn negative. Instead of feeling joy and satisfaction, the plant parent may feel disappointment and guilt because their plant has brown leaves, isn't flowering, or got infested with spider mites. But challenges like that are inevitable, just part of the plant-growing process, and any such feelings are caused not by the plant but by the plant parent. Whatever problem the plant is displaying is due not to any emotion it has but rather to some deficiency in its conditions.

Plants, like the rest of nature, simply cannot lie—they show you exactly what they are going through. Instead of wasting time thinking about how you've let your plant baby down, focus on determining the actual problem and how to resolve it. Love your plants but love them for what they are without assigning an unrealistic value to them, and then watch your appreciation for them grow!

Alongside the habit of personifying plants, I find many plant parents convince themselves that their plant has an opinion about where it lives—that is, about the home where it lives. I can't tell you how many times I've heard a plant's death be explained with "Ugh, it just hated my new house!"

Stop Being So Hard on Yourself

Feeling inadequate when it comes to my intellect really bothers me. We all feel like we *should* be able to figure certain things out on our own, whether it's a project for school or work, how to help a loved one through a trying time, or even how to assemble a piece of furniture from a box. The truth is, and this is coming from someone who is very hard on themselves, you *shouldn't* be able to figure everything out, at least not at first. New ideas and concepts outside of your life experiences take time to weave into your brain and thought patterns until one day it all "clicks." This light-bulb moment of understanding may not come in your first attempt, or even in the first dozen attempts, but if it feels right to pursue, keep going. Your brain is an infinitely powerful and capable tool, though it can be lazy and willing to abandon any idea whose outcome it cannot immediately appreciate or find value in.

The truth is plants aren't picky about where they live. While they care very much about their conditions—how much light there is, the humidity level, etc.—as far as they're concerned, your house is as good as the White House. And even if a plant doesn't like the conditions you've put it in, it's your home, and to a certain degree, you have control over those conditions and can change them.

On the topic of plants and emotions, I also want to touch on what happens when you kill a plant. The reality is that when a plant dies and you throw it away, it'll probably wind up in a landfill. The garbage surrounding it and the trash bag protecting it will eventually break down, along with the plant. Once that plant decomposes, the nutrients that once kept it living will return to the earth, where they will become nutrients for the next generation of plants. So, the next time you kill a plant, remind yourself that you're doing your part to contribute to that cycle.

This is an important mindset when you have an emotional attachment to a particular plant. When that plant's life is over, you may feel sad or disappointed in yourself. But you're not mourning the plant; you're mourning what it represents—perhaps it came from a loved one's funeral. If that's the case, let me tell you this: If you believe in a higher power, then the place that special person is in gives them perspective, and they wouldn't want you worried or sad about a plant you got from their funeral. They wouldn't want you to be worried or sad about anything. Even if the plant was simply a gift from a friend or family member, I guarantee they wouldn't want you to suffer emotionally because you didn't keep the plant alive.

PAY IT FORWARD

There are few things that bring me more joy in the world of plants than seeing the next generation finding value in the hobby of growing them. My hope, however, is that they're equipped with the tools they need to rewrite the stereotype of houseplants being something to fret over and stress about. There are enough things to cause anxiety in the world that are far more important than keeping a plant alive.

I recently watched a video of an experiment to see if babies who had never interacted with snakes would be afraid of them. The babies were separated from their parents and put in a playroom, where they were allowed to crawl about on the floor, which was covered in toys—and snakes. It was amazing to see how curious and unafraid these six- to nine-month-olds were with these large, slithering creatures that so many people have a phobia about. I don't have a fear of snakes, but I watched with bated breath as their tiny hands grabbed the snakes with the same enthusiasm as they would their favorite toy. The defenseless infants were fearless in a playroom full of reptiles that would keep most adults from even opening the door. As the video explained, this was because children look to their caregivers for clues to determine how they should react to new situations, but since their parents weren't around, the babies had no idea that the snakes were something to fear.

Plants are not snakes and we certainly don't need to be afraid of them, but there's a lesson here. Instead of holding on to and modeling our own insecurities around houseplants for our kids—or our friends, for that matter—we can teach them to have a healthy relationship with plants by normalizing the perceived negative and disappointing side of it. In that way, we are setting them up for success not just in plants but in the disappointing sides of any aspect of life.

CHAPTER TWO

Why You Can't Keep Your Houseplants Alive

Among my biggest hopes for you in reading this book is that you make peace with the reality of keeping plants, which will free you from the frustration, stress, anxiety, and guilt of past failures. I've been in the very same spot you may be in right now—or have found yourself in before. I've wondered what went wrong when I woke up to a dead plant that I just purchased and then felt guilty about the money I spent on it. And I've been frustrated when I purchased a second plant and then failed a second time! It's not a coincidence. Plants aren't meant to be kept indoors, and by making them houseplants, we are literally challenging nature. But this is not out of spite. It's out of admiration.

If you're reading this book, you intuitively understand and feel the difference in a room without plants, perhaps even noting its cold, sterile ambience. Yet despite your best intentions—and efforts—to live alongside plants, you just can't seem to make them happy. I want you to live in harmony with your plants so you can reap all the benefits of a hobby that's natural to gravitate toward and that enriches the lives of millions of people around the globe. To do that, I want to recalibrate your mindset about plants and how to take care of them.

In this chapter, I'll share insights into the most common reasons people fail with their houseplants, including industry secrets you may not be aware of, common pitfalls and their solutions, and my houseplant buying guide to start you off on the right foot. I'll even share my top five picks for the best beginner-friendly plants.

SOCIAL MEDIA IS KILLING YOUR PLANTS

Beautiful photos of houseplants living among decor and posted to social media are just that—beautiful photos! And it's not just social media but all media, including TV shows, movies, the Internet, and magazines, if you still read those. All too often, aspiring plant parents reference pictures found while scrolling their Instagram feed or watching their favorite interior design TV show and look to these photos for care advice or examples of where a plant should grow, forgetting or not even realizing that these shots are styled to look nice and are not necessarily accurate when it comes to depicting where plants will actually thrive in a home.

Consider this scenario: The aspiring plant parent heads to the store, buys a plant, and brings it home to be placed in an Insta-worthy location, which probably isn't right in front of a window, because backlit photos are obviously a no-no. If they're feeling extra inspired, they might even pick up repotting supplies while they're at the store and immediately transplant their new plant purchase before snapping a photo of their beautiful living decor. Spoiler alert: It's usually the ones who skipped the repot who end up doing the best with their first plants. Within a few weeks, that once beautiful plant, positioned twenty feet from the nearest window, starts to decline and ultimately meets its demise. Oddly enough, the plant parent almost always blames the plant for being "finicky" rather than considering their own possible missteps in caring for a living organism—one that naturally grows, without human intervention, thousands of miles away in a tropical environment.

When folks come into our store looking for the more popular home-decor plants, like the fiddle-leaf fig, which has been constantly featured in home decor for the past ten years, we always ask qualifying questions to determine if the plant will be in conditions conducive to success. The scenario laid out in the previous paragraph was happening so frequently that my wife, Erika, would often joke that it was her full-time job to tell customers that they couldn't get a fiddle-leaf fig upon showing her where they wanted to put it. I fondly remember one customer saying, "I've been in your store five times now, and you've never let me buy a plant!"

Part of having success with houseplants is getting rid of the noise. By "noise," I mean the unrealistic expectations that come from constant comparison to what other people's plants look like online. You must remember that the Internet is a wild place full of possibilities, and many of those possibilities are based on highly staged photos focused on aesthetics and have no connection to proper houseplant care. If you truly want to grow plants that fulfill you and give you all the good feelings you're striving for, then I recommend taking most plant-care advice you find in pop culture and any media source with a grain of salt. And yes, that even applies to my advice. This is not because I'm unsure or have anything but absolute confidence in my methods but because the pathway to concrete confidence in plant care comes, more than anything, by way of trial and error—*your* trial and error. Take what you learn from any resource and tweak it to suit your environment, lifestyle, and personality, making your plant-care approach a product of you coming to your own conclusions.

"IT'S NOT YOU, IT'S THEM!"

There's no shortage of retailers selling houseplants. From your local nursery, plant boutique, and home-and-garden center to your grocery store or even coffee shop, the allure of leafy, green, life-giving purchases are all around us. But are all the plants being sold from various locations of the same quality? I'd posit that they are not all equal. I don't mean to say the plants themselves are different. After all, a plant on the shelf of a boutique plant store often comes from the very same grower that supplies big-box stores. The difference comes in the care the plants receive once they arrive at the retail location.

Employees at your average big-box store aren't required to know how to care for plants or to even learn plant care on the job. You don't need a horticulture degree to work in the gardening section of Walmart, nor do you need to have any particular interests beyond the prospect of a job wielding the store's watering hose. Prior to hiring employees to work at our plant shop, I assumed that workers in the garden centers of these conglomerates at least had a special interest in plants and likely brought seasoned experience to the table in lieu of a degree, but I have since learned that no such interest or experience is necessary.

Up to this point, we've hired only two people who have previously worked in the garden centers of big-box stores, but neither had any previous interest in plants or experience in caring for them. Upon landing their big-box jobs, the only instructions these two new hires received was to water all the plants every day. Do I think this is the case at every big-box garden center? No. Can you get healthy plants from anyone who sells them? Absolutely!

When I talk about this idea on social media, employees from big-box stores often respond with statements like "Yep, I was told to water the houseplants every day" or "We were told to just keep the plants sitting in water." Once you read chapter 4 (page 80), which is a deep dive into watering, you'll realize that this is shocking advice when it comes to watering plants. And I don't mean shockingly good. Unfortunately, this is bad advice that those employees are passing on to their store's massive customer base.

I've also had big-box store employees tell me "No way! We were trained to let the tropical plants go completely dry before we watered!" or "They only hired experienced gardeners at my location!" I love hearing these responses and hope they are true more often than not. But I share all this to explain that the health of a newly purchased plant can vary dramatically depending on whether it was cared for by someone who is simply working for a paycheck or by someone who has experience in caring for plants or whose livelihood depends on keeping their investment alive—that is, an independent plant shop.

Here's one of those industry secrets I mentioned earlier: Whether you're buying your plants from a big-box store or a boutique plant shop like mine, most of them come from the same growers. But although the plants in both situations might be the same on the outside, it's what's going on beneath the soil at the time of purchase that plays a massive role in your chances at houseplant-growing success. Hint: You don't always get what you bargained for when shopping for plants.

When plants are cared for with haphazard watering, as in daily watering or being kept in water constantly, root rot can run rampant. You'll learn all about root rot in chapter 7 (page 141), but if left unchecked, it can kill plants faster than almost any other common houseplant issue. The problem for you, the unassuming consumer, is that signs of root rot aren't apparent in the early stages, which means the plant can look perfectly fine above the soil when it's rotting below. I cringe to think how many people have unknowingly purchased a plant that secretly had root rot, then gave up on plants completely when it died. Another point to keep in mind is that many big-box stores still use the "pay by scan" policy, which means the greenhouses growing the plants don't get paid until their plants are scanned at the checkout line. That's right, nurseries ship thousands of dollars' worth of inventory to stores but don't get paid unless the plants sell, which means the store has no incentive to keep these plants alive, because if they die, the store loses zero dollars. Thankfully, this practice is becoming less common, but it's an unusual part of the industry that isn't widely known and at least worth keeping in mind when considering a new plant purchase.

Don't get me wrong: If you accidentally kill a plant, it is 100 percent your fault. Even for the person who unknowingly bought a sickly plant, the blame is on you. Few things will lengthen your plant-growing learning curve

40 FOR THE LOVE OF HOUSEPLANTS

more than refusing to take responsibility for your own plant's decline. All too often I hear "That plant just *hates* me!" This, of course, isn't true. Plants don't hate people. However, they might hate the conditions people are putting them in. Blaming the plant for dying under your care is like blaming your car for running out of gas. The reason this distinction is important is because the sooner you take responsibility, the sooner you can really look at what went wrong, learn from it, and do better the next time.

"I WANT TO WATCH IT GROW!"

Beginners to the houseplant hobby often fall prey to the romantic desire to buy a small houseplant and watch it grow from a tiny plant to a large plant. Snapshots of the baby plant's transformation play in their mind, alongside visions of an upward trajectory at work, a growing family, or moving into a first home. But the reality about houseplants is that the smaller they are, the more difficult they can be to grow. This is true not only for the four-inch potted golden pothos you got from the store but also for the plant cuttings your friend gave you.

Small plants simply aren't as robust as their more established, usually larger, and older counterparts. They don't have extensive root systems, they haven't developed thick stems or branches that allow them to withstand damage, and they likely have never experienced pests, which would increase their tolerance to them. All these factors make caring for a smaller plant more challenging than caring for a larger one.

Speaking of the importance of robust roots, you must stop beating yourself up over cuttings that don't take root. I regularly encounter people who lament not having a green thumb and claim to be unable to grow anything. When I ask about their experiences, they go on about their friend who keeps giving them cuttings of this plant or that, and although their friend's plant is thriving, they're unable to make a plant from the cuttings. This scenario has one major problem: The health of the roots is the health of a plant. If you're starting your plant journey with a cutting, you're starting with a huge disadvantage—it has no roots! If you judge your ability to keep houseplants alive by how successful you are at growing plants that don't have roots, you're doing yourself a major injustice. (If you want to learn more about cuttings, we'll discuss them in part two, page 174.)

Root Rot, Stress, and Pests, Oh My!

While root rot is a problem all its own, it also means a plant is undergoing stress, and stressed plants are more likely to have pests, which can quickly derail your plant-parenthood journey—another topic we'll tackle in chapter 7 (page 141). Most people think houseplant pests are going to be easy to detect while shopping, but the truth is that even industry experts can have a tough time spotting these little buggers and often have to bust out a magnifying glass to find them. I'm willing to bet that most people don't go plant shopping with a magnifying glass—although it might be a good idea. Don't worry: Later in this chapter, I'll share my best advice for shopping for plants, so you can set yourself up for success with a healthy one and feel secure in your purchase.

HOUSEPLANT GUESSING GAME: A RECIPE FOR DISASTER

I'm often surprised at how self-deprecating most people are when it comes to their plant failures. Every day, folks readily admit to me how many plants they've killed, how they're terrible plant parents, or the ever-popular "I could kill a cactus!" Everybody can kill a cactus. Put it in a closet and water it every day, and I promise it will be dead in a few weeks. But does that mean you have a brown thumb? Absolutely not! Saying you have a brown thumb because you guessed how to take care of a plant and then failed is no different from saying you can't bake because you failed at making a soufflé without a recipe.

The reality is that when it comes to caring for plants, you can't just wing it and expect a magical connection with nature to tell you what your plant needs. While caring for plants is not difficult, it's much easier if you learn to understand how plants work and your role in their survival. When I mention this to clients, you can almost feel the weight lift off their shoulders. Their demeanor changes and they are instantly more relaxed. Stop being so hard on yourself! There are tons of things you didn't originally know how to do, but you do them now with expert skill. Houseplant care is no different.

Consider the following chapters as your recipe book for houseplants. This isn't the only time I'll relate houseplant care to cooking and baking, as I believe plant care, like much of the culinary arts, is simple but specific. When I call this book a "recipe book for houseplants," I mean the step-by-step, follow-the-directions approach you most often find in cookbooks. We won't be blending any orchids or frying up cacti here—although there is a place for that!

HOUSEPLANT HYSTERIA

If I were writing this book prior to the explosion of houseplant popularity that took place in 2020, I wouldn't need this section. In part, I'm happy that houseplants have gained so much attention, as I'm obviously a huge proponent of plant ownership. But then there's the other part of me, the part that sees the negative side of what happens when there's a huge influx of people sharing their ideas on the same subject. I deal with this downside so much that I came up with the term "houseplant hysteria," which I use to describe the scenario in which a new plant parent becomes completely consumed with all the things they "must do" to care for their plants, at least according to all the popular social media channels, blog articles, and online forums that have popped up in recent years.

The list of "must dos" includes but is not limited to growing your plants in water or using pon, LECA, or perlite exclusively. Here are some other non-negotiables you might stumble upon: If you want healthy plants, you *need* this fertilizer, that soil, and this brand of grow light. You'll never be able to grow calatheas without a humidifier, and so help me, if you don't use this exact spray, your plants will always be infested with pests! The pessimist in me thinks the people writing or saying these things are preying on vulnerable plant parents to sell a product, while the optimist thinks they're just trying to help by sharing what has worked for them. It's likely a mixture of both. (And don't panic if you're unfamiliar with pon, LECA, or perlite—we'll cover them in chapter 5, page 102.)

To explain this a bit more, let me share a scenario that pops up frequently in my houseplant consultations. An eager new plant parent brings home a new plant, perhaps guessing where it should go and how often to water it. Committed to keeping the new plant happy, they watch it closely, checking its leaves every day to look for signs of any negative change. Before long, they indeed see some changes. "Is that a yellowing leaf? Do I see a brown edge? What could these things mean?"

Committed to keeping the new plant happy, they start their Internet research. Et voilà! This person on Instagram keeps their plants in nothing but water, and their plants are beautiful! Naturally, the plant parent transfers their plant to water, relieved that they'll never again have to guess when the plant needs water. It worked for the person in the video, so it must be the answer! But after a while, there's a bit of mold growing on the plant's roots that you can see through the vase, that vase is now dirty with algae buildup, and the plant seems a bit "sad."

Still committed to keeping their new plant happy and convinced they must be doing something wrong, they once again consult the Internet for answers. This time, they learn about this thing called "pon," a type of substrate that an influencer uses to grow her plants, and her plants are gorgeous! A few clicks later and a bag of pon is set to deliver in two days' time. By day three, the plant is freshly potted in pon and hopes are running high.

Fast-forward a few more weeks, and once again the plant is declining, and the plant parent is puzzled as to why these solutions aren't working. I'll spare you the details on the next try, the next, and the next, all of which typically take place within a few days or weeks of each other. A lot of people give up somewhere along this plant-care roller coaster, which is understandable, but also such a shame because the positive intentions are there in spades!

The truth is, although houseplants can adapt to and sustain an incredible amount of stress, they can only take so much. When we constantly fuss over our plants by way of repotting, changing environments, and ultimately preventing them from settling into their new environments, we can surpass their abilities to recover and cause them to spiral into decline as a result. There are endless soil compositions and care methods you can utilize to successfully grow houseplants. Instead of jumping from one approach to another to another, my advice is to find one you like and stick to it. It's great to experiment with new ideas, but rather than going all in and ruining your fun with a host of unhappy plants, take it slow, introducing one new technique, product, etc., at a time.

Even if you don't make your plant unhappy (or kill it!), trying too many things all at once or in very close succession means it will be hard to know what works. Think about it this way: If you're sick and you bombard your system with a bunch of different medicines, you might feel better the next day, but you'll have no idea which one of those medicines did the trick. In other words, you'll have learned nothing.

Before you come for me, I want to share a bit more perspective on this. Prior to 2020, caring for houseplants was a popular hobby and gaining steam quickly. But the COVID lockdowns propelled the hobby into the stratosphere, and with that rise in popularity came an equally speedy change in how people cared for their plants, or at the very least, it highlighted approaches to plant care that were once considered niche.

When I first began caring for houseplants in 2017, everyone was using a few basic products. All the hobbyists and professional growers I knew exclusively used some ratio of peat moss and perlite or a combination of commercially available "houseplant soil" and "cactus soil" to grow their

collection. Most also used a single fertilizer for all their plants. The idea of purchasing a dedicated humidifier for your plants was just starting to gain popularity.

The landscape really changed when the houseplant hobby turned into the houseplant craze and took hold on social media, which underscores my theory about social media being the downfall for so many people in their plant-care journeys. My issue with social media—and this applies to so many areas of life—is that it can make you feel like you're missing out, that what you have isn't good enough, and that others simply have it better than you. There's a grid of curated photos with hundreds and thousands of "likes" as proof! Putting aside all the social media hoopla, the truth about houseplants is that they care very little about what they're planted in, they don't have brand loyalty to a certain fertilizer, and most will adapt to average household humidity within a couple of months. Houseplants do, however, care about what type of light they're getting, if their roots have enough oxygen, and that they are watered when needed—all topics we'll explore in this book.

YOU CAN'T (OR SHOULDN'T) ALWAYS GET WHAT YOU WANT!

Nature always wins. Humans have grown accustomed to having control over every aspect of their lives, especially within their homes. From paint color and finish work to cabinetry and furniture, all our spaces are curated to our liking. It's no surprise that we also want to control which plants we bring into our homes and where they'll go. However, problems arise when our ideas about where a plant *should* live clash with where a plant *needs* to live.

Something that surprised me when we opened our plant store was how adamant many customers were that they wanted a particular plant to live exactly where they wanted, and they expected the plant to "adjust to their home." Although plants can adapt to new environments, they have their limits. Don't expect a bright-light plant to adjust and thrive twenty feet away from any light source. In nature, when seeds fall on infertile soil or in a spot with inadequate light, they don't make it. Similarly, if your new houseplant is placed in improper light, it won't make it!

Plants can grow only where they can grow, and the rest die off! We can't assume that any amount of money, status, or decor dreams will force a living plant to thrive where its needs are not being met. There's a life lesson here, but I'll leave that for you to ponder the next time you're dusting your leaves. Expect plants to provide more life lessons as we progress through this book.

THREE THINGS TO CONSIDER BEFORE BUYING A HOUSEPLANT

Now that we've covered some common mistakes to avoid and you've girded your loins against social media hysteria, I want to set you up for success before you even walk through the door of your favorite plant shop.

If you want to experience houseplant-growing bliss, you must keep an open mind about which plants you're going to own and where you're going to put them. Keeping houseplants is meant to be an enjoyable experience, and that enjoyment can be achieved more easily by choosing plants whose care requirements fit most closely with your home's natural environment, your lifestyle, and your caring tendencies. For example, I wouldn't suggest a water-needy fern to an airline pilot who's gone for days or weeks at a time, just like I wouldn't suggest a drought-tolerant succulent to a new empty nester who wants something to take care of every day! This may sound a bit like what I said earlier—that "you can't always get what you want"! But trust me, even if your conditions can't grow your dream plant, you can still reap all the benefits you desire from other plants better suited to those conditions. You'll get much more satisfaction by having a thriving plant you didn't think you wanted than a dying plant you were obsessed with owning.

When it comes to matching a plant with your environment, there are three main factors to consider:

- **Light:** The first thing I want you to consider is your home's light conditions. Is your house or apartment full of windows and brightly lit? Do you prefer to have the shades drawn for most of the day? Homes built in hotter parts of the country often utilize covered patios and large trees to block the sun's heat from the windows, resulting in lower light. People living in cooler climates may not need to consider excessive heat and therefore build homes with big windows—what a dream! Or maybe you're lucky enough to have a home built in the '70s with a rad skylight. Side note: Please bring back skylights—signed, all plant parents. If you want to know definitively what type of light a given space has, please refer to chapter 3 (page 53). It's *so* easy to get lighting wrong, but I have a trick for getting it right every single time, without guessing!

Humidity: Second, what's the humidity like in your home? Plants deemed "houseplants" have been shown to adjust to average household humidity (30 percent to 50 percent). But maybe you live somewhere that requires you to have the heat on for most of the year. Wood-burning fireplaces and central heating can suck the humidity from your tropical houseplants, in which case desert cacti and succulents that prefer dry air would be a smart addition to the home. If not, perhaps you'll need to consider options that raise the average indoor humidity, such as a humidifier or grouping your plants together during the dry months.

Lifestyle: Finally, do you have ample time to dedicate to plants and want some green friends to tend to frequently, or do you travel for work and your home is more like a place you just sleep at four or five times a month? The former might enjoy air plants, ferns, or special orchids for their frequent watering needs. The latter should consider something more drought tolerant, like snake plants, ZZ plants, or a variety of succulents that prefer their soil to dry out completely between waterings. The idea is to work with what you've got, not against it!

HOUSEPLANT SHOPPING GUIDE

Understanding the conditions of your home, and more specifically the conditions of the space where you want to place a plant inside your home, and how the plant is going to fit into your lifestyle is of the utmost importance for setting yourself up for success. But when you head to the plant shop in search of a plant that fits those conditions, there's yet another essential element to keep in mind: You need to be sure you're purchasing a healthy plant. Avoiding a plant with rotting roots or one riddled with pests is just as crucial as or perhaps even more crucial than knowing your home's conditions and considering your lifestyle.

The prospect of adding new plants to your space is an exciting one, but don't make the mistake of falling in love with the first plant you see! Finding a completely healthy plant, like finding a good watermelon at the grocery store, can be a bit of a process, one that requires a touch of patience, so use the following tips to ensure you take home the most robust plant(s) in the store. These are the exact things I look for when browsing the plant aisles.

New growth: Fresh new leaves are one of the first and most obvious signs that you're looking at a healthy houseplant. That's not to say that a plant can't produce new foliage under the stress of pests or disease, but when a plant is really suffering, it often won't produce new leaves—at least not healthy ones! You'll learn more about this in chapter 7 (page 141), which covers troubleshooting, but no new growth may indicate that a plant is currently not living its best life. Also: If the newest leaves have blemishes, such as browning, put that baby down and step away. Healthy plants will have new leaves that are true to form and without blemishes. Even if the new leaf hasn't fully developed, inspect it closely to ensure you've got a healthy one.

Pests: Before heading to the checkout counter, do yourself a favor and inspect the plant for pests. This process shouldn't take long—just a minute will do—but taking the time to be thorough could play a huge part in your success as a plant parent, not to mention potentially saving you the headache of treating other plants already in your collection if you accidentally bring pests home on your new plant. Make sure you have adequate lighting, then select a few leaves and gently turn them over to reveal their undersides—this is where most pests hide. You'll learn more about pests in chapter 7 (page 141), including what to do if you do bring them home, but for now, keep in mind that many houseplant pests are very small, so look carefully! If you see anything suspicious, consider using the macro setting on your phone's camera to inspect more closely. If you don't know what you're looking for, it'll be a huge help to research what houseplant pests look like so your brain knows what to search for when the time

My Top-Five Beginner-Friendly Plants

For a plant to make this list it must tolerate a wide range of average indoor conditions and, most important, a wide range of lighting conditions. Here are five plants that I've found most people to be successful with, even beginners:

- Aglaonema
- Golden pothos
- Heartleaf philodendron
- Snake plant
- ZZ plant

While these are excellent plants for newbies, the best plant for a beginner is one whose needs are a good match for the person's space, habits, and lifestyle. If you'd like to learn more about these plants and see if they're a good fit for you, part two has all their care guides and more.

Plant Semantics

"Root-bound" is the most common way to describe roots growing out of the pot, but that condition is more technically called "pot-bound." "Root-bound" actually describes a plant that has grown so many roots they start to grow around one another to the point they're choking each other out, sort of like when you're on a road trip with all your kids in the same car—sooner or later the small space drives everyone crazy. Pot-bound is the same thing, except it hasn't gotten to the point of damaging the plant. I have never seen a houseplant become truly root-bound. If you think your plant is declining from roots coming out of the drainage holes, it's more likely you're not keeping up with the increased watering and fertilizing demands rather than the roots causing harm.

comes. Also: Be on the lookout for sticky deposits, which can be a sign of pests.

- **Healthy roots:** You're first going to notice signs of an unhealthy plant by what you see above the soil level—think yellow leaves or leaves with crispy edges—but generally, the true health of a plant happens beneath the soil in the roots. When shopping, don't be afraid to pick up a plant for a peek at its bottom drainage holes. If you spot roots, then you're dealing with a plant that has grown healthy roots all throughout the soil. How wonderful! If you don't see any roots, that doesn't mean the plant is unhealthy, just that it doesn't have as many roots. As long as it checks all the other boxes in the houseplant buying guide, feel confident that you're purchasing a healthy plant.

IS IT GOOD OR BAD TO BUY A ROOT-BOUND PLANT?

This next idea will ruffle some feathers, but I'm OK with that. When someone says a plant is root-bound, what they mean is that there are so many roots in the pot that they have nowhere else to go and are climbing out of the pot in search of more soil. You'll usually see roots coming out of the bottom drainage holes in this case, but they can climb out from the top of the pot as well. Many experts will tell you this is a bad sign and that you don't want to buy a root-bound plant. I disagree. The health of the roots is the health of the entire plant. When I see a root-bound (a.k.a. pot-bound) plant at the store, I know that plant has been well cared for and has maximum ability to take up water and nutrients from the soil with all those roots. If you want to give yourself the best chance at houseplant success, start with a vigorous root system.

To further illustrate my point, I'm going to let you in on another industry secret: You can't always trust that the potted plants you find at the store have adequate roots. In fact, checking for strong root systems is something we practice at our store when our weekly plant shipments arrive from wholesale suppliers. Several times a month our team finds dozens of plants that come right out of the soil when given a gentle tug, indicating a shallow root system, or no root system at all! If there aren't enough roots to sustain the plant, you may notice early, rapid decline due to the roots' inability to take up enough water and nutrients to keep the plant healthy. Imagine if you had to get all your food through a tiny straw, but you could use the straw only while the sun was shining. If you think of that straw as a plant root, you can see how it would be difficult to get all the nutrition you need on a daily basis. If you were unable to consume the calories you needed in that time frame, you would become weaker and weaker, inviting illness and more. A solution to this problem would be to use multiple straws (roots) at the same time, increasing your nutrient uptake in the same window of opportunity, while the sun is out. If plants need water and nutrients to stay healthy and fight disease and pests, it stands to reason that the more ability they have to take in that water and those nutrients, the better.

One of the reasons people say it's bad for a plant to be root-bound is because the roots "need room to grow!" That's fine, but is the plant showing any signs of distress because roots are coming out of the bottom drainage holes? No. Can you give it a bigger pot when you get home? Yes.

Nutrient deficiency is another common rebuttal to my love for root-bound plants. It's true that the more roots there are in the pot, the less growing medium (soil, generally) there is in the pot. Since soil is your main source of nutrients for the roots, it stands to reason that the more root-bound your plant is, the more prone it will be to nutrient deficiencies that can cause a host of problems, including stunted growth. However, as you'll learn more about in chapter 5 (page 102), most houseplant soil isn't soil! In fact, the ingredients that make up most houseplant soils on the market have little or no nutritive value. This means it's up to us to provide plants with nutrients, which is why fertilizer is so important. My argument here is that if I have a root-bound plant and there are no longer sufficient nutrients in the "soil," I'll just continue to water my plant with fertilizer that meets all my plant's nutritional needs.

Watering issues are yet another reason root-bound plants have a bad reputation. If you take a root-bound plant and give it a good soak, the water runs right through it with little to no delay. Won't this cause dehydration issues? I'm not saying these are the most convenient houseplants, but that doesn't mean being root-bound is unhealthy for the plant. Sure, a root-bound plant is going to need to be watered more frequently than one that's not root-bound, but that's a much easier problem to combat than overly saturated soil that takes too long to dry out. Don't get me wrong—repotting is not a bad thing, but plants don't decline from being root-bound. They may exhibit signs of dehydration and nutrient deficiency, but those are water and fertilizer problems and not a direct result of an abundance of roots.

A Quick Recap

- Beautifully curated plant photos in the media should not be used for care advice, especially when it comes to plant placement.
- Where you buy your plant may play a bigger role in your success than you think.
- Mature, established plants are more hardy and easier to grow than baby plants.
- Randomly guessing in plant care is a bad idea.
- Getting wrapped up in all the "must do" plant advice you see online is also a bad idea.
- Your success will grow when you prioritize the plants' needs instead of where they'll look best.
- When buying a plant, look for healthy roots, new growth, and clean leaves.
- A root-bound (pot-bound) plant has so many roots that they are growing out of the pot, but since the health of the roots is the health of the entire plant, being root-bound isn't necessarily a bad thing.

CHAPTER THREE

See the Light!

When it comes to houseplant care, there's no technical aspect more important to understand than light. To explain just how important light is for your plants, I'm going to tell you about my very first houseplant, an aloe vera. I watched my dad grow aloe at my childhood home in Oregon, and I figured a nice medicinal plant would not only add to the decor and warmth of my first home with Erika but also be easy to grow, and practical too. My dad kept his aloe near a window and didn't water it very often. With only these vague memories from childhood, I got my own aloe, repotted it into a large wooden pot, and placed it near our living room window with more confidence than I deserved.

Week after week my poor plant looked more and more pitiful. Leaves would wrinkle, and I'd water. Leaves would yellow, and I'd water more. We've all seen those videos where a sad-looking plant is watered and it springs back to life, but despite my best efforts, that aloe looked worse and worse. It was time to consult the Internet, like any self-respecting millennial would.

Upon googling "aloe vera care," I was pleased by how many articles and blog posts had been written on the matter. However, my excitement soon turned to dismay. The first article recommended my plant be in full sun. "Full sun outside?" I thought. I knew for sure I'd never seen my dad's aloe outside, so that couldn't be true. I clicked on the next article, which said to put my aloe in "bright, indirect light" and to "let the soil dry between waterings." That kind of made more sense. I still had questions, though. The location my plant was in seemed bright to me, and there definitely weren't any direct light rays hitting the plant. That had to mean it was in bright, indirect light, right?

"If the light is right, then it must be a watering issue," I thought. That second article said to let the soil dry between waterings. Did that mean *all* the soil in the pot should dry out between waterings, or did it mean only the soil I could see? After all, how could I know if the soil at the bottom of the pot was dry if I couldn't see it or touch it? I assumed it had to be the soil I could see.

All my effort was for naught, as each day the plant continued to look worse, until one morning I found my aloe completely tipped out of its pot without a single root attached to the leaves. All of them had rotted away, leaving nothing to anchor the plant in the soil! There was also a foul odor coming from the pot—I would later realize that was the distinctive, unpleasant smell of root rot. Frustrated with my failure, the waste of money, and the fact that all my Internet research left me with more questions than answers, I threw out the plant, washed the wooden pot, and filled it with some decorative balls we had lying around.

Does this sound like you? Have you experienced similar frustration with plant-care instructions and just how vague they are? In the days following my first plant failure, I couldn't get out of my head the fact that I wasn't able to keep this plant alive. Mostly, I couldn't believe how much plant-care advice differed from article to article. Instead of giving up under the guise of "plants hate me" and "I must not have a green thumb," I set out to learn how plants work and how to take care of them. If humans have been tending to plants for hundreds of years, there must be absolute answers out there somewhere! What I found in my research and then confirmed through my own experience is what this chapter is all about, and in hindsight, it's what inspired my work with plants and led us to open our shop and teach others what I learned. It changed my life.

THE ROLE OF LIGHT

I want you to imagine a factory—a sugar-making factory. This factory has a bunch of moving parts, people coming and going, all working in harmony toward a common goal: making sugar. At a very basic level, this is what plants are—sugar-making factories! But instead of producing sugar to sell, they make it for themselves. It's their fuel. That's right—our green friends are basically like the character Buddy from the movie *Elf*. Sugar is their food source. Lucky for them, and us, plants make their own food—their own sugar—by way of photosynthesis. An important part of plant care is understanding that if plants don't get enough sunlight to produce sugar, they will eventually decline. In fact, light drives *all* functions of a plant, which is why I started this chapter by stating that light is the most important aspect of plant care to understand.

If you're following along closely, you may have realized that plants are not only sugar-making factories but also solar-powered sugar-making factories. Are you thinking what I'm thinking? Plants were "going green" way before the rest of the world! Back to serious talk. Do you see why light is so important to plants? Light is the energy source that drives the engine that makes the food that helps keep a plant healthy.

PLANT DIETS

Although there are similarities among all plants, each has its own unique diet or dietary needs. And when I say "diet," I'm talking about their light diet. This is where the terms "bright light," "direct light," "bright indirect light," "medium light," and "low light" come into play. There are some plants that tolerate living only in the brightest light. That is, the brightest light

we can offer in a typical indoor environment. Anything other than right in front of a window, with no obstructions on the other side of that window, and a bright-light-diet plant will decline, or at least not grow true to its natural form.

The fiddle-leaf fig is a great example of a plant with a bright-light diet. Unfortunately, fiddle-leaf figs have earned a reputation for being difficult. This is because design magazines, social media, TV, and movies often depict them in areas where they couldn't possibly thrive long-term, such as tucked in a corner or next to a staircase twenty feet from a window. These images in the media lead people to think their fiddle-leaf fig can live in similar spots in their own home. They won't. And when these trees start to decline as a result, the owners blame the plant for being fickle or hard to grow, when they most likely weren't giving their plant enough light. Word to the wise: Don't trust interior designers with your plant care! Their job is to put plants where they look aesthetically pleasing, not where they'll thrive over a long period of time.

Other plants will tolerate low light. I use the word "tolerate" because there's a common misconception that when a plant is deemed a "low light" plant, it must live in low light. This is not the case. In fact, many plants that the houseplant industry calls "low light" plants grow in full sun in their natural habitat. Full sun is what the roof of your car gets as you're driving down the highway—a far cry from the amount of light a plant would receive anywhere indoors. It's important to keep in mind that in true low light (I'll explain exactly what that means soon) plants will not maintain their shape and vigor, and sometimes even their color, long-term. This even includes snake plants, which are known to be one of the most low-light-tolerant plants in the world!

To further illustrate this idea, I like to relate bright light and low light to something we humans are more familiar with—calories. Calories come from food, and we need them to survive. They are our energy source. There's some wiggle room in exactly how many calories you should eat per day, depending on factors like gender, activity level, and current state of health. But according to the most recent dietary guidelines issued by the Office of Disease Prevention and Health Promotion, adults should generally consume between 1,600 and 3,000 calories per day.

What would happen if you restricted your intake to only five hundred calories per day? Over time, you'd lose weight. Keep it up even longer and you might find yourself getting weaker. If this calorie restriction went on for too long, your body's ability to fight off disease and illness would also be compromised.

Plants are like us in this way, as they also have benchmark requirements for daily light consumption. What we call daily calorie intake, plants call daily light integral, which is the amount of light that hits a certain area (leaves in this case) over a twenty-four-hour period. When given enough light, plants can grow, thrive, and more easily fight off pests and disease.

Give them too little energy from light for a long enough period, and plants' ability to thrive and fight off pests and diseases diminishes. They might live with less light, but they won't flourish like they would in bright light.

HOW TO DETERMINE THE RIGHT LIGHT FOR YOUR PLANTS

Remember my aloe vera? One of the many things I got wrong with that plant was not giving it enough light. Following the recommendations I read online, which suggested that it needed "bright, indirect light," didn't help me, because from my perspective, it *was* in a bright area and light rays weren't directly hitting the leaves. The problem I have with using terms like "bright" without offering further explanation is that they are subjective. An area one person might consider bright might not be thought so by

the next person. There's a bit of debate on the subject, but it's generally believed that people with light-colored eyes are more sensitive to light than people with dark-colored eyes. I have blue eyes, which means I'm likely going to perceive any given well-lit area as being brighter than someone with brown eyes—like my wife, Erika—will.

If we all have different perceptions of how bright any given light is, how can we be expected to get the light for our plants right using the same terminology? I'd argue that we can't, at least not consistently. I'd also argue that most people end up guessing what "bright" means, and when you're guessing whether your plant is getting the right light—the most critical aspect of plant care—you're going to get it wrong from time to time. This is why I choose to use foot-candles (fc) to determine whether my plants are getting enough light. Most likely, you've never heard of foot-candles, but discovering foot-candles changed the houseplant game for me. I went from having a few plants that were doing OK to having dozens of plants thriving inside our home.

A foot-candle is a unit of illumination; it's how we measure light intensity. A single foot-candle is the amount of light you would get from a candle that is one foot away. Candles have become outdated as a primary light source, so there are other ways to measure light intensity, such as lux and lumens, but in the world of plants, foot-candles are still a common unit of measurement. This is especially true at colleges and universities across the United States where plants are being studied, as plant scientists need to record accurate light data to grow plants successfully.

Understanding Foot-Candles

I learned about foot-candles when I was researching care for my little aloe vera and stumbled on a university study describing proper light for aloe vera in a way I'd never encountered before. They recommended 1,000 fc for vigorous growth. I quickly searched for "plant light fc" and found the answer I'd been looking for all this time. Not only did I learn that there's a way to accurately and objectively measure light but I also discovered that my suspicions were right. People were studying how to take care of plants, and if they were studying them, then there must be science involved, and science is all about data. Listed out, right in front of me, were dozens of common houseplants and exactly how many foot-candles each plant needed to produce healthy growth, all based on university research. And while different foot-candle measurements correspond to terms like "bright light," which is 1,000 fc or more, rather than being vague and subjective, foot-candles are specific and objective.

"Why are houseplant enthusiasts guessing about light if there's a tool that measures light definitively?" I wondered. "It must be a super-expensive instrument only well-funded institutions can afford." With some trepidation, I searched the Internet for how to measure foot-candles. The first hit was an ad for a light meter that would measure my light in foot-candles, guaranteeing I would put my plants in the appropriate lighting, and for $34.95, I couldn't resist.

People have obviously been successfully owning plants for eons without a light meter, and many people may not want yet another gadget in their home. The last few sentences may have even triggered an eye roll. I understand! But like guessing with your houseplant lighting, you can also guess if the chicken you're cooking has reached an internal temperature of 165°F, making it safe to eat, or you could get a $10 meat thermometer and know for sure.

When the light meter arrived, I was off to the races, checking light exposure all over the house. It was at this moment that a huge weight lifted off my shoulders. All the confusion and frustration that had built up inside me from every article, blog post, and video on plant lighting that I'd consumed just melted away. Up to this point, keeping plants had felt like something that should be easily understandable, and yet for some reason I couldn't wrap my brain around how to get it right. But armed with my new light meter, I no longer felt like my plant goals and visions of beautiful, thriving greenery around the house were out of reach.

How to Choose and Use a Light Meter

There's no shortage of light meters on the market today, so I'll guide you through what to look for when shopping. Let me start by saying that phone apps for measuring light aren't a great idea. Current phones simply don't have the technology required to give an accurate reading, so for now, I recommend avoiding them.

When looking for a light meter for plant care, the only thing you absolutely need it to measure is foot-candles. You'll see light meters that

measure lux and possibly even lumens, but those are not important measurements for houseplants, and those meters will often cost more than ones that measure only foot-candles. Humidity, on the other hand, is a useful measurement to have on your light meter. Although it has nothing to do with light, humidity does affect the health of plants—we'll talk about this in chapter 7 (page 141)—so it's helpful information to have. One final note on choosing a light meter: The ability to measure more than just foot-candles tends to drive up the price of light meters, but so does accuracy. In other words, more expensive light meters tend to give more accurate readings.

Once you've selected your light meter, it's important to use it properly. I often find myself saying this when giving advice or helping people with plant-care issues, as it's the theme behind most aspects of plant care: It's simple but specific!

Start by holding the sensor of your light meter on top of the canopy of your plant. This is where most of the available light will hit the leaves, and it's a great spot for getting an idea of the type of light your plant is receiving. However, you can also measure light hitting other parts of the plant if you want to record more data. From there, I recommend tilting the sensor toward the nearest light source, typically a window. I like to move the sensor around a little to ensure I'm getting an accurate picture of the light reaching my plant. You want to avoid pointing the sensor at physical objects that obstruct light, such as blinds, curtains, covered patios, trees, or your neighbor's house.

This reading will give you a sense of the kind of light your plant receives at that particular time of day under those particular weather conditions. For that reason, I want you to take light readings at different hours to paint an even clearer picture of the light your plant is working with throughout the day. I recommend taking a measurement in the morning, just as the sun is fully visible in the sky; at noon; and in the evening, before the sun begins to set. The most valuable reading you can take is during the four hours of the day that you feel your plant is getting the most amount of light—that is, when it's receiving the most foot-candles. This four-hour block of time will differ depending on what time of year it is, where you live, and what direction your light source is coming from. Let's break down each of those elements so you have a clear understanding of why they matter.

Light Throughout the Seasons

When it comes to how much light your plant is getting, the time of year is important to consider. During the spring and summer months, our days are longer, and you can expect, at most, about fifteen hours of light, which leaves about nine hours of darkness. During the fall and winter months, our days are shorter, leaving us with, at most, about nine hours of light and fifteen hours of darkness. Keeping this in mind will better prepare you for the changes your plant might endure as light exposures become greater during certain times of year and diminish during others. The practical application here is knowing that your plant might benefit from being moved to a different location depending on the time of year.

To demonstrate what I mean, let's return to the daily light integral I mentioned earlier. I'm going to give you an example that isn't exactly how it works, but it's an easy way to understand the concept without getting too far into the weeds. Let's say your plant has a daily light integral of 4,000 fc per day, which means it needs to get that much light most days to stay healthy. It doesn't matter if your plant meets those needs by being in 2,000 fc for two hours, 1,000 fc for four hours, or 500 fc for eight hours, as long as the total amount adds up to 4,000 fc, thereby meeting the daily light integral requirements.

During the long days of summer, your plant may produce healthy growth farther away from the window, because even though it may be in lower light, it's *sustained* low light. This is the "500 fc for eight hours" example. In the winter months, your plant may still get 500 fc in this location, but the days are shorter, and as a result, your plant may not have enough time to reach the daily light integral of 4,000 fc. By moving your plant closer to the window, you're allowing it to gorge on brighter light so it can reach the daily light integral within the shorter time frame that winter allows.

In reality, your plant is absorbing photons, but in my example, I've simplified this scenario in two ways—first, by using foot-candles since they're easy to measure, and second, by applying terms like "bright," "medium," and "low" to those foot-candles. When you read about a plant needing bright, medium, or low light, that's based on an expert's estimate that if your plant is in that amount of foot-candles, you're likely to reach its daily light integral.

Guess the Foot-Candles!

Ready for a nerdy plant game? I call it "Guess the Foot-Candles"! Position your face among the leaves of your plant and peek out the window. Can you guess how bright the light is just by looking outside? Make your guess, then measure the light with your light meter. Bright light is 1,000 fc or more, medium light is 250–999 fc, and low light is 100–249 fc. Playing this game will train your brain to understand the different light levels with a science-backed understanding. Before long, you likely won't even need a light meter to get the lighting right for your plants.

But a word of caution: Don't play this game in public. It might even be a good idea to only play this game at home or in the company of other planty friends. Non-plant people already think we're crazy, and they don't need more evidence to back that up!

Seriously, though, being able to accurately determine light simply by looking at a plant's view of the sky from its perspective will alleviate so much of the stress and doubt that can come from determining whether your plant is getting enough light. The trick to ascertaining this critical information may make your friends and family question your sanity, but it will also help you derive lasting joy from this beautiful, rewarding hobby.

In much more infrequent cases, your plant might benefit from being moved away from the window during the winter months because it's receiving more intense light. The first reason to consider moving your plant is trees outside losing their leaves, which means brighter exposure. During the spring and summer, when your outside trees are full of leaves, they might block just enough sunlight to keep your green babies inside from getting leaf scorch, something we'll talk about in chapter 7 (page 141). Once those leaves fall, your plant might not be able to handle such intense light, resulting in damaged leaves. This isn't likely to kill your plant, but it's nice to be aware of the possibility so that you can avoid damaging your plant at all.

The second reason you may need to move your plant away from the window during winter is the position of the sun. In our plant store, we have two large south-facing windows on either side of the front door. For most of the year, any plants we put in front of these windows thrive in the bright light, but as winter approaches, the sun gets lower and lower in the sky, which can negatively impact plants. One day those plants in front of the window are doing great, and the next, they all get leaf scorch! Again, these two examples aren't terribly common, but they are helpful to know about, just in case.

Light and Where You Live

Regardless of where you live, the sun always rises in the east and always sets in the west, so if your plant is in an unobstructed east-facing window, you can expect it to receive higher levels of light in the morning than in the evening. The reverse is true if your plant is in an unobstructed west-facing window: It's going to receive higher levels of light in late afternoon and evening than in the morning.

However, light exposures differ depending on where you live. In the northern hemisphere, because Earth is tilted, sun exposure is greatest in the south and never actually hits the north. That's not to say there's no light coming from north-facing windows, but if you live in the northern hemisphere, you'll never see the physical sun from a window facing directly north.

The opposite is true if you live in the southern hemisphere. There, north-facing windows have the longest exposure to the sun, while south-facing windows have no exposure to the sun. Knowing this comes in handy when you're deciding where to put plants that need bright light. You can usually take the exposure that never sees the sun right off the list of possibilities.

The Direction of Your Light Source: S>W>E>N

I touched on this earlier, but here's a tad more insight on the direction of light. In the northern hemisphere, it's easy to remember the light hierarchy as S>W>E>N. South is our longest sunlight exposure, and often the brightest, followed by west, then east, and, finally, north. North exposures generally do not get enough light year-round to keep your "bright light" plants thriving. One of the nice things about S>W>E>N is that it is consistent throughout the year. However, remember that light exposures do differ depending on where you live; this changes the light hierarchy, but in a very simple way. If you're in the southern hemisphere, you simply flip the first letter with the last letter. In other words, the southern hemisphere light hierarchy is N>W>E>S.

While this system is quite straightforward, it's important to use it more as a guide, not a rule. A south-facing window with a covered patio that blocks out the light on the other side will not receive as much light as an east-facing window with no obstructions, so don't assume that the best light in your space is always going to be south facing.

THE LESS SCIENCE-Y APPROACH TO MEASURING LIGHT

Despite my enthusiasm for my light meter, I know gadgets aren't for everyone, and sometimes it's just nice to be able to get a ballpark idea of the type of light your plant is getting without using any tools but the ones on either side of your nose. This is the method I teach most often, because it has immediate impact and is so easy to understand. It's also completely free.

When I developed "the plant's view of the sky," it made perfect sense! The light meter's sensor is basically an electronic eyeball that gathers data and relays it on a screen. That "eyeball" detects higher numbers when pointed at the sky and lower numbers when pointed away from the sky, or when an object like a tree comes between the window and the sky. It's so obvious. The light source, our sun, is in the sky, which means that is where the light comes from, so when a plant sees more of the sky, it receives stronger light. There's a common misconception that "houseplants" are suitable for anywhere in the house, but the truth is that all plants are meant to be kept outdoors, a small number of them can thrive on our windowsills, and only a handful will survive in locations that don't have wide exposure to the sky.

Although the idea of plants looking at the sky isn't as scientific or as accurate as actually measuring foot-candles, you can get close enough to judging proper light simply by putting your eyes at the plant's level and looking out the nearest window. This doesn't mean standing in front of your plant. It means putting your eyeballs in a position to see what your plant sees, whether it's on the floor, on a table, or even hanging from the ceiling. The more sky the plant is looking at, the brighter the light it's receiving. If you position yourself at the plant's perspective and can turn your head to either side and maintain a view of the sky, that's really bright light!

"ENOUGH" LIGHT AND WHAT THAT MEANS TO YOUR PLANT

As a plant parent, you've likely read or heard the same light descriptions I mentioned at the beginning of the chapter: bright light, bright indirect light, direct light, etc. There's a reason beyond their subjective nature that I don't use these terms without the context of foot-candles to further explain what they mean, especially when it comes to "direct light." If I had a dollar for every time I made a video describing light needs for a specific plant or discussed light in our plant shop and got the response "So it needs direct light?" I'd have at least several hundred dollars.

Direct light doesn't happen indoors unless you have the windows open, because light always has to pass through something to reach a plant inside. I delineate the difference because "direct light" can be very deceiving. Let me give you an example of a scenario I see play out way too often.

An excited plant parent buys a plant. On the way out of the garden center, or during their online research, they discover the plant they purchased needs "direct light." It's late afternoon, and the sun is about to set.

They begin moving the plant around their home searching for the spot that gets hit with direct rays of sunlight and looks good with a plant. After a short search they find a spot twenty feet from a window, where the afternoon sun's rays are peeking through the blinds. They set the plant down and snap a photo of their new, gorgeous plant basking in the golden light.

Unfortunately, this is often the last photo of their plant looking so healthy, because after a few weeks and several watering attempts, the leaves start to droop, yellow, brown, and ultimately fall off. The plant parent is going through an experience like the one I had with my aloe vera, but it's even more confusing, because every evening they're seeing direct light rays hit their plant! They try changing everything except the light because obviously it's perfect light—direct light, just as the Internet said. This often continues until the plant's eventual demise. Dejected, the plant parent starts to believe they have a "brown thumb" or are just unable to grow plants.

Does this sound like an experience you've had? As I mentioned in chapter 1 (page 20), there's no genetic predisposition to being able to take care of plants. Plants do not hate you, and they're not finicky. Plants need certain things, and if we get close enough to giving them those certain things, they will live.

The problem with the type of "direct light" described above is that it's fleeting. As the sun moves throughout the day, there will be dozens of places inside a home that get hit with light rays, but that doesn't mean a plant will live or thrive there, because in another fifteen, thirty, or sixty minutes, the light rays will be gone, and that small window of "direct light" is not enough exposure to keep your plant thriving.

Let's return to the calorie analogy. Imagine each light particle represents a caloric value. For every plant there is a certain number of calories—let's call them "light calories"—that they want to consume each day to remain healthy. This is totally not science, but it illustrates light needs in a way that's easy and familiar. Earlier I mentioned that humans generally need about 1,600 to 3,000 calories per day to maintain health, so let's give that imaginary plant we put in "direct light" the same caloric needs, just to keep things simple. If the direct rays are hitting that plant for thirty minutes, it's unlikely the plant will be "eating" long enough to consume their two-to-three-thousand-light-calorie minimum to maintain good health.

It takes a long time to chow down on all those light particles, which is why I recommend placing your plant in a spot where it receives the recommended brightness of light for at least four hours per day. This should be seen as a general guideline, and not a rule. Some plants need longer exposures to their desired brightness, while others don't need as much, but four hours gives you a solid jumping-off point from which to monitor your plant's health and adjust its placement accordingly.

WINDOW TREATMENTS

There are a variety of things people do to keep the sun out of their home, reducing indoor temperatures and the air conditioner's workload. Not everyone has the heat we deal with in Texas, but most people have one kind of window treatment or another, and each one affects the light that gets to your plants.

- Sheer curtains diffuse light so that the rays coming through the window aren't as intense. They aren't the best option for heat reduction, but it's nice that light can still get in, especially when you have plants in the room. Sheer cur-

tains reduce the number of foot-candles reaching your plants, but not nearly as much as other window treatments do.

- Shutters and blinds are thicker than sheer curtains, so they provide better insulation from heat. They're also adjustable, which provides more control over the light let into a room. You can manipulate the angle of the shutter (or blind) blades to be completely closed, letting in no light, or closer to a ninety-degree angle to let in a lot of light. It's common for shutters and blinds to be manipulated throughout the day to create a comfortable environment, but if you want your plants to be healthy, you may need to angle your shutter blades toward your plants' leaves. This is when remembering to check your plants' view of the sky is so important!

    In the morning, people often choose to angle their shutters and blinds to be about ninety degrees, flooding the room with light. If the room is bright, that must also mean the plants are getting enough light, right? But think about where plants are usually displayed. They are typically on the floor, maybe on a low shelf, or hanging from the ceiling, and all largely near a window. When your blinds are angled at ninety degrees, they are potentially blocking the plants' view of the sky, because the sky is located upward from the plants. What else is located upward from the plants? The bottom of the blinds or shutters angled at ninety degrees. Did you get a light meter yet? You'll be surprised to see the foot-candle reading jump as you angle the blades of your shutters toward the plants, letting your plants truly bathe in sunlight while also keeping the room plenty bright for humans.

- Solar screens are a dark material that's placed over windows to reduce the heat and sunlight that comes indoors, and their effect on your plants will vary, depending on the material used. Solar screens are typically made of fabric and roll down like a shade, but there are also films that adhere directly to windows. These materials are advertised to block only harmful UV rays, but they also block some visible light, which can reduce your plant's ability to photosynthesize. Plants can absolutely live perfectly fine lives with solar screens and films, but it's something to keep in mind when considering these window treatments for your space.

COMMON MISCONCEPTIONS ABOUT LIGHT

Before we wrap up natural lighting, I want to touch on a few common misconceptions about light.

Direct Light

What does "direct light" mean to you? When I ask this question to new and seasoned plant parents alike, I always get the same answer, something like this: "Direct light is when the light touches the leaves, shining directly on them." Visually, that's correct, and for most applications in our daily lives it's accurate, but when it comes to plants, I would argue that description doesn't tell the entire story, because we're talking about plants that are being kept indoors.

The easiest way I can illustrate how outside direct light is different from inside direct light is by asking this question: Have you ever gotten a sunburn indoors? I know that if I'm in direct sunlight outdoors without a protective layer or sunscreen, for even a short period of time, my skin is going to burn. However, I've never gotten a sunburn from exposing my skin to direct light indoors. This is because the sun loses a lot of intensity when it passes through glass and into our homes. The very fact that sunlight must pass through glass to reach the plants inside means that it's no longer direct light. I realize this seems nitpicky, so I'll explain why this distinction is so important in plant care.

If you've ever observed the sun as it's rising in the morning or setting in the late afternoon, you may have noticed light beams streaming into the interior of your home. These light beams are usually narrow, due to the sun's low position in the sky, and can reach far beyond the window, depending on the height of that window. New plant parents see this far-reaching, narrow light, which they consider direct light, hitting a spot fifteen feet from their window and deem that spot a perfect place for a houseplant that needs bright or direct light. It seems simple. The plant needs direct light, and the light is hitting the plant directly on the leaves, so it should be happy there, right? Unfortunately, no. If you've seen the light beams in the morning or late afternoon, you also know that they move relatively quickly as the sun rises and sets, which means that direct light is not going to shine on that plant fifteen feet from the window for very long—and almost certainly not long enough for healthy growth. The conclusion? Ditch subjective terms that allow for error and use absolute measurements, like foot-candles, resulting in fewer or no errors at all. Or at the very least, check your plant's view of the sky.

Plants Adapt to Household Lighting

We call them "houseplants," but somewhere in the world, they grow outdoors. When this is pointed out, you can almost see a physical light bulb go off in a person's brain. "Of course houseplants grow somewhere outdoors!" Because of the name we give these plants, many people believe they can put their houseplant wherever they want and it will adapt to whatever conditions exist, because, duh, it's a houseplant—it can live anywhere as long as it's in a house!

If you're thinking to yourself right now, "Tanner, nobody *actually* thinks there are plants only meant for indoors!" know that this is an extremely common belief. The truth is, it's up to us to adapt to the needs of nature and not the other way around!

Plants *Thrive* in Certain Windows

Although they're trying to be helpful, plant parents habitually give advice that leads to more frustration than anything else. Let me paint a scene for you…

A person gets a plant and starts soliciting advice. Next, someone successfully growing that same particular plant offers their guidance: "Mine does really well in a south-facing window, and I water it once a week!" The new plant owner heeds this advice, placing their own plant in their own south-facing window and watering once a week, but over time, the plant declines. The new plant parent has done the exact thing the successful plant parent did and yet they still failed. What's the problem?

Everyone's home has different conditions, and not all window exposures are the same. In this scenario, the successful grower likely has an unobstructed south-facing window, providing enough light for the plant to grow and to require water about once per week. The unsuccessful grower, on the other hand, has a big, mature tree right outside their south-facing window, creating a huge obstruction for light getting to the plant, as well as causing the soil to dry out at a slower pace. In other words: If light is responsible for processing water, and there are differing levels of light, this means that plants receiving varying amounts of light are going to dry out at different rates and therefore need to be watered at different intervals. So, the direction your window faces isn't nearly as important as the obstructions your window has.

Same Space, Same Light—Right?

Here's something I hear all too often: "I don't know what's happening with my plant! It sits right next to my other plant in the same window, and that one is doing fine!" Don't be fooled into thinking that just because a plant is sharing a surface with another plant that they're receiving the same amount of light. Remember: It's all about how much sky the plant is looking at! Always be wary of obstructions outside your window and how they can hinder the light your plant receives.

GROW LIGHTS

I'm a huge advocate for grow lights, especially if you live in a hot area like I do, where we're trying to keep the sun and heat out for most of the year. Sure, there are plants that are better suited to lower-light conditions, but grow lights dramatically open up the possibilities of what you can grow in your home. This is because they effectively replicate the characteristics of the sun that a plant needs to grow. In other words, if your plants are living in what they might consider a cave, a grow light will improve their conditions. Think of them like mini low-powered suns you can keep indoors for your plants! From cacti to ficus and even fruits and vegetables, the right grow light can grow just about anything.

An entire book could be written on grow lights, and in fact, there are books already written on that exact subject. Between light colors, types of light, proximity, how light affects certain plants, and the deep dive into the science of it all, there's a lot to cover! But I'm going to walk you through what you really need to know to make an informed decision when considering purchasing a grow light.

Do You Need a Grow Light?

There are a few questions to consider when kicking around the idea of getting a grow light for your houseplants. Most homes are going to have adequate light to grow houseplants. The question of whether you need a grow light depends on the plant you're trying to care for, as well as whether the natural light where you want to place it is enough to keep that plant happy. If you want to put a bright-light-diet plant like the fiddle-leaf fig near a staircase located fifteen feet from the closest natural light source, a grow light is your best option for keeping that plant happy. But if you want to put a plant that is more tolerant of low light, such as a snake plant, in the same location, you likely won't need to invest in a grow light. That's not to say a low-light plant wouldn't benefit from a grow light; it's simply easier to meet their light requirements, so grow lights aren't typically purchased for them. While grow lights are mostly used to supplement natural light, their technology is so advanced that they can replicate it closely enough to be a plant's exclusive light source. In fact, you can use a grow light to grow any houseplant you want in complete darkness!

What to Look for When Buying a Grow Light

Grow-light specifications can be confusing, but they're important to understand to avoid making a bad investment. The confusion is due to the fact that a grow light's quality and effectiveness aren't detectable to the human eye. In fact, a highly effective grow light could be installed right next to a regular light bulb, and you wouldn't know the difference! A variety of light colors play different roles in plant growth and it's not always obvious to our eyes if a plant is getting the light colors it needs to photosynthesize and grow as it should. A quality grow light will offer specifications in its product information or on its packaging as proof that its light will replicate natural sunlight closely enough to produce healthy growth in your plants. Here are some terms grow-light companies will (hopefully) have on their packaging to help you find the right one for your plants' needs.

- Watts are how we measure the amount of energy being used—in this case, to power a bulb. Higher wattage numbers indicate that it will take more energy for the bulb to work, but it doesn't indicate if a light will be more effective in growing plants.

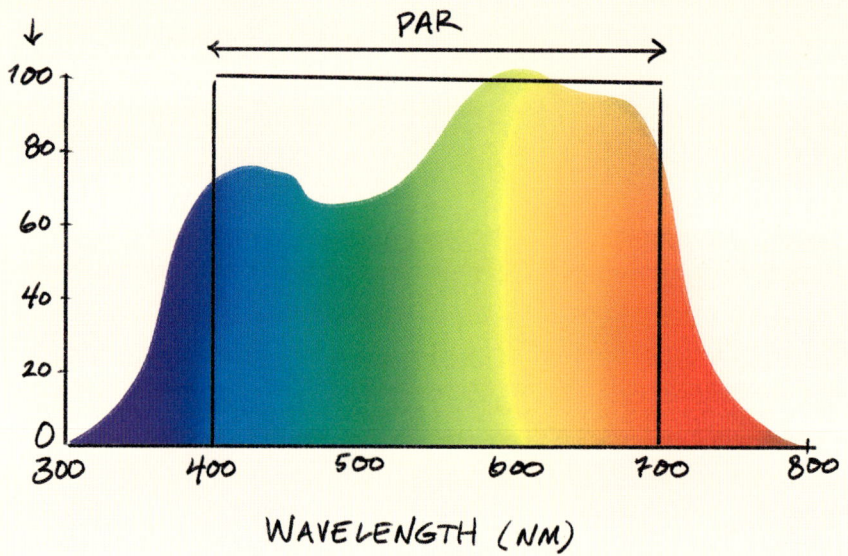

❦ PAR (photosynthetically active radiation) refers to the colors of light being emitted from a bulb that a plant can use to grow. Plants mostly use colors that fall between 400 and 700 nanometers (nm) on the light spectrum.

When a grow-light company claims their lights are "full spectrum," they're saying that the lights produce all the colors a plant needs to grow—blue, green, yellow, orange, and red. Plants are most sensitive to blue light and red light, which is why many grow lights will look purple to the human eye. PAR is nice to know for context, but it isn't the most important aspect of a grow light. Every light bulb in your home already falls somewhere within the PAR wavelengths, which is why your friend claims their ivy has been growing in a windowless bathroom for years without getting light. It has been getting light—every time your friend turns on the bathroom light.

❦ PPF (photosynthetic photon flux) is how PAR is measured and shows how many of those usable light photons are leaving your grow light every second. Imagine each light particle falling from a bulb is a tiny drop of blue, green, yellow, orange, or red paint—the colors a plant uses to grow. PPF is described in micromoles per second (µmol/s) and tells us how many of those tiny paint drops are leaving the bulb every second. Quality grow-light manufacturers will have this data available to you, and it is often in the 100–1,500 µmol/s range. PPF is nice to know for context and to calculate if your bulb is energy efficient. Higher-quality grow lights will usually use less energy (watts) to produce higher PPF numbers, whereas cheaper grow lights will often use more energy (watts) to produce the same or less PPF. You might see PPF described as "total PAR," and "PAR value" as well. When it comes to PPF values, the higher, the better!

- PPFD (photosynthetic photon flux density) measures how many usable light photons make it to the leaves of your plant. While it's good if the PPF number (usable photons leaving your light) is high, what's important is knowing how many of those photons make it from your grow light to the surface of the leaves. If we measure your grow bulb PPF and it shows one thousand drops of paint falling from it every second, PPFD is going to tell us how many of those drops hit the leaves every second. After all, what good is a grow light emitting one thousand paint drops per second if only ten of those drops make it to the plant?

A grow light's PPFD is the most important measurement for your houseplants, because it tells you how much usable light is hitting the leaves. And the more usable light that hits the leaves, the better growth you'll see in your plant. A quality grow-light company will have this data available on their website, and many will have it displayed right on the box. It's even better if this data is given for different distances, because the farther your plant gets from the grow light, the fewer paint drops will hit the leaves. You can then take the data provided by the grow-light company and compare it with the needs of the plant(s) you want to grow. If you've heard great things about a particular grow light and they don't display this information, I'd avoid it altogether. Having a high PPFD and not displaying it or offering it as part of the product specifications would be like a restaurant receiving three Michelin stars but not telling anyone!

How to Use a Grow Light

Information on how to properly set up a grow light to benefit your plants should be included with any grow light you purchase, but there are two basic concepts to keep in mind: how many hours per day your grow light needs to be on and how far away it can be from your plant.

Using our calorie analogy from earlier, we know it's important to reach the "caloric" intake necessary for growth. The problem is that unless someone has already recorded the number of calories your plant needs per day, figuring out the best position for your light will be a matter of guessing and checking.

If the grow light you purchased has its PPFD readings charted, consult that chart to determine how far away your plant should be from the grow light. I like to start with the farthest distance they've measured. From there, I recommend keeping the light on for twelve hours per day. If your plant produces new, healthy growth, maintain these parameters. If your plant isn't producing healthy growth, you'll need to either move the plant closer to the light to increase PPFD or leave the light on for longer periods of time. I've found the general range for different plants to meet their requirements to be twelve to twenty-four inches away from the leaves and ten to sixteen hours per day.

THREE SIGNS A PLANT NEEDS MORE LIGHT

Plants provide visual clues to their health; you just need to know what to look for! Saying your plant *needs* more light isn't totally correct. What I really mean is that your plant will show signs that its current lighting conditions aren't giving it what it needs to thrive. "Thriving" is a bit subjective, but for these purposes, let's define thriving as a plant growing without showing signs that it could benefit from a change in environment. Here are three signs that your plant would prefer more light:

- "Slow growth" simply means a plant is not growing as quickly as it used to. A lack of light may be the culprit. We see this on display most commonly during the winter, when the sun isn't in the sky for as long as it was in the summer. Since light drives all functions of a plant, shorter days can result in slower growth or no noticeable growth at all.
- "Leggy" describes a plant with a lot of stems but few leaves. This is also called being stretched out. Its real name is "etiolation," and we'll talk about that more in chapter 7 (page 141), but for the moment,

what's important to know is that a leggy plant is screaming for more light. Have you ever noticed the direction that leggy plant is leaning toward? That's right, they lean toward the light.

- Lack of flowers from a plant that is supposed to flower can happen for many reasons, but the most common is lack of light. Producing a flower takes a lot of energy, so a plant must be able to consume a lot of energy to make that happen. If your plant isn't flowering, start by checking the light.

MUSICAL CHAIRS, BUT FOR PLANTS

What happens in a situation where you have the *perfect* place for a plant, aesthetically speaking, but that space doesn't get enough light to keep a plant happy, and either you don't want to use a grow light or the space isn't suited for a grow light? If you like and enjoy decorating your space with plants, this will happen quite frequently. The truth is most interior spaces simply aren't naturally suited for plants to thrive in. I know, what a bummer! However, I do have one suggestion, a concept Erika refers to as "musical chairs, but for plants." I'm not sure where the game musical chairs and this idea overlap, but for some reason when I explain the idea to my clients, they totally get it. Here it goes...

I want you to get at least two plants that are tolerant to low light and have similar care needs. My favorite plants for this application are snake plants and ZZ plants, but other low-light-tolerant plants like golden pothos, *Philodendron cordatum*, Scindapsus, cast-iron plants, and certain types of ferns are also great options. Just make sure the plants you get have similar watering requirements.

The idea is that one of these plants will be on display in that perfect spot you've always dreamed of having a plant, while the other will be in a bright-light area. I call this "the recovery zone." Every couple of weeks, or whenever the plant in the poorly lit area needs to be watered, rotate the plants. This allows you to always have a plant adorning the spot that satisfies your decorative eye, but that plant will also have the chance to thrive for years to come—because it gets time in bright light.

I recommend waiting to swap the plants until the plant in the poorly lit area needs watering, because you don't want to saturate the soil of a plant and then immediately put it in poor light where it won't be able to process water efficiently—that will only increase the likelihood of root rot. This means that watering should take place only for the plant experiencing bright light, which is why I prefer to use snake plants and ZZ plants for this method, as they can go weeks without needing to be watered.

My clients often choose two or more identical-looking plants for their musical chairs so that the look is always consistent, but occasionally, a client will choose starkly different plants to keep the look fresh and new. Either approach is perfectly fine, but I like the idea of my space changing on a regular basis, and it may help your brain more easily remember a care timeline.

A Quick Recap

- Light drives all functions of plants, including their ability to produce their own food, and is therefore the most crucial aspect of plant care to understand and provide for your plant!
- With the help of a light meter, light can be measured in foot-candles (fc), which will help ensure your plant is getting the light it needs to thrive.
- You can determine the amount of light your plant is getting by observing the amount of sky your plant is looking at. The more sky it sees, the brighter the light!
- A plant should get its recommended light exposure for at least four hours per day.
- Be mindful of objects inside or out, such as trees and window treatments, that may come between the leaves of your plant and the sky. Each obstruction minimizes the amount of light your plant receives.
- During the shorter days of fall and winter, your plants may need to be moved closer to the window to receive enough light each day. Supplement with a grow light if you can't provide enough light.
- Grow lights can be used as your plant's exclusive light source or for supplementing natural light.
- When choosing a grow light, first determine your plant's light requirements, then find a quality grow light that can meet those needs.
- Your plant may benefit from brighter light if it has slow growth, has become leggy, or isn't flowering.

CHAPTER FOUR

Watering with Confidence

As I mentioned in the previous chapter, my first plant was an aloe vera. When I brought home that little plant, I was very concerned about watering. I was afraid to overwater. I was afraid to not water enough. I even questioned the quality of my water.

At that point, my houseplant-watering philosophy was that water is life-giving, so how I handled this aspect of plant care would make or break my success. Can you blame me? Overwatering is one of the most common problems you hear in conversations about houseplant care. When my aloe vera started to decline, I immediately blamed improper watering. I didn't know if I was watering too little or too much, but the aloe's droopy leaves made me think it was the former. Little did I know that my watering was making the situation worse, which is so counterintuitive!

Keeping houseplants is often portrayed as this very Zen and calming activity. Pinterest and Instagram are full of photos depicting beautiful in-home jungles, with their caretakers peacefully watering plants. The photos create an atmosphere of serenity that is so thick you might think it's a painting you can reach out and smear. Instead, your thumb double taps and scrolls to the next post. With each flick of the thumb, you can leave that feeling further behind. However, social media algorithms are incredibly good at learning what we want to see, and you're bound to have another one of those photos pop up any minute. Double tap enough times and eventually you're going to find yourself in a plant shop, excited to curate your own indoor jungle and start sharing your own vibey social media posts.

Maybe this isn't everyone's experience. Heck, it wasn't mine! My point is that the act of watering your plants is a romanticized activity that elicits as many beautiful feelings as the plants themselves. As a result, one of the most common causes of houseplant demise is overwatering. The truth about watering, as with all aspects of houseplant care, is that it's not done by intuition. An observant person might notice their plant looking dehydrated, but as you'll soon learn, you don't need to look for clues from your plant that it needs water.

Watering your houseplants should be everything you've ever dreamed it could be. It should bring a sense of calm and make you feel such a deep level of being present that every other worry is forgotten. I want you to look forward to that time with your plants and cherish that short escape, when you can appreciate something living and the part you play in its life. I'm confident we can get you there, and I hope you tag me in your inspirational jungle-watering photos when you do!

THE ROLE OF WATER

The health of a plant's roots has a direct correlation to the health of the plant. Roots need a few things to survive, and one of those things is water. A plant can have perfect lighting, but if its roots aren't getting the water they need, the plant will decline. Water is sucked up by the roots and dispersed through the plant's vascular system, reaching its trunk, stems, and leaves, keeping them hydrated, nourished, and rigid. Excess water is then released as water vapor through stomata, which are similar to the pores of your skin. This is what we call transpiration. If you've ever noticed little droplets of water on the ends of your leaves early in the morning or late at night, that's the result of the final stage of transpiration. To me, it's a cheerful reminder that I'm caring for a living creature and a welcome sight at the start of my day. However, I do recommend wiping or shaking off those water droplets to avoid possible leaf spots, which can happen when stagnant water rests on leaves for too long.

One of water's most important jobs is that it carries the nutrients that plants need to thrive. In nature, when it rains, water runs down into the nooks and crannies of the soil and picks up available nutrients along the way. Once the water reaches a plant's roots, it's packed with all the nutrients the plant needs. At home, we can mimic this process by adding fertilizer directly to the soil or to the water we add to the soil.

Watering your plant also provides cooling, which is less important when your houseplants are indoors but useful if your houseplants are like mine and get regular stints outdoors when the weather allows. This is the motivating factor that gets me to water my porch plants during those hot months.

Most important, water is a key ingredient in the sugar-making process we discussed in chapter 3 (page 53). Without water, plants cannot produce their own sugar and will eventually decline. Can you imagine trying to make chocolate chip cookies without chocolate chips? It doesn't work!

WATERING TECHNIQUES

Start by holding your wrist at a ninety-degree angle. While maintaining control of the tip of your watering can spout, slowly relax your wrist muscles and allow a gentle stream of water to flow from the spout. Circular motions around your soil are necessary.

Just kidding! Plants don't care *how* they're watered; they only care that they're watered when they need to be.

When it comes to watering techniques, there are two main methods, but the goal is always the same—thorough saturation of every speck of soil in the pot. The reason we want complete saturation is because this is your plant's opportunity to take up all the vital nutrients it needs. Plus, remember, water is a key ingredient in how a plant makes its own sugar. Imagine your plant has a mouth, which is easier to do if you think of a Venus flytrap, because they kind of do have mouths. Imagine your Venus flytrap has no roots. Instead, clenched between its teeth are five straws that each lead to a small glass of nutrient-filled water. When your flytrap is ready to suck up that concoction, would you fill only one of the glasses with water or all five?

When you fail to saturate your plant's soil, you miss the opportunity to fully "feed" your plant, because unless the soil is fully saturated, you can't be sure that your water hits all the roots in the pot. Does this mean that if you don't fully saturate your soil with each watering that your plant won't do well? Absolutely not. But when your plant is getting enough light and is potted properly in appropriate soil, giving your plant a full soak with every watering will help it grow a robust and healthy root system, and that's a good thing!

Should I Water from the Top or the Bottom?

Watering your potted plants from the top is the most traditional approach. And it makes sense, as plants growing outside also get watered from the top every time it rains. You simply pour water on the soil and gravity pulls it down, causing it to trickle through all the pockets in between the soil particles and then eventually exit through a drainage hole (or holes) in the bottom of the pot. To ensure complete saturation when top watering, I recommend not using a watering can and instead putting your plants in a sink or tub so that you can completely soak the soil. If the weather allows, you can do this outside and use a hose.

The top-watering approach allows the soil to absorb what it needs and the rest can drain off. Repeat this process several times, letting the excess water drain into the sink, tub, or ground each time. Pour water over the topsoil, let it sink in, let it drain out. Pour water over the topsoil, let it sink in, let it drain out. You cannot do this too many times! Remember, the goal is to completely soak all the soil with each watering session. Although we can't be 100 percent sure we've achieved complete coverage, three to five repetitions of watering, allowing it to sink in, and letting it drain off should do the trick and get pretty darn close.

Watering from the bottom, better known as "bottom watering," is a less traditional method but every bit as effective as watering from the top. If you want to bottom water, you'll need a few things: a pot with one large drainage hole or several small ones to let water in, a moisture-wicking medium like soil, and a separate reservoir for the pot to comfortably sit in. This is where those plastic plant "drip trays" come in handy. I also like to use decorative pots with no drainage holes, a.k.a. cache pots, for bottom watering. You'll learn more about soil composition and cache pots in chapter 5 (page 102), so don't panic if you don't know what I'm talking about.

In bottom watering, when your plant needs water, you simply pour water into your chosen reservoir—like a drip tray or a cache pot—and set your potted plant in it. When the water comes in contact with the moisture-wicking medium via the drainage holes, capillary action begins to pull the water upward. If you've ever used a paper towel or rag to clean up a liquid, you've witnessed capillary action. It helps to imagine water as a bunch of molecules that are friends. These water-molecule friends like to connect with one another, and they also like to connect with other friendly materials like paper towels, rags, sponges, and, in this case, soil.

Bottom watering is particularly effective in ensuring complete soil saturation, because it doesn't rely on gravity for disbursement. When you water from the top, water will always take the path of least resistance, and sometimes that path runs right past dry soil particles. But when you water from the bottom, capillary action ensures that nowhere gets missed. Water molecules don't skip friends—they connect with each soil particle on their way to the top of the pot.

For bottom watering, I recommend letting your plant sit in the reservoir of water until the topsoil is damp. That way you know the water has traveled from the bottom drainage holes all the way to the top, ensuring complete soil and root saturation! This process can take minutes or hours, depending on the size of the pot your plant is in and the composition of its soil. I usually wake up in the morning and fill the reservoirs of any plants that need water, then leave for work. When I get back, eight to ten hours later, all the plants have completed their watering. If it takes longer than eight to ten hours for your plant to complete its watering, you may need to check soil conditions, as compacted soil and hydrophobic soil—two things you'll learn about in chapter 7 (page 141)—can drastically slow down the bottom-watering process.

There is no "better" way to water your plants. Like I said, plants don't care how they're watered; they only care that they are watered. However, there are advantages and disadvantages to both methods.

Top watering your plant is fast and effective. You see a plant that needs water and you take it to the sink, spray it down and let it drain out a few times, then place it back in its spot. The entire process takes less than five minutes. The downsides to watering your plants from the top are minimal, but they are worth mentioning. Remember how I said water travels from the topsoil and trickles down until it escapes through the drainage holes? It's not just water that's draining but all the nutrients it picked up along the way. Every time you water your plant from the top, the soil is losing nutrients through the bottom drainage holes. Luckily, these nutrients can be easily replaced with fertilizer, but it's good to keep this in mind.

Perhaps the worst thing about top watering is the risk of leaves getting wet. I know I'm guilty of wanting to replicate rainfall for my plants, but getting water on the leaves of a houseplant can invite all sorts of harmful bacteria that can damage the leaves, even to the point of no return. This might seem ridiculous, as plants get rained on in nature and their leaves obviously get wet, but houseplants aren't in nature. They're indoors, and our homes don't provide as much light, heat, and airflow as nature does! When a plant is in its natural environment, the elements usually dry the leaves of stagnant water before problems occur.

I'd like to take this opportunity to remind you that your houseplants aren't going to be perfect. They're living creatures and they will have flaws! It's easy for us to compare ourselves with other, seemingly "better" plant parents out there, or the unrealistic (staged) photos we see on social media. But the next time you're outside, observe some of the native plants. Are they perfect, even when growing in the environment they were meant to grow in? Look at the leaves. Are any of them broken or blemished? Do you see traces of browning or yellowing? Your houseplants are living far away from their natural habitat, in a pot instead of in the ground, and with a person in charge of their every need instead of Mother Nature. Your houseplants will have flaws, but don't let those minor blemishes steal any amount of joy from your houseplant hobby!

Personally, I love bottom watering my plants, both at home and at the shop. It's passive and super effective in making sure my plants are fully watered. I mentioned earlier that I simply put my plants that need water in water-filled reservoirs before leaving for work. When I get home, I dump out any water that wasn't sucked up by the plants and is left in the reservoirs. This allows me to water a dozen plants in just five to ten minutes, which is incredibly efficient.

The biggest draw of bottom watering—passiveness—is also its biggest drawback. Watering from the bottom takes such little effort and requires such a long time to complete that it's easy to forget that a plant or two might still be sitting in water! I know this from my own experience. I also know that while it's OK to leave your houseplants sitting in water for a workday, most will suffer root rot if they're left for too long. What constitutes "too long" depends on the type of plant and the conditions, so it's impossible to give you a specific maximum time. However, what I do know, from the hundreds of plants I've bottom watered in my personal collection, along with the thousands we've bottom watered in the store, is that none of them have suffered adverse effects when left in water for a typical nine-to-five workday.

Another potential issue with bottom watering is that it's quite easy for minerals and fertilizer salts to accumulate and build up. Minerals are great for your houseplants, but too much of a good thing can cause decline. Plants are all about balance. When bottom watering your plants, there is no draining. Because the water that's now in the pot "climbed" into the soil and wasn't poured on top, there's going to be more minerals and fertilizer salts stored in that soil. This buildup will manifest itself as a white haze on your topsoil, almost like a very light dusting of powdered sugar. If your pots are made of a breathable material, such as terra-cotta or unsealed ceramic, mineral buildup can also show up there. Have you ever seen a terra-cotta pot with white hazing on the outside? That's mineral buildup.

Mineral buildup isn't likely to kill your plants, but it has the potential to burn plant tissue and hinder nutrient absorption if left unchecked. Regardless of the method you choose to water your plants, every one to three months, I recommend watering from the top with distilled water to flush out excess minerals and fertilizer salts. Distilled water contains few to no minerals, so a proper flushing will act as a reset for your plants.

HOW OFTEN SHOULD YOU WATER YOUR HOUSEPLANTS?

When I stumbled upon the idea of foot-candles to determine proper plant lighting, I was overjoyed. Having a definitive method to ensure my plants received the right amount of light was a huge piece of the plant puzzle for me. The next bit I had to tackle was the mystery of watering. I was already aware of traditional methods used to determine whether a plant needs water, including the "finger test," where you jam a finger a couple of inches into the soil and feel for moisture. If it's dry, you water; if it's wet, you leave it alone. I'd also witnessed experienced houseplant parents simply pick up their plants by the pot and wave them up and down, judging by feeling their weight. And at my local garden center, they recommended a moisture meter, which is a tool with a metal probe on one end that you stick in the soil to get a moisture-level reading.

The idea of using a moisture meter was exciting, as I had had such a breakthrough experience with a light meter. However, I soon learned they can be quite problematic, because multiple factors that have nothing to do with moisture can skew the actual moisture reading.

Again, like the good millennial I am, I consulted the Internet for answers. Suggestions such as "water when the top inch of soil feels dry" seemed like a good idea, but I couldn't see how different types of plants could have the same watering needs. Plus, the volume of an inch of soil changes with each pot size, so how could this "one inch" rule apply to all plants regardless of pot size? As soon as an article used phrases like "keep the soil damp but not wet," or my favorite, "don't overwater," I immediately stopped reading. I didn't want subjective advice; I wanted specifics so I would know for sure if a plant needed water—like the light meter telling me exactly where to place my plants in relation to the sun! I was shocked and a bit dismayed to find no scientific data on the matter. Even the academic articles I read, including ones that recorded specific light levels and sometimes even soil pH levels, used only subjective terms when mentioning water—if they mentioned it at all.

Determined to make some headway, and driven by curiosity, I decided to do my own "experiments." I use that word lightly, because it was just me in my home with a bunch of unsightly plants, using my best observational skills to find clues to a more concrete understanding of plant watering. I didn't—and still don't—have a degree in anything, or even a white lab coat!

What I did have was a basic understanding of what water does for plants and how plants use water, as well as what happens when plants get watered too often and when they don't get watered often enough—two topics we'll explore in chapter 7 (page 141). Using these tidbits of knowledge, along with a certain cake-baking experience from my past, I developed a method for determining when to water potted plants, and it's helped me to never overwater again.

The "Baking Method"

Erika calls me a "hobbyist"—not of any one thing in particular, but just a hobbyist. I prefer to describe myself as curious. There are just so many things I'm interested in learning about and experiencing! When something captures my interest, I tend to obsess over it, achieve proficiency in it, and then move on to the next thing. Plants, however, are one of those hobbies that stuck, due in large part to the fact that I find plants endlessly fascinating, which drives my never-ending desire to learn more about them. Oh yeah, and the plant business Erika and I started is our entire livelihood!

In sixth grade, my obsession was chess, which began when I saw *Searching for Bobby Fischer*. Before the closing credits, I knew I needed a chess set, and within a few months, I'd studied all the books on chess at my local library. I picked up a few tricks to win games against unsuspecting friends and family members, so the next obvious step was to hold a tournament at my grandparents' restaurant. The grand prize? A cake baked by me, a sixth grader, who had never baked a cake in his life.

That chess tournament didn't turn out as my childhood heart had hoped—I was tricked by the easiest trap in the book and lost—but what I learned while baking the grand prize cake would change my adult life forever. That might sound like an overstatement, and to an extent it is, but keep reading and I'll explain what I mean.

After mixing the batter, preheating the oven, and licking the spoons, I put my cake in the oven. When the oven timer sounded, I had to make

sure the batter had been cooked all the way through. An easy way to do this is to insert a small knife or toothpick into the center of the cake, then remove it. Wet batter on your knife or toothpick indicates your cake needs to bake for longer, while a dry knife or toothpick means the cake is cooked all the way through. Years later I realized that this very same method could be utilized to determine how far down into the pot your plant's soil is wet. This is how I came up with what I call "the baking method," though I recommend using different tools for your cakes and plants!

As I was thinking about ways to measure soil moisture, my mind wandered to that first cake-baking experience. I'd used a knife or toothpick to determine if the batter was cooked dozens of times since and decided to try it with my plants. Using a wooden chopstick from our last takeout meal, I shoved the blunt end about four inches into the soil of my prized *Monstera deliciosa*. When I removed it, I found what I was looking for: wet soil clinging to the chopstick! What was even better was that the wet soil was only sticking to the bottom inch or so, which told me that the first three inches from the top were dry. Or put another way, the soil wasn't wet until three inches down into the pot. I spent the next hour checking all my plants, if for no other reason than it gave me a little thrill.

I hesitate to say I invented this method, because it's so simple that I'm convinced other plant parents have used the same or a similar approach. But the baking method has become an integral part of my teaching via social media, and it undoubtedly helped grow my following. It's also an idea that has spread. In fact, if I don't mention the baking method when I talk about watering in an online video, I always get a bunch of comments from folks suggesting the approach. I've been teaching this method for the last six years, so it's amusing and heartwarming to have others recommend it to me!

These days I use aluminum or plastic knitting needles to check the moisture levels in soil, mostly because I have a habit of leaving them in the soil and wooden chopsticks eventually rot. However, feel free to use anything with a blunt tip and a diameter similar to a pencil. No matter what object you choose, it'll be just as thrilling.

And sometimes, all you need is a little thrill, something to get excited about. Plants do that for me with every intentional interaction. Isn't it funny how plants can blend into the background of our lives? They're the most incredible life-giving creatures on the planet, yet it's so easy to forget to appreciate them. Even the most showy and vibrant plants can seem invisible, but I'm telling you that there is magic and wonder to be found with every plant if you take a few really conscious moments to be grateful for them. I like to put everything down and get up close with a plant. I touch the leaves and turn them over in my hands. I bend them to see how they move and how they look in different lighting, hoping to discover something new—new to me, at least. I like to ask myself questions about the plant, like "Why does this plant have so many colors?" and "What advantage does this leaf shape give the plant?" I challenge you to spend one minute being curious with a plant and see how you feel afterward.

Back to watering: Using my trusty chopstick, I was able to discern, with surprising accuracy, the moisture levels in my plants' soil, but I still wasn't quite sure how to utilize this information to determine when to water my plants. Since I was still in the mood for experimenting, I decided to do more "research."

In my attempts to uncover the secrets of plant watering from the Internet, I learned about wilting and how drooping might indicate that a plant needs water. Using this built-in communication from the plant, I figured I could see how wet the soil was when a plant began to wilt. To be totally transparent here, this part of my plant-parenthood journey included a lot of plant abuse, mostly in the form of dehydration.

Different Plants, Different Watering Needs

The experiment was simple. Following the readings from my light meter, I would put a plant in the correct amount of foot-candles, soak the plant's soil in water, and then wait for it to wilt. Some plants wilted within the first week, while others took several weeks. Some even went more than a month before showing any signs of decline! As soon as I saw a plant begin to wilt, I'd bust out my chopstick and check its moisture level, then record my findings.

My ferns and calatheas wilted very quickly—most would droop when the soil was about one-quarter to one-half of the way dry. My succulents lasted the longest. After a month of no water and no outwardly visible changes, I used my chopstick to find absolutely no moisture in their pots. My *Monstera deliciosa* and philodendrons were somewhere in the middle;

they wilted when their soil was about one-half to three-quarters of the way dry.

Thanks to the data I'd collected, I now had a foundation for knowing when to water my plants. Wilting causes stress for plants, which slows down growth and invites pests, among other things. If I knew when my plants would wilt, then I could routinely check moisture levels and simply water before they reached that point. The next question I needed to answer was how dry the soil should be before I watered. If a plant began wilting when moisture was found three-quarters of the way down the pot, should I water when moisture reached halfway down the pot? A quarter of the way down the pot?

Succulents were the first to be checked off my list. At 100 percent dry, they showed no signs of wilt or any other stress, so I watered them only when all the soil in the pot was dry. My succulents thrived with this method, and I've never looked back. The non-desert-dwelling plants required more trial and error... and a lot of dead roots!

Since I knew my monstera would wilt with moisture levels measuring about three-quarters of the way down, I went ahead and watered it when the moisture was halfway down the pot. The plant didn't wilt, and it also showed no signs of root rot. I then watered when the moisture was one-quarter of the way down and there were still no signs of decline or root rot. I pushed it one step further by watering just as the topsoil dried. After a few weeks of watering my monstera every few days, only as the topsoil dried out, it began showing signs of decline by way of new leaves yellowing—a classic sign of root rot, as we'll discuss in chapter 7 (page 141).

Testing the watering needs of all my different plants went on for some time until I had them all figured out. My recordings looked something like this:

Monstera deliciosa. 800–1,300 fc. Wilts at ~3/4 dry. OK to water between 1/4 and 1/2 dry.

Furry feather calathea. 500–1,000 fc. Wilts at ~1/2 dry. OK to water when topsoil dries.

How Plants Store Water

I was ecstatic to develop a watering method that worked for me. However, there was one little issue still nagging at me: Why can some plants go longer than others without watering, and is there a way to know how dry a plant's soil should be before watering that doesn't involve testing? I thought about my succulents and the fact that they can go several weeks without watering. I also remembered learning in elementary school how cacti in the desert can store water to survive periods of drought and wondered if other plants have water-storage systems.

When I looked at the succulents on my windowsill, it was apparent that their plump leaves stored water. The ferns sitting nearby, however, had very thin leaves. There couldn't be much water storage in those paper-thin leaves, which led me to think about whether my ferns needed more frequent watering simply because they didn't have as much water storage built into their anatomy.

Over the following weeks and months, I observed and tested dozens of plants. I noted points of possible water storage by just looking at each plant. The thicker the roots, stems or trunks, and leaves of a plant, the more water storage it had and the longer it could go without watering.

If a plant had no points of water storage, it would wilt when the soil was just below 25 percent dry—or dry one-quarter of the way down. To avoid wilting, I watered the plant just as the topsoil completely dried out. This prevented wilting and didn't cause any overwatering issues like root rot.

For plants with only one point of thick anatomy for storing water, I watered when the soil was about 25 percent dry. When a plant had two points of thick anatomy, I could get away with watering when the soil was between 25 percent and 50 percent dry. When a plant had three points of thick anatomy, I would wait until the soil was 75 percent to 100 percent dry. Each of these percentages is based on letting the soil dry out enough to avoid root rot but also not letting it dry out so much that the plant wilts.

There are additional features that allow plants to store or hold on to their water longer, like their cuticle and rhizomes, but most plants you'll encounter have roots, stems or trunks, and leaves, so I rely on these three common points of anatomy and their relative thickness or thinness to give me clues to their ability to store water, which influences how much they need to dry between waterings.

What I love about watering plants this way is that it's super simple to determine how dry your soil is. It doesn't take skill, intuition, or a degree, and you don't need a fancy tool. Most important, it's effective!

Seven Reasons Soil Dries at Different Rates

While a plant's anatomy can tell you a lot about how often it needs to be watered, there are conditions unrelated to the thickness or thinness of a plant's roots, stems or trunks, and leaves that can also play a part in how frequently it requires water. As you develop and adjust your approach to watering, keep these seven things in mind:

- **Light:** Brighter light causes plants to work harder, increasing their water consumption.
- **Temperature:** Increased temperatures, whether indoors or out, accelerate soil's water evaporation process. Remember that indoor temperatures can increase in the fall or winter when home heating systems, or even a fireplace, kick into use.
- **Pot size:** The more soil that surrounds the roots of a plant without actually coming into contact with the roots, the longer the soil will retain moisture. And in a larger pot, there's going to be more soil.

- **Pot material:** Some pot materials, such as terra-cotta, are porous, allowing oxygen to pass through to the soil, which causes it to dry more quickly. Materials that don't breathe, such as plastic, will keep your soil wetter for longer.
- **Ambient humidity**: Dry air causes soil to dry faster, while increased humidity causes soil to dry more slowly.
- **Airflow:** Whether indoors or out, increased airflow from a fan or wind dries the air as it passes over the surface of the soil, drying it out more quickly than stagnant air.
- **Soil composition:** Soil is composed of ingredients that shed or retain water, and some blends will dry faster than others depending on the ratio of water-draining to water-retaining ingredients.

WATER QUALITY

Because we refer to plants that we keep indoors as "houseplants," we often forget that these plants are meant to grow outside and in different parts of the world, which means that in their natural environment most of them are being watered by natural sources, including rivers and lakes, but mostly rainfall. It may come as a surprise, then, to learn that the quality of the water you use can affect their health. If you only ever water your plant with water from your tap, in most cases your plants will likely be fine, but there are a few things to keep in mind about quality. Here's what you need to know.

Tap water, the most common water folks use for their plants, varies in quality from city to city. Municipal water must be treated for bacteria, salinity, and turbidity, among other things. What's important to remember here is that your tap water is treated for human consumption, which is a far cry from what rainwater offers to plants. Think of it like gasoline for your car. Sure, it'll run on the cheapest gas—we're all guilty of filling up with "regular"—but the overall health and performance of your vehicle may improve with premium gas.

The same is true for your plants. When you soak them with water that is closer to what they would get in nature, the water they're designed to use, they can experience less stress and better performance. Water from your tap isn't likely to have immediate negative effects on your plants, but if you notice browning on the tips or edges of your plant leaves, poor wa-

Humidity and Misting Your Houseplants

"Houseplants" as we know them actually grow outdoors somewhere in the world, mostly in tropical or subtropical climates. But not every plant found in nature can be a houseplant. What makes a houseplant a houseplant is its ability to adapt to average in-home environments. In other words, these are plants that will grow under the conditions that a typical indoor environment would provide, including lighting, temperature, and humidity. In fact, before they are considered for commercial growing, plants are tested under these conditions for weeks or months to ensure they'll be a good product for us crazy plant people—I mean, for the consumer.

Because most houseplants grow under tropical conditions, which includes higher-than-average humidity, an old wives' tale about the value of misting your plants has stood the test of time. The basic idea is that misting the leaves of a plant will increase the humidity around the plant, mimicking their natural tropical environment. This is actually true…sort of. The problem is that for misting to increase humidity to the point of being effective, you'd have to do it so dang often it would be near-impossible to keep up with for the average person. This is because the effects of misting only last as long as the water droplets are present on the leaves, which isn't long enough to make a difference in the health of your plant. To make sure your plant always has water droplets on its leaves would mean visiting your plant a dozen or more times per day to administer a few pumps from a spray bottle. If you're able to keep up with that schedule, you're a lot more diligent than the average plant parent—and your forearms are probably a whole lot more toned too!

Now, don't get me wrong: Increasing the humidity for your tropical or subtropical plants is a wonderful idea and absolutely beneficial, but unless you have very dry air in your home, rest assured that your houseplants will adapt to your home conditions. If you want to give a humidifier a try, I suggest a top-filling machine for convenience. Don't add any oils to it and use a cool mist setting to avoid heat damage to leaves.

Despite the fact that misting your houseplants will not have a directly positive effect on them, I do actually recommend doing it. Misting, done at any rate your current schedule allows, helps you be more in tune with the needs of your plants. It's an activity done up close and personal, which gives you a better chance of noticing any abnormal changes in your plants' leaves or soil conditions. Being attentive in this way also makes it more likely you'll notice pests before they've had the chance to get away with seriously harming your plants. We'll get into pests in chapter 7 (page 141), but if you've ever had to treat an advanced case of spider mites or mealybugs, then you know how advantageous it is to catch an infestation in its early stages, when it's *way* easier to eradicate!

ter quality could be the culprit. Consider using a higher-quality water if you want to help avoid these brown tips and edges. Collecting rainwater in a barrel is the most economical way to harvest this liquid gold from the sky. I've been known to gather buckets, vases—pretty much anything that holds water—and set them outside during a heavy rainstorm to catch water. So, the next time you see your crazy neighbor in their slippers hauling their Pyrex dishes and empty bathroom garbage cans onto the driveway during a downpour, mind your business. They have plants to water!

If you're not ready to commit to collecting rainwater, there are other options for giving your plants higher-quality water. My two favorites are reverse osmosis (RO) water and distilled water. Both are quite affordable, especially if you're only caring for a few plants, and can likely be found at your local grocery store.

OVERWATERING

I've found there's nothing plant parents fear more than the dreaded overwatering. I can't tell you how many social media videos, blog posts, and articles I've seen that recommend watering plants with a single cup of water to avoid overwatering, but this won't do your plants any favors. That's because overwatering does not describe the quantity of water. It only describes how frequently you water a plant.

As we discussed earlier, plants vary in how often they need water, according to their ability to store it and how fast their soil dries. Let's go back to my little aloe vera. It was overwatered because I didn't let the soil dry out 100 percent before I watered it again. When I noticed it was wilting, I watered way too often, which is a common beginner mistake. I know this explanation is obvious to some, but the misconception around what is and isn't overwatering is one of the most prevalent errors I come across in all my social media interactions, in day-to-day conversations with customers, and in troubleshooting plant issues for folks across the globe.

If your plant is receiving enough light, if the soil is appropriate for the plant, and if your pot has adequate drainage, you can use a gallon of water or a hundred gallons of water on that single plant and it will thrive, because the soil will hold on to only so much water, and the rest will drain away.

Plants Need Moisture *and* Oxygen

How is it that you can grow plants with their roots sitting in water full time (known as "water culture" or "hydroponics"), but those same plants can die from overwatering? This question comes up so frequently in the comments of my social media videos that I have a response saved in my phone's notes that I can copy and paste whenever it comes up, which is a challenge with a 150-character limit! We have endless characters available here, so let me give you the slightly extended version.

It all comes down to oxygen and the fact that roots need oxygen to live. When a plant's roots are kept in water full time, they have constant access to the two things that are most immediately important to them: moisture and oxygen. After all, the water molecule is H_2O, meaning it contains two hydrogen atoms and one oxygen atom. As long as the water your plant is in has not become stagnant and has plenty of oxygen, it will be a perfectly acceptable medium to grow plants in. To avoid stagnation, you can add fresh water to the vessel as it evaporates or consider adding an aeration stone or bubbler to the water, which does the same thing but keeps you from having to add water so often. As long as the water is disturbed on a regular basis to increase the available oxygen to the plant's roots, they'll remain perfectly happy for a lifetime.

To understand why a plant dies from overwatering, we need to take a microscope to the soil. When we look closely, we can see that there are tiny air gaps throughout the soil. These air gaps are providing oxygen to the roots and are largely responsible for keeping them alive. Therefore, dry soil is oxygen rich. But remember, roots need both oxygen *and* moisture. Too much oxygen without water (underwatering) will cause the roots to die, just like too much water without oxygen (overwatering) will cause the roots to die. When the soil is watered, all of those little air gaps are filled with water, which makes that dry, oxygen-rich soil low in oxygen and high in moisture. It's up to the roots and environmental conditions like light, heat, and airflow to dry the soil out fast enough to restore the air pockets around a plant's roots, otherwise they'll suffocate and die. This fact further illustrates why light is so important, because it drives transpiration, the process by which your plant uses and expels water. Light is typically also the main source of heat, which helps the soil dry out quickly and restores oxygen to the roots.

In case you're curious, here's the message I copy and paste from my notes when I'm asked about roots sitting in water full time:

Roots need oxygen to survive.
H_2O = high oxygen content
H_2O + soil = low oxygen content
Oxygen must be restored to roots before they suffocate.

I'm actually proud of how effective this is in explaining the concept.

Relax and Enjoy Your Plants

There's so much anxiety around watering houseplants, because the one thing everyone seems to know, regardless of their level of experience with plants, is that you don't want to overwater. Here's what I think: There is good anxiety, the kind that turns your stomach when you sense that an activity or situation is dangerous. This anxiety serves you and helps you navigate life when you don't have someone there to warn you or offer advice. Our ancestors used this anxiety to help keep themselves out of dangerous, often life-threatening situations.

Then there's bad anxiety. I hesitate to even call it "bad," because it's just less useful than it is "bad." Bad anxiety is the kind that makes you think you'll never get married because your current significant other just broke up with you.

To combat watering anxiety, it helps to keep perspective. When you got your first houseplant, was the idea to introduce more anxiety into your life? When your friend gifted you a baby plant, the card didn't say "Hoping this cactus causes years of uncertainty and disappointment!" No way!

Plants are meant to bring you joy, tranquility, purpose, connection, and fulfillment. They're meant to bring you positivity, and I want to encourage you, any time you're feeling negative stress toward this hobby or toward a particular plant, to rethink, recenter, and remember that it's not that serious! Killing a plant says nothing about you as a person. It doesn't mean you're bad, it doesn't mean you're cold and callous, it doesn't mean you don't know how to nurture, and it doesn't mean you'll be an unfit parent. It only means that you have a living creature in your home that is existing away from its comfortable natural conditions in your barely hospitable space and you're guessing how to take care of it by reading conflicting and subjective blog articles or listening to old wives' tales telling you to wipe the leaves down with mayonnaise and repot every time you see a yellow leaf.

When it comes to keeping plants alive and thriving in your home, the odds are against you. Sometimes I don't know if it's kind or unkind of us to force these tropical plants to live in our homes with comparatively terrible conditions, and yet there's that pull, that attraction to plants that can only be natural. I wonder if that magical draw we feel that invites us to touch the leaf of a plant or smell a flower is some adaptation plants have conjured to lure us back to a more symbiotic relationship once held between humans and plants.

This might sound a little kooky, but I like to think that each plant, no matter its size, is part of the same organism or idea of Mother Earth, and she knows that even when you're not successful with a plant, it'll eventually find its way back to the soil through decomposition and continue to be part of the same organism. The fact that you recognized the magic of a plant at a store and that the draw was so powerful that you brought it home is enough, because your intentions were pure. And even if you're not successful this time, that intention makes you the opposite of all those negative things you think about yourself for killing the plant for any reason—including overwatering.

A Quick Recap

- Water is a crucial ingredient that plants use to make their own sugar. Water also carries nutrients to the plant and fills up the cells, keeping the plants rigid, or "turgid."
- Plants differ in how dry their soil should be between waterings. Thicker plant anatomy equals more built-in water storage and the longer a plant can go without water. Conversely, thinner plant anatomy means less built-in water storage, resulting in a plant that needs to be watered more frequently.
- Use a probe, such as a chopstick or knitting needle, to measure moisture levels using the baking method.
- The goal of watering is to thoroughly saturate all of the soil in the pot. This is achieved by top watering or bottom watering—either is fine for any plant!
- The quality of municipal water varies and should be considered when watering your plants.

CHAPTER FIVE

Repot—or Not?

Repotting is one of the most daunting tasks for a plant parent—and for good reason! From using the wrong soil or increasing the pot size too much to inadequate drainage or repotting prematurely, there's a lot that can go wrong and quickly send your once-thriving plant into a downward spiral. The litany of problems that can arise during a repot is enough to cause even seasoned plant parents to avoid the chore.

There are two cures for this apprehension: understanding when, how, and why to repot, and, as with many tasks, flat-out repetition. I don't know if this is where the expression "get your hands dirty" comes from, but it definitely applies here. If you're avoiding a specific task—plant related or otherwise—the solution is to act. There are no consequences in this hobby greater than the loss of self-confidence that comes when we avoid the tasks we know we *should* do, and ultimately know we *can* do, but don't do.

WHEN TO REPOT YOUR HOUSEPLANT

I first want to say that if your houseplant's health is declining, it's very unlikely that its pot is the cause. For some reason, there's this idea that if your plant isn't doing well, the best thing you can do is repot it. However, this is sort of like performing brain surgery for a headache! Repotting when things aren't going well could fix your problem, but when you understand how plants work, you know that needing a new pot, or even a bigger pot, is almost never the reason your plant is experiencing stress.

Here's a common scenario that perpetuates the "repot when houseplant is dying" idea.

Most plant parents find comfort in watering their plants on a schedule. "It's watering day!" is a caption I see all too often accompanying plant photos and videos on social media. Watering day usually happens on a day off from work, when there's time to catch up on planty projects and chores. Days off tend to be the same every week, so a once-a-week routine is established for watering plants. As the plant grows, the soil fills with more and more roots. As the roots grow, the soil dries faster simply because there are more roots to suck up moisture from the soil. When enough roots have grown, the soil will dry out so quickly that by the time it's watering day, the plant looks super dehydrated and sickly with a few yellowing or browning leaves. To the plant's caretaker, what's happening can seem like a mystery. In their eyes, nothing has changed.

In a panic, this plant parent might do a repot. Why? Because a ton of the advice out there says that if something isn't looking right, hopefully a repot will fix it. Now that the plant has been put in a larger pot with more soil, the soil stays wetter longer, and by the time watering day comes around again, the plant is no longer looking wilted and sad. Because the

repot "worked," that person spreads the word to their plant-loving friends that if a plant has yellow or browning leaves before watering day, the cure is to repot.

In reality, all the plant parent had to do was water the plant more frequently to keep the roots hydrated, but you can see how rumors spread. The problem is that yellowing and browning leaves can be caused by several different factors—I'll discuss this in chapter 7 (page 141)—and repotting unnecessarily can cause more stress to the plant than taking the time to deduce the actual source of stress. When a repot doesn't help, the vast majority of concerned plant parents become frustrated and believe they're just not meant to have plants—they don't have a green thumb!

Repotting houseplants, and more specifically when to do so, is a controversial subject. Some experts say to repot only in the spring, while others say it can be done any time of year. Before we consider some reasons that your plant might benefit from a repot, I want to clarify that there are actually two kinds of repots.

In a true repot, you don't increase the size of the pot at all. You simply take the plant out of the pot, shake the soil off the roots, prune them, and replant it in the same pot with fresh soil. This type of repot is great for when you want to slow down the growth of your plant. After all, many houseplants under proper conditions can easily outgrow the average home, so at some point, this type of repot should become necessary. The best practitioners of this type of repotting are bonsai enthusiasts. To keep these potentially huge trees in tiny pots, their growth must be restricted, and this is done by repotting them in the same size pot. In fact, a bonsai tree might stay in the same size pot for a hundred years, receiving only root pruning and new soil every year or two before going back into the exact same pot.

The second type of repot is also called an up-pot, meaning you "up" or increase the size of the pot. This type of repot is done when you want your plant to get larger, because a plant can grow only as large as the pot it's in. The two types of repots have different goals, but in terms of process, they are largely the same.

Four Reasons to Repot

- **Root growth:** The most common sign that your plant could benefit from a repot is when the roots are emerging from the drainage holes of its pot. At this stage of growth, it's likely your plant has grown a mass of roots—what we call a "root ball"—to the point where the only place left for the roots to go is outside the pot! When a plant amasses a lot of roots, you may notice that it dries out more quickly. When the roots start to grow out of the pot, this is what we call "root-bound." However, roots coming out of drainage holes is not a bad thing at all, and it is not worth getting alarmed about (see chapter 2, page 50, for more on this topic). Remember, this is a sign that your plant *could* benefit from a repot; it doesn't mean it *needs* a repot.

- **Time:** If it has been two or more years since you last repotted your plant, it's a good idea to do a little refresh. Soil components break down over time, which can lead to the properties of the soil itself changing, and that can be harmful to your plant. Plus, repotting is a good opportunity to take a peek at the roots and get a better overall picture of the health of your plant.

- **Greenhouse soil:** While it's not always necessary, it can be tremendously helpful in the life of your plant to repot it soon after bringing it home from the store. You might assume that when you purchase a plant it is in the ideal soil, because these plants are grown by professionals, and they know what they're doing. They do know what they're doing … in a greenhouse! The best aspects of a greenhouse (perfect light, warm temperatures, and high humidity) are also the aspects that can present the most challenges to greenhouse growers. Brighter light and warmer temperatures result in faster growth, which is great when your growing plant needs to reach a certain size before you can sell it. But when plants dry out too quickly due to increased light and heat, they can decline very rapidly. One way greenhouse growers combat this problem is by planting in soil that retains moisture, which lowers the risks of plants drying out and growers losing money. However, when these plants grow large enough to sell, they're shipped

to retail stores in that same soil. When you put that plant in your home, which doesn't have greenhouse conditions, the soil may stay too wet for too long, increasing the chances of root rot.

Soils that retain moisture consist predominantly of either peat moss or coco peat. In either case, I recommend repotting plants that are in greenhouse soil and putting them in a soil that drains and dries more quickly, which will better suit the growing conditions in your home. Don't worry: We'll dive into soil compositions later in the chapter.

Emergencies: An emergency repot may be required at any time, although we most often see them in the fall and winter months, which I believe is due to watering schedules and shorter, less sunny days. Spring is one of the busiest seasons for our plant shop. The mild weather brings in droves of folks excited about growing plants and bringing some life into their space that might have been missing during the gloomier months. Upon purchasing their plant, they bring it home, set it where they envisioned, and establish a watering schedule, usually about once a week. They'll have success all through the long, sunny days of spring and summer by adhering to that watering schedule. Then, when winter comes, things often take a turn for the worse. The days are shorter and often overcast or cloudy, and less light means a plant has less time to process water, which can result in the soil staying wetter for longer. When the plant parent sticks to their once-a-week watering schedule, regardless of the fact that the soil is still wet, root rot develops, and an emergency repot is needed. The sooner you can rid your plant of root rot, the more likely the plant is to recover!

REPOTTING, STEP-BY-STEP

No matter the reason for repotting, I always like to start the same way—with preparation. Over my years of houseplant consulting, I've noticed that repotting is a task that induces a flurry of anxiety and procrastination for so many plant parents. Something that helps me get over those feelings is being prepared. I'll go so far as to put it on my calendar and give myself time to get right with it and organize my supplies. Once the day arrives, I'll pop in my headphones, then turn on my favorite podcast, an audiobook, or music and get to work. I never want an aspect of this hobby I love so much to become an obligation. I don't want to dread the tasks that might not be the most fun, or, worse, avoid them altogether. The only way to glean a lifetime of enjoyment from plants is to find a way to take pleasure in every aspect of plant care, even the aspects we don't love.

Step One: Gather Your Supplies

Here's a list of my most frequently used items, including a few bonus products if you really want to give your plants a proper spa day.

The Essentials

- **Clean workspace:** Potting mats help keep the mess contained. If the weather is warm enough, about 60°F for most houseplants, feel free to repot outside! Stay in the shade, though, as you don't want you or your plants getting sunburned.
- **Soil and soil scoop/trowel:** Soil may vary for each plant, but no matter the mix, you'll need a tool to scoop it into the pot. (We'll dive into soil specifics later in this chapter and again in part two, page 174.)
- **Pot:** I generally recommend increasing the size of your plant's pot so that it is one to two inches larger than the current root ball diameter. However, if you're repotting due to roots popping out through the bottom drainage holes, then you can assume you'll need a pot that is one to two inches larger than the current pot. This is because if the roots are coming out the drainage holes, then it's a safe bet that they've been swirling around the pot and have taken on the current pot size diameter. If you're repotting for any other reason, I recommend getting one pot larger than the current pot, as well as one smaller. You won't know the current size of the root ball until you actually start the repotting process, but you can avoid unnecessary trips back and forth to the store by preparing for the possibility that you may need to go down in pot size if there's significant root loss.
- **Pruners:** I always like to keep a pair of sharp, clean pruners on hand for repots. They come in handy for removing dead leaves and dead roots. A dedicated kitchen knife can also be helpful for removing roots.

A Few Bonus Items

- **Hydrogen peroxide:** A spray bottle filled with hydrogen peroxide is good to have on hand in emergency repot cases. You're often dealing with root rot, and a thorough misting of bare plant roots can stop the spread of the molds and fungi that cause rot.
- **Isopropyl alcohol:** I use isopropyl alcohol to clean my pruners. Cutting plant material can leave unwanted bacteria on your blades, and although the risk of cross contamination in an at-home setting is low, it gives me peace of mind to know that I took precautions to further mitigate the risk.
- **Mycorrhizae:** This type of fungus is added to soil to enhance its ability to take up water and nutrients. The fungus attaches to the plants' roots and trades water and nutrients for sugar, forging a very special—and beneficial—relationship. Using mycorrhizae may also help reduce transplant shock when repotting and can be an extra defense against root rot. You'll learn more about mycorrhizae (and worm castings!) in chapter 6 (page 121).
- **Worm castings:** This nutrient-rich material (worm poop) is an organic soil amendment with billions of beneficial microbes, enzymes, and bacteria. I add worm castings to all of my plants to boost soil health and, consequently, plant health.
- **Knitting needle or chopstick:** These blunt instruments are used to gently guide new potting soil into the small nooks and crannies between the roots that your fingers might be too large to reach.
- **Gloves**: Elitist plant enthusiasts will say you're not a real plant person if you wear gloves when repotting. I'm not one of them. I get it: Some folks want to avoid getting their hands dirty. I often wear gloves when I repot several plants in the same day to avoid having to wash my hands multiple times. There's no shame in my glove-wearing game!

Step Two: Remove the Plant from Its Pot

Once you've gathered all the necessary materials, it's time to get your hands dirty. Or not, if you're a glove-wearing rebel like me.

If your plant is in a plastic pot, you want to gently squeeze the pot between your hands. The goal is to loosen the soil from the inner wall of the pot, making it easier to remove the plant. If your plant is in a pot you can't squish, like a ceramic one, you'll want to slip your knitting needle, chopstick, or trowel between the inner pot wall and the soil, effectively accomplishing the same goal as squishing a plastic pot.

Once all the soil is separated from the inner pot wall, the plant should slide out with ease. Grab the pot with one hand and support the plant with the other. If the plant has trunks or stems, I'll grab as many as I can and, with the plant tipped upside down or parallel to the work surface, gently pull the plant out while jiggling the pot. Plants will usually pop out within a few tries, but if you feel resistance to the point that you're afraid you're going to damage the plant, stop—you may have to create more separation between the soil and the inner wall of the pot.

If your plant is too large to hold, I suggest all the same steps, but instead of holding the plant, lay it down on the ground, grip the pot between your feet, and grip the plant with both hands. If you have a helper, I suggest that one person hold the pot while the other tugs on the plant. An extra set of hands is always welcome when doing large repots.

Don't be too concerned about damaging some roots or losing a few leaves. Remember that plants are meant to grow roots and cling to everything around them for support, so resistance and damage are to be expected. If you've ever watched some of my repotting videos online, you'll notice that I'm pretty rough with the plants. I do this in an effort to show that you don't need to be apprehensive when repotting—just go for it! Plants are very tough. Also, plants will come out of their pots much easier when the soil is wet, so if you're having trouble getting a plant out, a good soil soak is in order.

In cases where a plant is severely root-bound, it can be less stress on the plant to simply break the pot it's in or to cut the plant out of the pot if it's made of plastic.

Step Three: Prep the Plant for Repotting

Once your plant is out of its original pot, remove the soil around the roots. Gently massaging the roots with your fingers usually loosens up the soil adequately and allows the roots to take on a new shape instead of the shape of the pot. This can also help your roots climb into their new soil more easily.

If the soil is super dry, making it hard to loosen, I recommend submerging the soil in water until it's thoroughly saturated. Most houseplants will be small enough to put in the sink, bathtub, or even a bucket. A quick thirty- to sixty-minute soak is typically enough for soil to fall away from the roots with ease. If the weather allows, a dousing with the hose outside is also a great option. Again, don't worry about damaging a few roots—it's an expected part of the repotting process!

Step Four: Choose Your Pot

We discussed earlier how houseplants are unlikely to decline due to the size of their pot. However, you can reduce the risk of root rot by choosing a pot that is only one or two inches larger in diameter than that of your root ball. With experience, you'll get good at eyeballing this, but early on, it helps to use a measuring tape to determine the diameter of your root ball. That way you can be confident you're choosing a pot that allows for more roots to grow without bogging down the existing roots with extra water-processing work.

Pot Materials

The material your plant is potted in can affect how your houseplant processes water. Here are some popular choices, and the pros and cons of each.

- **Plastic:** Houseplants are commercially grown in plastic containers called nursery pots, because they're effective, long-lasting, and reusable. Plastic pots are also the most affordable option and are readily available, making them a solid choice for potting and repotting houseplants. However, plastic is not a porous material, which means the only airflow is through the bottom drainage holes and the top of the pot. Oxygen getting to the roots is what lessens the risk of root rot, so if you opt for plastic, it's important to make sure the pot has enough drainage. Some cheaper pots come with only one small drainage hole and that's often not enough for many plants.
- **Ceramic:** Ceramic pots are popular for their decorative features. They come in just about any color you'd like and in endless designs. While some ceramic pots are unsealed, it's more common for them to be sealed. Sealing ceramic pottery results in a glossy finish, but it also means the pores of the ceramic are sealed, so as with plastic pots, the only airflow is from the bottom drainage holes and the top of the pot. Sealed ceramics are widely available, but they are often the

most expensive option. Unsealed ceramics can also be expensive, but they are porous, making them more like terra-cotta.

- **Terra-cotta:** This porous material is perhaps the most popular choice for potted plants because it's still relatively affordable, is easily available, and has the added benefit of airflow. With terra-cotta, air is able to get into the soil from every angle—there is airflow from the bottom drainage holes, at the top of the pot, and through the sides of the pot—providing oxygen to the entire root ball. As a result, soil planted in terra-cotta will dry out faster than soil in nonbreathable materials like plastic and sealed ceramics. Terra-cotta doesn't come in many color options, which is a downside if its natural color doesn't fit in with your decor scheme.

No matter which pot material you choose, there will be options that have drainage holes and options that don't. Pots with holes are meant to be potted in directly, whereas pots without holes are meant to be used as cover pots, also known as cache pots, slip pots, or drop pots. I love this method, and as I'll discuss shortly, I keep most of my personal plants in plastic nursery pots slipped inside decorative cover pots.

You can grow any houseplant you want in any of these pots, but some offer benefits and drawbacks depending on the plant you want to grow. For example, putting a moisture-loving plant like a maidenhair fern in a terra-cotta pot wouldn't be ideal, because the material will cause the soil to dry out faster, which means you'll have to water more frequently. A plastic pot or a sealed ceramic pot would make more sense for a maidenhair fern from a watering perspective.

On the other hand, planting a desert cactus in a terra-cotta pot makes perfect sense, because desert cacti want their soil to dry quickly. Although it's totally doable, planting a cactus in a plastic pot or a sealed ceramic pot makes less sense, because the soil is going to take longer to dry out. And the longer the soil takes to dry out, the greater the risk of root rot.

All professionally grown plants are grown in plastic pots, so you don't have to choose a certain pot material based on the plant you're trying to grow. As I mentioned, I keep all of my plants in plastic pots with drainage holes and slip them into cover pots. We'll talk more about that in a minute, but keep in mind that pot selection really comes down to knowing your-

The Cover Pot System

Keeping your plants in pots that have drainage holes and setting them inside a decorative pot without drainage holes is called a cache pot or cover pot system. Although it's very popular in Europe, the cover pot system is less known in the United States. It's how I keep most of my personal plant collection because it fits my lifestyle.

The traditional way of keeping plants is to plant them directly in pots with drainage holes. When the plant needs to be watered, you either stick a drip tray under the pot to catch the water being poured on the soil from the top, or you take the entire potted plant to the sink to be watered there. The plant gets the water it needs and drains the excess, and you either wait for the bottom of the pot to dry or rest it on something that protects your surfaces from water damage.

The reason I love the cover pot system is it makes watering very passive—and thorough! When I wake up in the morning, one of the first things I do is check on my plants. If I notice that any of them need water, I simply pour water into their decorative cover pot and leave for work. When I get back from work, the plant has taken up all the water and is happily hydrated. If there's any excess water, I simply dump it out, or if it's a big floor plant that I can't move, I'll just use my dedicated turkey baster to suck up the remaining water. Watering this way is great for the plant, it takes only a minute, and it means I don't have to worry about water damage on my surfaces. Another bonus is that you can water a large number of plants in a short amount of time, which is perfect for someone with a large collection. Just don't forget to remove the excess water!

self, your habits, your lifestyle . . . and your personality. Are you someone who tends to overnurture your plants with love—that is, water? A porous pot made of terra-cotta will help even out your tendency to water too often. Are you on the go and hardly ever remember to water your plants? A plastic or sealed ceramic pot might be a better option to help keep your plants from dehydrating while you tackle your busy schedule. Are we splitting hairs here? Kinda. Does pot selection make a huge difference? Not really. But do some people find way more success choosing one type of pot over another? Absolutely.

Step Five: Select Your Soil

When I brought my first aloe vera home, I immediately repotted it, using a fresh bag of houseplant soil and a fancy new wooden bowl. Unbeknownst to me, planting my aloe in houseplant soil was one of the biggest mistakes I could make. Honestly, I didn't put much thought into it. I had a houseplant, I needed soil, I got houseplant soil. What could go wrong? The problem was that houseplant soil retains a lot of moisture, and aloe vera, being a succulent, also stores a lot of water. What I didn't know at the time was that if your plant stores water, your soil shouldn't!

Choosing soil is an aspect of houseplant care that can increase or diminish your chances of keeping a plant alive. In other words, the right soil, just like the right light, watering regimen, and pot selection, can give you more or less room for error when it comes to keeping a houseplant happy. Choosing the right soil for houseplants is mostly about moisture retention, airflow, and how you balance both with the plant's natural ability to store water. In fact, many of the principles of soil selection can be taken from the discussion of watering in chapter 4 (page 80).

Before we get into what's in commercial houseplant soil, I should first explain that most of them don't contain any true soil. Most of the "soils" you can purchase are all mixes of soilless ingredients like moss, wood, and aggregate, which could include pea gravel, pumice, perlite, granite, sand, or other rock materials, in some form or another. Each soil ingredient is used for either its moisture-retaining or its moisture-draining capabilities. Moisture-retaining ingredients are going to decrease the frequency of your watering, but the tradeoff is less airflow to the roots due to the dense nature of materials that retain moisture. And that means increased risk of root rot. Moisture-draining materials can be called "sharp draining" or "fast draining." They increase drainage, but they also increase airflow, as the faster something drains, the faster it dries, which in this case restores the oxygen supply to the roots. Expect to water more often when the soil-ingredient ratio tips in favor of moisture-draining materials, but know that the mixture's ability to restore oxygen in the soil helps prevent root rot.

Although the soil mixture you use, in respect to moisture-draining or moisture-retaining capabilities, isn't going to be the reason a plant dies, customizing a soil blend that works with the plant's natural ability to store water can make your houseplant-hobby years exceptionally easier.

Common Moisture-Retaining Potting Materials

- Peat moss
- Coco peat
- Compost
- Vermiculite
- Long-fiber sphagnum moss
- Standard houseplant soil

Common Moisture-Draining Potting Materials

- Perlite
- Orchid bark
- Coconut chips
- Horticultural charcoal
- Horticultural sand
- Rice hulls
- Cactus potting soil
- Calcined clay

Before you choose which ingredients to mix together for your plant, let's revisit the plant's anatomy to help us decide which ones might be best to use.

There are several ways a plant can store water, but I use the roots, stems or trunks, and leaves to determine a plant's ability to store water, because just about all houseplants have those three points of anatomy. When the anatomy of a plant is thicker, we can safely assume that it stores more water. Going a step further, the thicker the plant's anatomy, the longer the plant can go without water. This isn't scientific, but if we know nothing about a plant, looking at its anatomy is an easy way to create a soil recipe that works with the natural properties of the plant. A succulent, for example, has very thick leaves and stems. It quite literally stores water in its leaves as a survival adaptation to withstand the weeks and sometimes months it may go without rain in its natural environment. Succulents are so adept at storing water that it's best to plant them in soil that drains very quickly. Standard cactus potting soil is a great idea. If you'd like to mix your own custom soil, then you might use something like one part peat moss, two parts perlite, and two parts calcined clay.

Monstera deliciosa is a popular plant—let's consider its anatomy! When looking at the leaves of a *Monstera deliciosa*, it's easy to see that they don't store water, especially when we compare them to the thick leaves of a succulent. Next, look at the stems. Even when this plant is young, it has quite thick stems. Now we have one point of water storage (stems) and one point of no water storage (leaves). Finally, the roots. This plant has both soil roots and aerial roots. Aerial roots are what some climbing plants use to attach to structures for support, usually a tree, and climb upward to compete for light. The roots of the monstera are also quite thick. In fact, even in a six-inch pot, the monstera often will have roots with the diameter of a pencil. This means the monstera has two out of the three points of water storage. For this plant, I like to use a soil recipe that contains one part peat moss, one part orchid bark, and one part perlite.

Finally, let's look at the maidenhair fern. Its leaves are even thinner than that of the monstera.

If you pinch them between your fingers, they offer almost no resistance. Next, examine the stems. The delicate stems of this fern are also very thin, resembling the whiskers of a cat. Finally, let's inspect the roots. The roots, although plentiful, are very thin and fibrous—this might be the thinnest anatomy on the entire plant! By my count the maidenhair fern has zero out of three points of water storage. With that in mind, for the maidenhair fern, I would use a standard houseplant mix, because it retains a lot of moisture and the plant needs that. If I were to create my own soil recipe, I would use one part perlite and three parts peat moss.

Did you pick up on any patterns with plant anatomy and how it relates to soil recipes? Each recommended soil counterbalances the plant's anatomy and natural water-storing capabilities. The succulent is huge on water storage, so we plant it in cactus soil that doesn't retain moisture. For the monstera, we use one moisture-retaining ingredient to balance the fact that its leaves don't retain moisture, and two moisture-draining ingredients to balance the fact that the stems and roots do. Finally, for the maidenhair, which has no built-in water storage, we use a soil recipe that retains moisture. You might notice perlite in the fern mix, and that's because no matter the plant's ability to store water, I always throw in one ingredient that will provide air to the roots and help the soil drain. Doing this gives a bit of security in the root rot department.

When selecting soil ingredients, it always helps to choose ones with different diameter sizes. Doing so will create more airflow. For example, if I need two moisture-retaining ingredients and one draining ingredient, it would be less optimal for me to choose peat moss and coco peat as my two moisture-retaining ingredients because their diameters are so closely matched. Ingredients that are similar in size will also cause soil to be denser, which means less airflow. For three specific soil "recipes," see part two (page 174).

REPOT—OR NOT? 115

Step Six: Check the Roots

Checking the roots when you're repotting isn't necessary, but if you've already taken the plant out of its soil, you might as well. After all, the health of the roots is _____ _____. Hopefully by now you're able to fill in the blank with "the health of the plant."

Healthy roots can look the same as unhealthy roots, so the best way to check is by giving them a little squeeze. Healthy roots will be firm, while unhealthy ones will be mushy or crunchy. Healthy roots will also have some resistance when given a little tug. It's good practice to get rid of all the unhealthy roots, as they can spread unwanted diseases. Grab a pair of pruners or sharp scissors and snip away any roots that aren't firm to the touch and throw them in the garbage. It's unlikely that a personal plant collection will face cross-contamination of bacteria, but any time you cut a plant, I recommend disinfecting the blades. I keep a spray bottle of isopropyl alcohol handy at my potting bench and spritz my blades before and after cutting. Cleaning between each cut is a bit overboard, but if you like being really thorough, more power to you!

There are cases where you might want to cut away healthy roots too. This is called "root pruning." As I alluded to earlier, root pruning is most commonly used in bonsai care to help keep the trees small, but it can be applied to any potted plant and is very handy for maintaining a plant's size. If you don't want to increase the size of the pot, you can simply cut away a portion of the roots and put the plant back in its pot with fresh soil for the roots to grow into. Some plants can withstand nearly the entire root ball being cut away, while others will go into massive shock and temporarily stop growing, remain wilted for days or weeks after pruning, or even drop all their leaves even with a light pruning. My general rule of thumb is to cut away no more than 25 percent of the root ball. You can do this with a clean set of pruners, but my favorite way is to lay the plant on its side and, using a dedicated kitchen knife, cut the bottom 25 percent of the roots off in a sawing motion. You will likely see a few of those symptoms of shock, but the plant should stabilize within a few weeks.

Soil Amendments

If the mentions of pon, LECA, and perlite in chapter 2 had you scratching your head, don't panic. These are soilless mediums and amendments that can be used to grow plants. All three have recently become more popular.

- Pon is a mixture of lava rock, pumice, and zeolites and was originally created to be used in conjunction with self-watering planter pots.
- LECA is an acronym for "lightweight expanded clay aggregate." It's basically small clay balls that have been fired in a kiln, which causes gases in the clay to expand to make the balls porous. LECA was originally used in construction but is now very popular in plant care.
- Perlite was invented before LECA and created with a similar process. It's volcanic glass that has been exposed to high temperatures, which eliminates any trapped water inside and causes it to expand.

While their compositions vary, all these materials aim to provide a balanced ratio of water to oxygen for the roots by using them as either soil amendments or the exclusive growing mediums.

REPOT—OR NOT? 117

Step Seven: Get Ready to Repot

You've determined your plant needs a repot and you've got your supplies, removed the plant from the pot it was in, and done your root maintenance. It's finally time to see how your plant is going to look in its new home.

Toss about an inch of soil in the bottom of the pot, level it with your hand, and set your plant inside. This is a test fit. You want to maintain the soil level the plant was previously at, and you want that level to be about half an inch to an inch below the rim of the new pot—because if you fill the soil to the top of the pot, when you give your freshly potted plant its first drink of water, the water will run off the side. Repotting is already a messy job, so don't give yourself more to clean. This test fit will help you determine how much soil needs to be at the bottom of the pot before filling in the rest.

One trick you can use to test fit without actually having to pick up the plant is to use the old pot. You follow the same steps of adding an even layer of soil at the bottom of your new pot, but instead of using the plant to perform the test fit, you simply grab the old pot and set it on the layer of soil in the new pot. When the old pot rim and new pot rim are even with each other, you'll know you have the right amount of soil. This trick can be utilized for any size plant, but it really comes in handy when you're repotting large, heavy plants, because you don't have to pick them up several times for test fitting.

Once you have the right amount of soil in your pot, place the plant in the center and begin filling in the empty space around it with the soil you've carefully selected. For every couple of scoops, I like to make sure the soil is settling in around the roots. Depending on the root ball and the soil ingredients you chose, the task of filling in the empty space can offer some challenges. This is especially apparent when using large pieces of material like orchid bark, because they might not fit between the roots without a little encouragement. Cue the uncomfortable, prolonged eye contact and SLAP THAT POT!

You have no idea how long I've been waiting to write that in this book. Many of you likely know what I'm talking about, and the fact that I'm Internet famous for SLAP THAT POT. For all of you who are reading this and thinking I've lost my mind, allow me to explain.

I film a ton of plant-advice videos for social media, and a large portion of that content demonstrates how to repot different plants that customers drop off at our store. In an effort to help settle in the soil around the roots, I tell the audience to SLAP THAT POT, then I stare directly into the camera while it slowly zooms in on my face as I'm gently slapping the pot. It's totally awkward for everyone involved, but it's so popular we started selling SLAP THAT POT merch!

Slapping the pot isn't just for show. It's very effective at getting soil to settle in all around the nooks and crannies of the roots, and although prolonged eye contact isn't required for this technique, I do highly recommend it. Repotting often happens when you're concerned for the plant's health, and it helps to keep things lighthearted with a bit of nonsense.

If pot slapping isn't for you, there's another way: Using a chopstick, you can poke and prod around the roots, guiding soil into all the hard-to-reach places. This method is very effective, and I'll often combine it with pot slapping to ensure the soil is reaching all the empty spaces.

As you fill the pot, you can also "firm in" the soil by using your hands to press down on it around the plant. Press firmly enough to keep the plant upright but not so hard that you risk breaking roots.

Step Eight: Water Your Repotted Plant

The very last step is to give your freshly potted plant a good soak! This will further settle the soil in and around the roots and get your plant on the right track to recover from the shock of a repot. Remember that your goal, whenever you water a plant, is to saturate all the soil in the pot, so soak it. And yes, even if you're repotting due to root rot (from overwatering), you still want to soak your plant after repotting. Water is a key ingredient in a plant's ability to make its own food. Depriving your repotted plant of water is like being injured in the hospital and the doctor forcing you to fast. Our bodies need food to aid in recovery, and so do plants.

YOUR POST-REPOT PLANT

Some plants are more sensitive to repotting than others. Ficus, for example, are notorious for showing signs of stress after a repot. They'll often respond by dropping leaves and looking wilted for a few weeks. Remember that in their native environment, these plants would never be repotted. They grow their roots in one spot their entire lives, so it's no wonder that they kick up a fuss when something so foreign happens to them. This doesn't happen with all plants, or even all ficus, but having that expectation sets you up for success. With proper care, the shock of a repot will subside and the plant will continue to thrive.

Repotting can bring on all sorts of feelings, like excitement, anxiety, and doubt. These feelings can make you hyperaware of your freshly potted plant, prompting you to frequently check every leaf and scrutinize any detail you might construe as negative or worthy of worry. But if you've done your best, then there's nothing else you can do! If the plant doesn't do well as a result of a mistake, you have the opportunity to learn from the mistake. Next time, your best will be better, and if Mother Nature is wise enough to withstand what's been thrown at her so far, she's wise enough to **not be** offended by you killing a few plants in your effort to learn how to **better nur**ture her.

CHAPTER SIX

Feeding for Growth

Over the years, I've done hundreds of consultations with folks looking for help identifying and fixing their potted-plant problems. These conversations start many different ways, but a common theme involves the plant parent readily admitting that they don't fertilize their plants consistently, as often as they should, or even at all, and their belief that this is likely the cause of their plants' decline. I'm here to tell you that a lack of fertilizer is hardly ever the cause of plant issues. However, that doesn't mean fertilizer is not important!

If I made a list of aspects of houseplant care from most important to least important, fertilizing would be near the bottom. Most people are shocked to hear this, but if your plant isn't getting proper light and water, it doesn't really matter if you give it the most perfect, super-amazing, ten-out-of-ten fertilizer in the world—it will still decline. But boy howdy, when all of a plant's needs are being met, and you couple that with the right fertilizer, your plants will *explode* with growth!

Let's take a deeper dive into the "X factor" of houseplant fertilizing!

WHY FERTILIZER IS IMPORTANT TO PLANTS

Plants need several chemical elements to produce healthy growth—seventeen, to be exact. The most important ones—oxygen, hydrogen, and carbon—are found in the air and water, but the other fourteen must be added to potted plants by way of fertilizer. These fourteen chemicals are split into three groups: macronutrients, secondary nutrients, and micronutrients.

While all the chemical elements play a role in producing healthy plant matter, the macronutrients—nitrogen, phosphorus, and potassium—are the most important. The secondary nutrients—calcium, magnesium, and sulfur—are needed in lesser quantities than macronutrients but in greater quantities than micronutrients. Micronutrients are found in much lower quantities in commercially available fertilizers, and they include boron, chlorine, cobalt, copper, iron, manganese, molybdenum, and zinc. It's not important that you memorize any of this, but I mention it to help you better understand fertilizers, and so you can make informed decisions when it's time to shop.

To understand why fertilizer is important to your plants, once again, I want you to imagine that your plant is simply a sugar-making factory powered by the sun. Light, water, and oxygen are combined to make the sugar that's used as fuel for the plant. The roots of your plant are the workers at the factory, making sure water and nutrients are being dispersed properly throughout the plant. When you add fertilizer to your plant—your sugar-making factory—you're giving it building materials to grow bigger and the tools required to function more efficiently, as well as increasing its natural defenses against pests that are out to steal the plant's sugar.

Let's take a look at how fertilization occurs in nature. Plants growing in their natural habitat get fertilized in many ways, including from nutrients found in the air, but most commonly through nutrients found in the soil. How do nutrients find their way to the soil? Cue the *Lion King* soundtrack: "It's the cirrrrrrrcle of liiiiiife!" In this Disney classic, Mufasa, voiced by the great James Earl Jones, is the lion king of the Pride Lands, and he explains to his cub, Simba, how the world works and the role that they, as lions, play in the world: "When we die, our bodies become the grass, and the antelope eat the grass, and so we are all connected in the great circle of life."

All living things, including plants and animals, eventually die. And once they die, the decomposers of the world—fungi and bacteria—move in and break down the decaying matter, releasing all the stored nutrients that were once found in the living creature. This step is crucial, as plants can't feed on dead matter alone—it needs to be broken down. The exception, of course, being carnivorous plants like the Venus flytrap. Although many carnivorous plants require special circumstances to thrive indoors, there are several that do well in the average home. What fascinating plants they are!

Once the decomposers have done their job, they leave behind tons of beneficial nutrients in the soil, and once the rain hits them, they can be taken up by the roots of plants and dispersed to where they're needed. That is, until the plant dies, and the circle of life continues. Isn't nature beautiful?

There are times in my life where I get really overwhelmed with work or tasks that need to get done. I get so wound up in the things I "need" to do that anything else going on that isn't contributing to those things being done is completely disregarded. But if I can shake myself from that narrow focus long enough, I will often find comfort in remembering that I'm just part of that circle of life, and whether I get my job done or not, I'll be in the ground one day, alongside everyone else. Perspective elevates my life in all things, including plant care.

NPK

On the package of every fertilizer product, you'll find three numbers, usually displayed prominently. It'll look something like this: 10-4-16. These three numbers represent the percentages of nitrogen (N), phosphorus (P), and potassium (K)—the three macronutrients essential to healthy, thriving plant life. In this example, 10-4-16 means the product is 10 percent nitrogen, 4 percent phosphorus, and 16 percent potassium. You might be thinking, "What composes the remaining 70 percent?" It depends on the specific fertilizer, but it can generally be lumped into the category of "filler," which includes anticaking ingredients and other compounds that make the chemicals stable and usable to plants. We wouldn't want to add pure potassium to our soil, for example, as it violently combusts when it comes into contact with water. Although these "fillers" don't directly affect plants, they play a huge role in making the chemical elements that plants need actually usable.

Each plant in your collection may benefit from different ratios of these nutrients, depending on their individual goals and priorities, or even their native environment. A golden pothos, for instance, is a foliage plant and concentrates its energy on producing leaves. Leaf production is largely supported by nitrogen; therefore, a golden pothos would benefit from a fertilizer containing a higher concentration of that chemical. Other plants, such as roses, orchids, and fruit, prioritize flowering, a goal supported by phosphorus, which is why fertilizers with higher levels of phosphorus are often recommended for these types of plants. Potassium is important for all plants, but especially for fast-growing plants. They tend to use up more nutrients and water, and a healthy supply of potassium is needed in order to distribute these crucial building blocks throughout the plant. And then we have plants like cacti and succulents. Their native desert habitats might offer very little in the way of nutrient-rich soil, and they have adapted to thrive in that very environment. It's better to work with rather than against nature, so plants that aren't accustomed to a heavy dose of nutrients in their native habitat should get minimal fertilizer in their new habitat, your home.

To break it down in a very basic way:

- Nitrogen is used by your plant to grow leaves and stems.
- Phosphorus is mainly for root and flower growth.
- Potassium supports your plant's vascular system, moving nutrients throughout the plant.

While I just explained that different plants can benefit from different fertilizers, it's important to understand that the vast majority of houseplants are going to live long, happy lives if given a simple, balanced fertilizer, usually 10-10-10, 15-15-15, or 20-20-20. As you learn more about your plants and evolve your planty goals, you may choose to customize the nutrient ratios to better suit those goals. But if you have a large collection like I do, it's easiest to reduce the number of fertilizers you have on hand and simply give all your plants, or at least most of them, the same fertilizer.

Early on in my plant-parenting days, I used a different fertilizer for each plant in my collection. It soon became a task that required recordkeeping, and I found myself skipping the headache of tracking it all, which ultimately meant that only my favorite plants (I'll admit, it's the orchids—don't tell the others) got fertilized. Even if it's not perfectly curated for each plant, using a simple, low-dose fertilizer for all your plants is better than overwhelming yourself with the task to the point of paralysis. Erika has a life motto: Better done than perfect! I find this helpful for plant care and in general, as I'm often a perfectionist even when I know I don't need to be.

TYPES OF FERTILIZER AND HOW TO USE THEM

When it comes to choosing how you fertilize your plants, you first need to decide if you want to give your plants synthetic fertilizer, organic fertilizer, or both. There is no wrong answer here. I encourage you to experiment and see what you prefer. Here's what you need to know.

Synthetic Fertilizers

Synthetic fertilizers are manufactured chemicals, and they work very quickly, resulting in rapid growth. I like to think of them like steroids for plants, because as long as all other care needs, like light and watering, are being met, synthetic fertilizers offer fast growth in a relatively short period of time.

If you've purchased a plant online, from a big-box store, or even from most boutique plant shops, the plant was almost definitely fertilized synthetically. Simply put: Synthetic fertilizer produces the fastest growth, which is advantageous when you're selling a living product that must grow to a certain size before you can sell it! Another advantage of synthetic fertilizers is that they're quite affordable, at least compared with organic fertilizers. They're also readily available. Next time you go to your local garden center, take a look at how many synthetic fertilizer options are available—there will be several.

Synthetic fertilizers come in two main forms: slow-release and liquid-soluble. Slow-release fertilizers are usually found in the form of small granules, pellets, or little stakes that you shove in the soil. Each time you water your soil, a small amount of that fertilizer is picked up by the water, which is then picked up by the roots and dispersed throughout the plant. If you have a plant that's still in its original soil from the store, go ahead and take a look at it. See those little round balls in there? They're usually purple or green. Those are slow-release synthetic fertilizer granules.

During the busiest times of my life, or when I've accumulated more plants than normal, I'll often switch to a slow-release fertilizer because they're just so simple to use. Each product will differ, but most slow-release fertilizers work anywhere from three to twelve months at a time. Using a slow-release fertilizer gives me peace of mind that all my plants are getting what they need, even when they're not my top priority. Most of these products even offer a "no burn" guarantee, which simply means your plant is protected from the effects of overfertilization, such as leaf scorch.

Liquid-soluble fertilizer is perhaps the most common method I see the average hobbyist using to fertilize their plants. This method allows you to mix a dose of liquid fertilizer into your watering can. It combines easily with the water, which you can then pour on your soil for the roots to take up. Of course, you can also use this mixture to water your plants from the bottom, as long as you're diligent about flushing your soil with pure water on a regular basis to avoid any buildup. One of the great things about liquid-soluble fertilizer is that you can adjust the strength of the dose you're giving your plant. This is beneficial for maximizing growth during times of the year when your plant is growing the fastest, and for protecting your plant from overfertilizing during times of the year when growth may be slower.

There is no one recommended dosage chart for different plants. However, every fertilizer product you buy will come with varying dosage recommendations based on frequency of use and the strength of the product.

Call me paranoid, but I dilute my liquid-soluble fertilizer even further than what the manufacturer suggests—because I can always add more fertilizer in the future, but once the concoction is poured on the soil, I can't take it back.

Organic Fertilizers

Organic fertilizers are derived from organic materials that are broken down in various ways, such as through composting, then blended together to create different NPK ratios. Compared with synthetic fertilizer, organic fertilizers more closely replicate what a plant would experience in its natural habitat. While they've long been popular in backyard food gardening, organic fertilizers have only recently taken hold among houseplant hobbyists. Don't worry, I'm not suggesting a DIY project! Organic fertilizers are commercially available. You can definitely find them online and likely even at your local garden center.

If synthetic fertilizers are like steroids for your plants, organic fertilizers are like a well-balanced diet and exercise routine. Your plants are going to get everything they need from an organic fertilizer, but they're not going to grow as quickly as plants being given synthetic fertilizer. However, organic fertilizers are going to create a healthier soil environment for your roots in the long run, so there's an added benefit for your patience.

Organic fertilizers are available as powders, liquids, and slow-release pellets, and they are applied the same way as synthetic fertilizers. Always adhere to the product recommendations for usage, unless you're like me and prefer to err on

FEEDING FOR GROWTH   127

How to Shop for and Store Fertilizer

With the Internet and the ability to ship just about any product anywhere in the world, you'll no doubt have endless fertilizer options. But, when possible, I strongly recommend shopping for fertilizer in person or at least from a reputable online retailer. Shelf life is an issue with fertilizer, and having the ability to ask when the product was made can keep you from buying a stale and ultimately less-effective fertilizer that has been stored in a boiling-hot warehouse for who knows how long. Whichever fertilizer you choose, store it in a cool, dry place for best results.

the side of caution; then you can dilute the fertilizer slightly more than the specified dosage.

Which Fertilizer Should You Choose?

Which fertilizer you choose is going to depend on the goals you have for your plants, your lifestyle, and what's readily available to you. If you want your plants to grow as fast as possible, synthetic fertilizers are the way to go, but if you'd rather cultivate healthy soil and more closely replicate what your plant would experience in nature, then consider organic fertilizer. Does life have you on the go, but you still want to make sure your plants are getting what they need? I've found that slow-release fertilizer is the best option when I'm busy. Simply sprinkle the pellets on the topsoil or mix them in when you repot. Et voilà, you won't have to remember to fertilize for three, six, or even twelve months, depending on the product you chose. If you go this route, I recommend setting a calendar reminder so you know when it's time to reapply.

HOW OFTEN SHOULD YOU FERTILIZE YOUR HOUSEPLANTS?

In the online houseplant community, how often to fertilize is one of the most popular topics, so I'm grateful for the opportunity to address it here. The frequency of fertilizing is going to depend on the plant you're fertilizing and its growth stage, as well as the product you're using and the time of year. Earlier in this chapter, we learned that plants are going to differ in their need for fertilizer, which mostly depends on where the plant naturally grows. Because plants grow in such diverse conditions, you may consider researching the specific needs of your plants before diving in, but there are some general guidelines to steer you in the right direction. Desert cacti are accustomed to low levels of nutrients and may not be able to handle frequent fertilizing, simply because that's not what they're used to. On that same note, a tropical cactus that naturally grows on a tropical forest floor teeming with nutrients isn't going to perform optimally if we fertilize it at the same rate as we do a desert cactus.

Furthermore, certain plants may not be able to effectively utilize fertilizer depending on their current stage of growth. For most plants, this occurs when the plant is in its dormancy cycle or when it's flowering. If nutrients are the building materials plants use to grow, and the plant is not actively growing due to dormancy or a shift in energy focus, it may benefit your plant to reduce or even cease fertilizing until your plant continues growing. Phalaenopsis orchids, for example, may cease or slow down their leaf and root growth while flowering. Further diluting your fertilizer or fertilizing less frequently during that time may be beneficial to your orchid while it focuses on the reproductive cycle (flowering) and not the building cycle.

It's a common belief that houseplants go dormant in the fall and winter months; however, the truth is that most houseplants neither have nor require a true dormancy period. The word "dormancy" is a term most folks understand even if they don't own a single plant, so it's easier to describe a period of slower growth in houseplants by calling it dormancy instead of what it really is—energy conservation due to less sunlight during those months. The reason most houseplants don't have a true dormancy period is because a significant change in temperature or a significant change in the number of hours of light they receive is what's responsible for triggering dormancy in plants. But most houseplants grow near the equator where these fluctuations aren't great enough to trigger a dormancy response.

I think of it like this: When your plants are focused on leaf production (we call this "vegetative growth"), the sugar-factory workers are on the main floor. The nutrients are coming in and they're using these nutrients to grow the factory. But when a plant is ready to produce flowers, priorities shift. For plants, flowering is kind of like expanding the brand. The hope is that the flower will be pollinated, resulting in seeds that drop on the ground nearby and start a whole new factory. During this flowering period, the plant is either not as focused on vegetative growth or not concerned with it at all, so the workers leave the main floor for the flower room where they work on growing the flower. At this point, if you continue adding fertilizer to the now-unmanned conveyor belt, there's going to be nowhere for that fertilizer to go. Enough fertilizer buildup can lead to leaf scorch and possible detrimental effects on your houseplant.

You also need to consider the strength of the fertilizer you're using. If its NPK is quite high, say 20-20-20, during flowering, you may not need to fertilize as frequently as you would if you were using a weaker 5-5-5 fertilizer.

FEEDING FOR GROWTH

Finally, let's consider the time of year. This topic is debated quite heavily among houseplant enthusiasts. Some experts recommend you cease fertilizing in the fall and winter months, while others urge you to fertilize year-round. Plants growing in their natural habitat aren't suddenly removed from the nutrient-rich ground they're growing in come fall, so what logic could there be in discontinuing your fertilizing efforts during this season? Answering that question requires understanding how your plant processes fertilizer. For that, let's take another trip back to the sugar-making factory!

We've already established that in our sugar-making factory, the leaves are the solar panels, collecting sunlight and converting it to energy for all the factory operations to run on. The roots are the workers, making sure all of the building materials (the water and nutrients) are being properly distributed throughout the factory. I want you to imagine the building materials moving through the factory on a conveyor belt, and the workers (the plant's roots) taking those materials off the conveyor belt and using them

to make the factory larger, sturdier, and more resistant to intruders. The more light that the solar panels are able to capture, the faster the entire factory operates. The workers have more pep in their step, the belt is running at high speed, and the factory quickly grows larger and larger!

But what happens when fall comes around? Well, for everyone in the northern hemisphere, fall coincides with fewer hours of daylight, and often fewer sunny days altogether. Fewer hours of daylight means factory operations slow down. The workers don't work quite as quickly, the conveyor belt moves more slowly, and the factory isn't adding more branches quite as often as it was during the long, sunny days of summer. In fact, sometimes expansion ceases altogether.

During this time, when our sugar-making factory is experiencing less production, we can avoid burnout (leaf scorch, a.k.a. leaf burn) by giving the workers less work, since they're forced to move more slowly. One way we give them less work is by drastically reducing the amount of building materials (the nutrients provided by fertilizer) we put on the conveyor belt for them to process. If we continue to give them the same workload in the gloomy, short days of fall and winter as we did in the long, sunny days of spring and summer, it may be too much work for them and can actually lead to the demise of some of the solar panels (leaves).

This is all well and good, but who in nature is giving the plants less fertilizer during the fall and winter months to avoid leaf scorch? Well, nobody, because the plants in nature very often don't get a break! Most "houseplants" come from tropical regions of the world, and those regions are all relatively close to the equator, and the closer you get to the equator, the fewer fluctuations there are in the number of hours of daylight. Additionally, the types of fertilizer plants get from the soil in their natural environment are much easier for them to process and don't overload them.

Signs of Overfertilizing

If you got a little overzealous with the fertilizer, like I did with my *Monstera deliciosa* early on in my houseplant-keeping career, you may find yourself with signs of leaf scorch. This is a buildup of the soluble salts that contain the nutrients for your plant—think of them like little nutrient gifts wrapped in boxes made of salt. When there's significant salt buildup, you may notice the edges of your plant's leaves turning brown and crispy. This is leaf scorch, and if left unchecked, it can destroy entire leaves and even entire plants! This salt buildup can also leach water from the roots, causing your plant to dehydrate, even if there's water available in the soil, and that will inevitably lead to wilting or puckering of the leaves, less nutrient uptake, and stunted growth.

In severe cases of overfertilizing, you may notice a crusty buildup on the top of your soil that has a white, hazy look and is dry to the touch. A white, hazy appearance can also come from a mineral buildup due to watering with tap water. The good news is that whether the buildup is from excess minerals from water or from fertilizer, the protocol is the same—FLUSH IT! Hold on, don't flush your plant down the toilet. Flush it with water—pure water! Grab a gallon of distilled water from the grocery store and water your plant with it. This pure water will wash away the buildup so that no harm comes to the plant from said buildups. I perform this task preventatively whenever I think about it, which is usually when I'm shopping for something near the distilled water and happen to notice it. I take that as a sign to flush my soil, although if you're more organized than I am, once a month is a good schedule for this task.

Signs of Underfertilizing

As I mentioned before, there have been times in my life, and I'm sure in yours, when the time required to take care of your plants is taken over by more important tasks, you're just not in the mental space to take the extra steps to fertilize, or you just flat-out forget! When life hits you with the illusion that something else is more important than self-care (plant keeping), you may see slower or stunted growth (not to be confused with slow growth during the short days of winter, which is totally normal and expected!), leaves that lose their original color saturation, less flower production, or an overall weaker plant. You might especially recognize this "weakness" in the stems or branches of your plant, which will look thin and often won't have the strength to hold up the leaves they're meant to be supporting. It's worth noting that for established plants, signs of underfertilizing happen over the course of several months and are hardly ever the first thing I look at when troubleshooting the cause of plant decline.

The remedy for underfertilizing is, of course, to start fertilizing more! If you've got a hunch that you haven't been giving your plant enough fertilizer, I want you to take it slow on reintroducing fertilizer, especially if it's derived synthetically. Going from zero to one hundred too quickly could overwhelm your plant, so go ahead and dilute your fertilizer by twice the recommended amount, just to be on the safe side.

ADDITIONAL WAYS TO "FEED" YOUR PLANT

There are several ways you can improve the health of your plant by adding amendment products, such as compost, worm castings, and mycorrhizae to your plant's soil. Plants can also receive some nutrients through their leaves with a foliar-feeding spray. But keep in mind that all of these products are meant to supplement or enhance your fertilizing practices and are not replacements for fertilizer.

Compost

Composting takes advantage of the natural decomposition process to make a nutrient-rich soil amendment for your plants. I don't claim to be an expert on the matter, but whether you can or should add compost to your houseplants is a question I get often, so it's worth a quick mention.

The great thing about composting is that you're basically recycling kitchen scraps. Instead of throwing those banana peels, eggshells, and coffee grounds in the garbage, you can recycle them in your compost pile. There are many techniques and guidelines to follow to make sure you're composting properly, but it doesn't take much effort, and you're left with a product that can be mixed into your houseplant soil to improve its structure, microbial activity (that's a good thing), and water retention. It also acts as a mild slow-release fertilizer for your plants that's sustainable and super cost-effective. Who doesn't love that?

The only word of caution I'll throw out about using compost for your houseplants—beyond the normal risks of using any fertilizer—is to be mindful of your compost's moisture-retaining properties. When you increase your soil's moisture retention, you also increase your risk of root rot and fungus gnats, which feed on organic material. Increased water retention may be one reason why compost is most commonly used on outdoor plants instead of indoor plants, as outdoor plants are less prone to root rot and fungus gnats because their outdoor environment has increased light, temperatures, and airflow, which dries wet soil much faster than plants kept indoors. When applying compost to your houseplants, it's best to mix it in with your soil during a repot, but it's also fine to add a layer on the topsoil and mix it in.

Worm Castings

Worm castings are another popular organic soil amendment and one I highly recommend. "Worm casting" is just a nicer way of saying worm poop, which is exactly what it is. The eighth grader in me chuckles at the fact that there are huge businesses out there devoted to harvesting worm poop. It reminds me of the scene from the movie *Dumb and Dumber*, when the character Lloyd (played by Jim Carrey) drives a woman to the airport and tells her about his future plans to own a pet store called "I Got Worms" that specializes in worm farms. "Ya know, like ant farms?" he says. As a young teenager watching that movie, I never would have thought my future self would consider building my own small worm farm to harvest poop, but here we are!

Worm castings blur the line between fertilizer and soil conditioner. Technically they're a fertilizer, because they contain nitrogen, phosphorus, and potassium, but in very small amounts, so I wouldn't use them as your only source of nutrients. The real magic of worm castings comes in their micronutrients, trace minerals, natural growth hormones, and beneficial microbes that protect plant roots from harmful pathogens. Worm castings also improve soil structure, which is going to improve the airflow in your soil, further protecting those roots! Worm castings can be mixed in with your soil during a repot, which is the best approach, but they can also be applied to the topsoil and gently mixed in to avoid breaking any roots near the soil surface.

Worm castings shouldn't produce much, if any, unpleasant odor, which sets them apart from manure. They're also becoming more readily available and, as they gain popularity, quite affordable—very affordable if you farm your own, although you might want to keep that hobby among gardening and plant friends. Farming worm poop is a weird hobby to have without some context.

Mycorrhizae

Mycorrhizae are fungi that have a symbiotic relationship with plants. Don't worry: You can't see them, and they don't have a smell. These fungi aren't technically fertilizer, but they can be added to soil to promote growth, so I couldn't leave them out. I also find mycorrhizae's relationship with plants completely fascinating!

When mycorrhizae are added to plant soil, the fungi seek out and attach themselves to the plant's roots. The roots give the fungi sugar in exchange for water and nutrients the fungi find in the soil, using their hyphae, which can be thought of as fungi roots. These hyphae are very thin—so thin you can't see them with the naked eye—which allows them to find nutrients in the soil that larger roots, like those of a plant, might miss altogether.

The really fascinating part about this relationship is how the plant and the fungi communicate. Exactly how they do so isn't fully understood, but let's say, for example, that your plant is experiencing a deficiency in nitrogen. The mycorrhizae are able to identify this need and will focus their efforts on finding nitrogen for the plant. These magical plant butlers also reduce transplant shock (my repot customers love this) and make it harder for harmful root pathogens to thrive. Some strains of mycorrhizae even possess antifungal compounds that are beneficial to the plant, which is absolutely wild to me. If you don't get excited about nature after reading about plants and mycorrhizae, you might want to check your pulse.

To start using these beneficial fungi, look for a high-quality product that's specifically for houseplants. Directions for application will be on the product packaging, which you'll definitely want to follow.

Foliar Feeding

In recent years, foliar feeding has grown in popularity by leaps and bounds. I've personally witnessed the dramatic rise in foliar-feeding products via Instagram and Facebook ads, which tells me I'm not as good as I thought I was at keeping myself removed from online houseplant content!

Foliar feeding is the act of spraying liquid nutrients on leaves so they can absorb those nutrients through tiny openings on their surfaces. It had long been thought that nutrients were absorbed through the stomata openings, but a recent study suggests they are more likely absorbed through even smaller openings on the leaf cuticle. Although accepting nutrients is not the main function of these microscopic openings, certain nutrients—mostly micronutrients—are able to be absorbed in this way. At the end of the day, most of us just want to know: Does it work, what do I buy, and how do I use it? I appreciate that, so let's dive in!

Yes, foliar feed does work! However, I do want to clarify what "work" means, because I've seen some wild claims (usually by product manufacturers) about how effective foliar feeding is and a litany of its benefits. The truth is that plants are not great at taking in nutrients through their leaves, especially compared with their roots' ability to take up and distribute nutrients. Some plants, due to their specific anatomy and adaptations they've made to their environment, are better than others at this task, but it's estimated that only about 15 percent to 20 percent of liquid nutrients sprayed on a plant's leaves are actually used by the plant. That's a lot of waste! So, foliar feeding does work, but maybe not to the degree that the growing number of foliar-feeding products says it does. On that note, if any plant product claims things that seem too good to be true, they're probably too good to be true!

Before you start foliar feeding, know that it's not a replacement for feeding your soil and should only ever be used as a supplement to fertilizer. Also, if you want to start using a foliar feed, I recommend using a product specifically formulated as a foliar spray, because it will be mild and will lean into the use of micronutrients over macronutrients, as the latter are shown to be less effective in foliar applications. Products specifically made for foliar feeding will also contain a surfactant, a crucial element in the effectiveness of the spray, as the nutrients must remain on the leaves

for an extended period of time for them to be absorbed by the leaf. This means that if you're trying to DIY your foliar feeding by mixing your regular fertilizer in a spray bottle, it will be only mildly beneficial at best. Also, be sure to follow the application directions on foliar sprays to prevent leaf scorching due to overuse.

In recent years, I have found myself buying into the hype of foliar feeding my houseplants—not so much for the benefits of the increased nutrient uptake but for the ritual of it. As I mentioned in chapter 4 (page 80), misting your plants with water is largely ineffective at increasing humidity, but I still like to do it, because it helps build the relationship I have with my plants. By simply adding nutrients to the spray bottle, I am adding to that positive relationship between me and my green collection.

In short, foliar feeding can be seen as an opportunity to inspect the sugar-making factory to find potential issues before they become big problems. It's an opportunity to clean the windows of the factory and do all the little things that, once the main needs of the building are taken care of, are nice to have, adding an extra glimmer that results in a better place to work and a greater chance at preserving the longevity and vigor of the factory.

DIY FERTILIZERS

It's no secret that a big part of my life is social media. I like to think I am mostly a content creator, but I can scroll mindlessly with the best of them! Between our plant business and all the plant-related content I create, my life is already so plant heavy that I try not to be on PlantTok, Plantstagram, and whatever the equivalents are for Facebook and YouTube. But my nature is to be curious, the algorithm knows that, and consequently, it takes a grip on me more frequently than I'd like to admit.

Despite my best efforts to shield myself from excessive plant content, every spring my social media feed is inundated with "new" natural plant fertilizers. These new ideas are hardly ever actually new, but rather recycled ideas that an influencer or excited plant parent newly discovered. I realize this might imply disdain, and there is some truth to that, but ultimately, I reel it back in and remind myself that I'm just grateful and excited that people are interested in plants and in doing a better job of feeding them. The dismissive thoughts that creep in when I see the annual posts touting the magical powers of banana-peel tea, eggshells, and coffee grounds are because I know my inbox is about to be flooded with questions regarding these methods, their effectiveness, and what I recommend. Don't get me wrong: I'm flattered that so many plant lovers value my opinion, but I get salty when people muddy the waters of plant care in an attempt to get more views. Plants already have a reputation for being difficult to care for, and if folks would just do the tiniest bit of research, they would find these methods to be mildly effective at best and detrimental at worst.

The idea behind recycling food waste to fertilize plants is definitely viable. We touched on this fact in the composting section. The conundrum lies in how effective these natural fertilizers are, when you consider the time it takes for these once-living organisms to break down into usable nutrients for your plant.

I never want to discourage anyone from using organic materials to fertilize their plants or shy away from experimenting with any number of methods to grow plants. To me, this is one of the aspects of plant care, and our relationship with plants, that is the most fun, thought-provoking, and exciting. I only aim to provide realistic expectations by laying out some basic information about these popular fertilizers and to hopefully spark further interest in how you care for your houseplants. Am I trying to make everyone a nerdy houseplant person because I've found that increases my joy and fascination with them? Maybe. But hey, there are worse things in life!

Fertilizing with Coffee Grounds

When considering a fertilizer, I always recommend looking at its NPK content, and for coffee, it's very minimal. Coffee grounds contain anywhere from 1 percent to 2 percent nitrogen, less than 1 percent of both phosphorus and potassium, and even lower amounts of the remaining nutrients needed for plant growth. When used properly, coffee grounds can provide some mild, slow-release fertilizer benefits, but with such low nutrient levels, they aren't considered a complete fertilizer.

It's also important to recognize the potential downside of fertilizing with coffee grounds. Coffee is one of the most popular drinks in the world, which means there are leftover coffee grounds being produced daily and just begging to be recycled. But the trace amounts of caffeine in coffee grounds have been found to slow the growth of some plants when added to their soil. If too much is applied, coffee grounds could be detrimental to your plant's health, because built-up caffeine may burn its roots, and as we've learned, the health of your roots has a direct correlation to the health of your plants! If you do want to use coffee grounds for fertilizing, the best thing you can do is to compost them, wait for them to be broken down by that process, and then use the compost as the final fertilizer product.

Fertilizing with Eggshells

Like coffee grounds, eggshells contain very low levels of the nutrients that plants need, with an NPK somewhere around 1-0-0. Not only are there not enough macronutrients in eggshells for them to be considered a complete fertilizer but, unless you crush them into a fine powder, it'll take a long time before they decompose enough for their nutrients to be usable to plants.

The redeeming qualities of eggshells are that they're high in calcium, and although that's not a macronutrient, plants do use it and therefore will benefit from it. Be careful, though, as eggshells are naturally alkaline, which your plants may or may not appreciate.

As with coffee grounds, the most practical way to use eggshells as a fertilizer is by composting them. And be sure to at least crush them up a little before adding them to your compost pile.

Fertilizing with Banana-Peel Tea

Banana-peel tea is made by adding banana peels to a vessel of water, sealing it off, and letting them soak in the sunlight. After a few days, the water will turn a different color—evidence of the banana peel breaking down—at which point you can discard the peels and water your plants with the nutrient-rich water.

Blog articles and viral social media videos make it look like banana-peel tea is a natural superfertilizer. But how effective is it, really? Let's take a look at the NPK and go from there. If your banana peels are dried, their NPK is roughly 0.6-0.4-11.5. I'm going to assume most folks aren't drying their bananas for their tea, as every example I've seen of banana-peel tea uses fresh banana peels, which have an NPK of 0.1-0.1-2.3. Again, this food scrap doesn't make a great showing as a complete fertilizer.

You also have to keep in mind that these values are based on the entirety of the contents of a banana peel, meaning you would get that value only if you're able to extract 100 percent of the nutrients from that peel. I'm not trying to dissuade anyone from using banana-peel tea, but steeping banana peels in a jar for a few days, or even for a few weeks, won't result in 100 percent extraction of the nutrients, which means the steeping water is going to be only mildly beneficial. Again, if you want to recycle banana peels for houseplant use, it's best to compost them.

MY HOUSEPLANT FERTILIZING RECOMMENDATION

Here's the truth about fertilizing: It's not *that* big of a deal. I've spelled out all of this information for the plant person who is genuinely curious about the how and why behind fertilizing, but I don't want you to get caught up in the endless products, methods, and suggestions from the ever-noisy world that is the Internet. I aim to make things as simple as possible, because simplicity helps keep me focused on the joy of the hobby, and for me, that means less measuring, less tracking, and more admiring—something I want each and every one of you to experience, because when you do, it feels like natural, organic magic.

I choose to go the organic route when it comes to fertilizing my plants. I'll admit that I resisted organic fertilizer for a long time because I wanted the rapid growth that comes with synthetic fertilizer. In hindsight, that may have been coupled with a bit of ego and excitement to prove to myself that I could grow plants. However, I've learned that joy doesn't increase by growing plants quickly as opposed to slowly, nobody is watching to see if I have the ability to grow them, and my "good human" meter doesn't move when I kill a plant or keep it thriving.

Go to your local garden center or plant shop and choose a general-purpose organic fertilizer. Any brand will do. Apply the fertilizer according to the directions and go about your merry way. Your plants will get everything they need and your plant-parenting career will be that much simpler.

A Quick Recap

- Fertilizing your plants is important, but not nearly as important as light, water, and soil—address those needs first!
- Plants need seventeen nutrients for growth, but three of them—nitrogen (N), phosphorus (P), and potassium (K)—contribute to growth more than the rest, and each plant will do best with different ratios of those three nutrients.
- Fertilizers can be organic or synthetic. Organic options don't grow plants as quickly, but they are safer and more natural for plants. Synthetic options produce faster growth, but they are more likely to harm plants than their organic counterparts. Both have their good and bad qualities and come in a variety of application methods.
- You can research the nutrient needs of your plants and choose fertilizers to address those needs, but it's often easier and nearly as effective to choose one general-use fertilizer for all your plants.
- If you're short on time, consider using a slow-release fertilizer that needs to be applied only every three to twelve months, but if you have the time and crave more active plant care, a water-soluble fertilizer you add when watering might be a better option for you.
- There are several soil-feeding amendments, such as mycorrhizae, worm castings, and compost, but a true fertilizer is going to yield the best results, especially when combined with the previously mentioned amendments!

CHAPTER SEVEN

Troubleshooting (It Doesn't Need to Be Troublesome)

Houseplant problems, including pests and disease, are every bit a part of the hobby as repotting and watering. Hopefully, you'll deal with these issues infrequently, but I don't want you living in a plant fantasy world where challenges don't arise. In fact, I believe that by accepting the fact of their existence, you help set yourself up for long-term plant ownership and enjoyment, as most things are easier to handle when you've accepted them as inevitable. After all, if plants are getting pests and diseases in their natural environment—an environment absolutely, perfectly suited for them—expecting perpetually perfect plants inside your home is just having your head in the sand. But your head isn't in the sand. I can tell, because you're reading this book! Dealing with plant issues can still be stressful, but by expecting occasional issues and by using the tips in this chapter and all the chapters before this one, you can mitigate that stress by having a plan of action.

In this chapter, you'll learn how to identify, prevent, and treat common houseplant problems, including issues with watering, light, fertilizer, diseases, and pests. This is where we troubleshoot. Dig in!

OVERWATERING (ROOT ROT)

No concept in the plant world has been more misunderstood than overwatering. Plant parents around the globe have fretted over the dreaded idea that giving their plant one and a half cups of water instead of one cup will lead to their plant's demise. This contributes to the idea that plants are difficult to care for and not worth having. The truth is that when plants are ready to be watered, you can empty an entire swimming pool onto their soil, and they will be perfectly fine. Let me clarify: As long as it's not a chlorinated pool, your pot has a drainage hole, and your plant is in proper lighting, if you are thoroughly saturating the soil, the quantity of water you give your plant does not matter.

An overwatered plant is actually one that has been watered too frequently, and when a plant is watered too frequently, it develops a disease called root rot (a.k.a. root suffocation). Unfortunately, you won't really know you've overwatered a plant until it shows signs of being overwatered—that is, until it shows signs of root rot. In short, overwatering is synonymous with root rot, has nothing to do with the quantity of water, and has everything to do with the frequency of watering. This is why I always recommend not watering on a schedule and instead checking the moisture levels of your plant's soil before watering. Conditions change throughout the year, and so should your watering habits—a topic explored extensively in chapter 4 (page 80).

SYMPTOMS: Overwatering happens. We've all forgotten a plant sitting in water for days or weeks on end or entrusted a family member or neighbor to water our plants, only to return home and find them declining. Don't beat yourself up! In most cases, plants can be salvaged. The fact that plants are contenders for the longest existing organisms on the planet should tell you that they know how to survive. Still, when we have plants in our homes, we may need to lend a helping hand, as they no longer have the hand of Mother Nature for assistance.

The first sign that you may be flirting with overwatering will be fungus gnats, which like to lay their eggs in soil that is always wet. With the exception of carnivorous plants, which would eat the fungus gnats anyway, there are no houseplants that require constantly wet soil. This means that when it comes to watering your houseplants, there's never any reason to create a fungus gnat-friendly environment!

As we'll discuss later in the chapter, these annoying critters are quite small, so you may not even see them. The first physical signs of overwatering that you can actually see on your plants tend to be new leaves turning yellow or mushy, or brown spots forming on the interior margins of leaves, meaning the brown spots aren't touching the perimeter of the leaf. These unsightly leaves won't recover from the damage, so feel free to prune them or just let nature take its course.

The most confusing sign of overwatering is wilting. When we see a plant droop or pucker, our minds automatically think the plant is dehydrated, in which case a thorough soaking is in order, right? You'd actually be right in thinking that wilting is a sign of dehydration, but it's dehydration of the plant cells and not dehydration of the soil. Remember that overwatering is synonymous with root rot and roots are responsible for distributing water throughout the plant, keeping it hydrated and rigid. If a plant has been overwatered, that means enough roots have died off to the point where there aren't enough of them—or, in severe cases, no roots at all—to keep the plant hydrated. It's a bit like the sugar-making factory is flooding, but there's no one there to do anything with the water. In this case, no amount of watering will fix the wilting, because there are no roots to take up the water and distribute it to the plant. If your plant is wilted and the soil is wet, you've most likely overwatered your plant. In other words, it probably has root rot.

If you suspect root rot, you'll need to remove the plant from the pot to verify that the visible signs do in fact indicate root rot. Upon removing the plant from the pot, you may be greeted with an unpleasant smell—the smell of root rot!—confirming your suspicions. This only happens in severe cases, so don't let the fear of an unpleasant smell keep you from doing the deed. In most cases, you'll have to inspect the roots to confirm root rot. The roots will be either mushy or paper-thin and crunchy. Remember: Healthy roots should always be firm to the touch and have some resistance when given a little tug.

TREATMENT: Once you've determined that your plant definitely has root rot, you can take different courses of action. The most passive way of treating root rot is to simply let the roots dry out completely. The fungi that are actually responsible for the rot brought on by unfavorable soil conditions are only able to survive in soil that remains wet, so by letting the roots dry completely, you're performing a sort of "reset" within your soil. The tricky part with this approach is letting the roots dry long enough to kill the fungi, but not so long that it causes permanent damage to the roots and, consequently, the plant.

I've typically had success by simply removing as much soil from the roots as possible—either with my gloved hand, by swishing the root ball in a bucket of water, or by spraying it down with a garden hose—and then letting the roots dry overnight. For most plants, performing this reset for the roots is simple, free, and super effective. Once the roots have all dried out, you can immediately repot your plant in fresh soil and give it a thorough soak—it's time to get your plant on the road to recovery!

If you want to increase the effectiveness of your root rot treatment, spraying the roots with 3 percent hydrogen peroxide is a great practice to employ. Diluted hydrogen peroxide is available at grocery stores and drugstores and typically costs just a few dollars. This method is similar to the passive root rot treatment, but instead of letting the roots dry out overnight, you rinse them, spray them with hydrogen peroxide, and then immediately repot the plant in fresh soil. There's no need to dilute your 3 percent hydrogen peroxide any further, and there's no need to wash it off after applying. A third option is to combine both methods, which means removing the soil from the roots, rinsing the roots, and letting them dry overnight, then spraying them with hydrogen peroxide and repotting the plant in fresh soil.

All these approaches are effective and simple to do, but there are some situations when I prefer to use one or the other. For plants that require more frequent watering, like ferns, peace lilies, monstera, and anthurium, it's best to get the plant out of the pot, wash off the contaminated soil, spray the remaining roots with hydrogen peroxide, and repot it immediately. This avoids the heavy wilting due to dehydration that can happen when the roots are simply left to dry overnight, and it gets the plant back on track sooner, which is always a good thing. Succulents store water in their leaves, so they can survive longer periods of drought without showing signs of stress, and this means you can let them dry out for a couple of days before cleaning them up and repotting them.

My Approach to Treating Overwatering (Root Rot)

Those are the basic ways to deal with a case of root rot, but before we move on to other plant issues, I want to share how I typically address root rot and go into a bit more detail about the different steps.

When I establish that a plant has root rot, I immediately remove the soil from the roots by hand and then more thoroughly with a stream of water from the sink, or a hose if it's warm enough to treat the plant outside. Two things here: I don't recommend rinsing a bunch of soil down your drain, so take precautions on that end, and be careful when taking your plants outside. Direct outdoor sun can burn a plant's leaves in just a few minutes, so be sure you avoid that type of exposure.

Once most of the soil has been rinsed away, I prune any roots that aren't firm when squeezed until only healthy roots remain. Next, I thoroughly spray the remaining healthy roots with hydrogen peroxide. Once I'm satisfied with my work, I assess the size of the pot needed for the new root ball.

In chapter 5 (page 102), which covers repotting, I recommend increasing pot size by only one or two inches more than the root ball diameter. Depending on the amount of root rot a plant sustains, it may even be necessary to decrease the size of the pot to maintain those standards. Pro tip: If a plant got root rot because it was watered too fre-

quently, consider using a pot only one inch larger than the diameter of the root ball. Smaller pots mean there's less soil surrounding the root ball, which results in the soil drying out more quickly, reducing the likelihood of root rot developing again.

If I'm able to use the same pot the plant was previously in, I thoroughly clean the pot inside and out with hot, soapy water or bleach to ensure no fungi are present. Once the plant is repotted, it's time to get back to proper care, starting with a complete soak of the soil. This may seem counterintuitive, as overwatering caused the problem in the first place. However, the issue was not that the plant got too much water but rather that it was watered too often. Now that the soil's been reset, we need to get the plant's sugar-making factory working optimally once again, which means the roots need to be hydrated.

The time it takes a plant to recover from the shock of being treated for root rot and then repotted will depend on the type of plant, how severe the root rot was, and the care it receives going forward. I always suggest placing a recovering plant in bright light, regardless of its tolerance to lower light, to help speed up the recovery process and get the plant back to its former glory more quickly. Keep in mind that this process requires patience, as it may take at least four to six weeks to see noticeable improvements.

EDEMA

This plant disorder isn't usually life-threatening to plants, but like fungus gnats, it's a warning sign that you may be watering too frequently. Edema happens when a plant is taking on water faster than it can process it through transpiration. The cells literally get so full of water that they burst, leaving behind some type of physical damage to the plant. In our sugar-making-factory analogy, this would be like rooms of the factory flooding to the point of visible evidence on the exterior of the factory, such as a broken window!

Edema can be caused by sudden changes in a plant's environment, like temperature and humidity swings, but the most common reason is simply watering your plant too frequently.

SYMPTOMS: Plant edema is not unlike edema found in humans and will manifest itself as blisters, watery patches, raised bumps, or tiny red dots on your plant's leaves. Because edema happens when a plant takes on more water than it can process before its cells burst, you may also notice your plant showing signs of overwatering.

TREATMENT: There's no way to "treat" edema in the context of erasing the physical damage. Whatever damage the plant sustained as a result of its cells filling up with water and bursting will only fade over time or be covered up by other foliage. However, edema is another one of those ailments that is often a precursor to more severe plant damage, especially root rot from overwatering, which you want to prevent. If your plant is experiencing edema, it's time to reconsider the following aspects of the care your plant is receiving:

- **Watering:** Watering too frequently is the number one cause of edema. I want to, once again, make a clear distinction between the amount of water you're using and how often you're watering. Edema is *not* a quantity problem; it's a frequency problem. For a more detailed explanation, return to the water discussion in chapter 4 (page 80).
- **Drainage**: Poorly draining pots hold on to water longer, and giving a plant's roots constant access to water will cause them to continually suck it up and distribute it to cells around the plant, increasing the risk that they'll fill to the point of bursting. Consider a pot with more drainage holes or larger drainage holes.
- **Lighting:** Plants that aren't receiving adequate light are at higher risk of edema, because the amount of light directly impacts how fast a plant is able to process water around its roots. If water isn't processed quickly enough, the plant's cells will fill up with water and burst!
- **Soil:** Soil containing an excess of fine moisture-retentive particles will hold on to more water, potentially prolonging the amount of time it takes for your plant to process that water, increasing the risk of edema. For more on soil composition, revisit chapter 5 (page 102).
- **Humidity:** Although it's not a common occurrence, you may experience edema due to unusually high humidity. This is only going to happen if you've gone to great lengths to provide much-higher-than-average household humidity. For example, terrariums have

consistently high humidity, which can elevate the chances of edema. Ensuring proper airflow for plants growing in any high-humidity environment will help reduce the risk of edema.

UNDERWATERING

In most cases, underwatering is far less detrimental to a plant's health than overwatering. I suspect this is because it's more common for plants living in their natural habitat to experience periods without rainfall than periods with constant rainfall, leading them to adapt to the former in varying degrees, depending on their climate. For this reason, as well as for other reasons like laziness and a seemingly endless number of projects and responsibilities I have at this stage of life, I tend to err on the side of underwatering my personal plant collection. This is why I gravitate toward plants that can handle underwatering, except in the case of ferns. Ferns are my kryptonite. Of all the plants my lifestyle prevents me from parenting, ferns are the ones I love the most. One day I aspire to commit the time and attention to all the ferns my heart desires, but for now, I'll stick to plants that won't kick up a fuss when I forget about them for weeks or months at a time.

SYMPTOMS: As easy as it is to water a plant too often, it's just as easy to not water it often enough. For most of us, houseplants are not the center of our universe. Heck, I own a plant business, and plants still don't get all of my attention, which is why I readily admit to frequently underwatering my own plants. But I'm not here to stress about my personal plant collection. While I want to see them grow, flower, and fulfill my aesthetic dreams, I'm not going to beat myself up over skipping a watering or two.

If you're like me in the watering department, you may find your plants displaying some dried-out, crispy edges. Your plants might wilt from time to time. Your soil could become compact, even to the point of cracking, and if any or all of this is left unchecked, your plants will most certainly grow less. Luckily for us, these symptoms are easily treated and quick to recover from.

TREATMENT: Wilting is often the first sign your plant hasn't been watered often enough. Plant cells that are filled with water are what keep your plant looking perky, so wilting tells us that the plant isn't able to take up any water—either because there's no water available in the soil or because, as mentioned in the overwatering section, you've watered your plant too frequently and have killed off the roots, resulting in wet soil but no roots to distribute the available water. However, if your plant is wilting and the soil is dry, it's due to underwatering, which means it's time to give the soil a thorough soaking.

But what happens when the soil is compacted and cracking, and the water you give the plant simply runs right through the drainage holes without really saturating the soil? It could be that your soil has become hydrophobic, meaning that it has dried so much that it no longer absorbs water and actually repels it. In hydrophobic soil, water takes the path of least resistance, and instead of absorbing into the soil, it will bead up and run to the edges of the pot. This happens quite commonly with houseplants, especially those plants that can go a long period of time without being watered. In such cases, I recommend a little soil maintenance to get the soil to accept water again. For this, I employ my trusty chopstick, but any blunt probing object will work. You're going to use your chosen probe to break up the soil by gently pushing it into the soil several times over the entire exposed surface area. Don't worry about breaking a few roots, especially when it's in an effort to improve your plant's circumstances.

Once the soil has been broken up, it's time to rehydrate it. Grab a bowl or bucket large enough to house your potted plant, fill that vessel about halfway with water, and place your potted plant in the water. If your cache or cover pot is large enough, it can act as your bucket, but if not, set that aside and place the nursery pot directly in the bucket of water. It's best to completely submerge all of the soil, so adding more water may be necessary. Yes, some of the soil particles will float to the top, but you can always replace lost soil later. For now, focus on getting the current soil to accept water so that you can hydrate the plant.

At first, you may need to hold the plant under the water for a minute or two to keep it from floating to the top, but it shouldn't take long for the soil to start accepting water again. Once the plant is able to stay underwater on its own, let it sit there and accept water for a few minutes. You'll see air bubbles floating to the top, but once the soil has been rehydrated, the bubbles will stop, at which point you can let the pot drain and put your plant back on display.

In cases when your plant is too large for a bucket, I recommend a combination of thorough watering and soil probing, repeating this cycle until the soil is once again accepting water. You'll know the soil is accepting water when the water is immediately absorbed by the soil. If the weather allows, take the plant outside in full shade and give the soil a good soak, then break it up as much as possible with a probe, repeating this process over and over until the soil starts accepting water again. In severe cases, or if you'd rather not deal with the soaking-and-probing process, consider repotting the plant. I often suggest this to customers when it's been a year or more since they last repotted their hydrophobic plant. If it could use a soil refresh anyway, there's no point in going through the trouble of rehydrating old soil.

I should note that some plants, despite living in absolute perfect conditions, with the best light and proper watering and fertilizing, will still get crispy tips. Ponytail palms and several types of dracaenas are well-known for this. And although crispy tips are a sign that your plant is suffering from underwatering, it can also indicate different issues, which we'll talk about later in the chapter. This is why using context clues and really thinking about the full scope of your plant care is important in deducing the true reason for any given symptom.

PESTS

I've said it once, or maybe twice, but I'm going to say it again: Having realistic expectations for your plants is going to be one of the best pieces of advice I can give when it comes to enjoying a positive relationship with them. You'll need to lean into these realistic expectations throughout your plant-parenthood journey, but never more so than when your plants get pests. Before we dive into identifying plant pests, the symptoms to look for, and how to treat them, I want to offer some guidance to see you through what's normally considered a negative experience. Allow me to offer a different perspective.

Let's be honest: You didn't purchase a living creature expecting zero issues, right? That idea doesn't apply when adopting a new dog or cat, or anything else that sustains its own life through biological processes. It's the intricacies of living creatures that give them the essence of life, and I find it incredibly exciting and completely fascinating that, despite my best efforts, and the efforts of all humanity, we may never completely understand plants from an academic point of view. And even still, we all seem naturally and mysteriously drawn to them. We humans are invisibly wired to plants through years of evolution, and anything that grips the human mind and spirit so firmly yet so gently for so long is inevitably going to come with challenges—if there weren't challenges, that connection wouldn't have as much power. If you just wanted something that looked nice, you would have purchased a fake plant, but you wanted something that both looked nice *and* felt nice, which only comes from the connection to something living.

When your plant gets pests, I encourage you to rebel against the instinct to feel dejected and the assumption that because there's something wrong with your plant, there's something wrong with you. Wallowing in self-pity, sadness, or frustration is doing you and your plant a disservice—and is the very opposite of how you should feel caring for plants. Instead, rejoice in the fact that you're experiencing life, and sharing that life with another creature that, until very recently in human history, you likely would never have known existed, let alone had the opportunity to cultivate a relationship with in your own home. We are spoiled with such magnificence, and that shouldn't be dulled by a relatively small problem, like pests.

I get it: You've made a financial investment in this plant, it's an heirloom, or it holds special significance. Do you want to know what I tell all my clients when they drop off a plant that needs to be rescued? This plant will not ruin you financially—you'll make more money. The person who passed this plant along to you, or the person you're fondly reminded of whenever you see this plant, would not want you to stress over it one single ounce, because this person likely loved you very much, and that is something that the health of a plant couldn't possibly change.

Keeping this renewed perspective in mind, let's get into the nitty-gritty of plant pests.

Where Do Pests Come From? And How to Avoid Them

Have you ever wondered, "If I keep my plants inside, how do they get pests?" I'm going to do my best to not sound like a broken record here, but I really want you to get comfortable with the fact that pests are simply part of the houseplant hobby. If you get pests on your houseplants, it's not a slight against you; it's not even necessarily anything you have or haven't done! Getting pests on your plants is like your car getting a flat tire—we can put in place all the precautions to avoid it like regular air checks and inspections, but drive long enough and chances are you're eventually going to get a flat tire.

Pests come from several places, most notably as hitchhikers on people, pets, and new plants. I don't expect you to give your pets and guests a once-over with the magnifying glass (although that would be hilarious), but it's helpful to know. Still, this is why inspecting your plants before purchasing is so important, as is purchasing from a reputable source—read more on this in chapter 2 (page 36). Don't be afraid to ask the plant shop about their pest-control efforts. That being said, pests are very easy to overlook, especially if you are overly excited to see a wish list plant in person and make an impulse buy. I'm speaking from experience on this one. If you're like me, you might occasionally throw caution to the wind and buy a plant without inspecting for pests. Hey, sometimes the risk is worth the reward.

If you have those tendencies, then a good habit to get into is to quarantine your new plant from other plants in your collection for two weeks. This allows the new plant to settle in and mitigates the likelihood of pests spreading from the new plant to your established plants, as well as from the old plants to the new plant.

Store-bought potting mix is also a common pest-carrying culprit. This is especially true with lower-quality soils. Potting mixes don't often contain pests like spider mites or mealybugs, but they frequently have fungus gnats at some life stage or another. This can be frustrating, because there usually aren't any good ways to know whether the potting mix you're buying has pests before you purchase it. Still, here are some tips: If the bag of soil is resealable, make sure it's OK with the store owner, then pop that baby open. Look for any small gnats that might come out. Give the bag a little shake while it's open—disturbing the potential pesky bugs into flight makes them easier to spot.

My second tip isn't as thorough, but it can reduce the risk of buying contaminated soil without even opening the bag. Fungus gnats lay their eggs in consistently damp soil, so if you pick up the bag and it's super heavy and obviously wet, dig around for a different bag that is lighter and drier. Fungus gnat eggs and larvae don't thrive in dry soil, so by checking for weight and moisture, you can give yourself a better shot at buying a clean product, which is weird to say considering you're buying soil...

If you want to be extra careful with your soil, consider sterilizing it. A simple and quick approach is to bake the soil, and all you need is a rimmed baking sheet, aluminum foil, an instant-read thermometer, and a 200°F oven. Next, make sure your soil is damp. You want it wet enough to hold moisture, but not so wet that you can squeeze water from it. Spread your damp soil evenly across the baking sheet—an inch or two deep is fine—then cover your forbidden cake mix with foil and bake it for about thirty minutes, or until it reaches 180°F when tested with the thermometer. Once the soil is sterilized, remove it from the oven and let it cool before using.

Finally, pests can come from moving plants from the outdoors to the indoors. This is very common, as plant parents often bring their collection indoors for the winter to avoid cold temperatures. Although this is the most obvious way to bring pests into your home, I find it's probably the least likely to happen, or at least less likely than you think!

Something most people don't consider is that when your plant is outside among pests, everything that kills and deters pests is also out there. The wind and the rain can make it difficult for pests to establish themselves on your plants, while natural predators will actually track them down and devour them. I can't tell you how many times I've been too lazy to treat a pest outbreak and stuck a plant outside for quarantine—with the blessing "Live if you're gonna live, die if you're gonna die"—only to return a week or two later to a squeaky-clean, pest-free plant. Sometimes you just have to let nature decide.

Before bringing my plants back indoors for the winter, I always do three things. Inspect, spray with water, and apply neem-oil. The first part is simple. I give any plant making the transition indoors a thorough inspection, paying extra attention to the undersides of leaves, where most pests hide. Next, I use the garden hose and spray down the entire plant with the goal of cleaning the leaves and blasting off any bugs I may have missed. I recommend spraying your plants down when they're outside just as often as you water them. Of course, you don't have to, but when you hose down the leaves of your outdoor plants, they're less likely to harbor pests. Just make sure the leaves are drying out each day to avoid leaf diseases that come from stagnant water. Finally, I wipe down the leaves with neem-oil. We'll discuss neem-oil in more detail in a bit, but for the moment, just know that it gives them a nice shine, so they're looking presentable to the indoor plants and decor, and because it kills most houseplant pests, it provides a layer of confidence that my home isn't about to be pest infested.

As long as you regularly check your plants and routinely clean their leaves, pests shouldn't be a big problem. It's when we neglect our preventative measures that plants tend to get pests, so do yourself a favor and make your plant-care routine part of your self-care routine. Also: Keep in mind that pest infestations are much easier to eradicate when their populations are small, which means it's best to act quickly.

Common Harmful Houseplant Pests

A ton of pests use plants as their food source, much to the detriment of the plants, but when it comes to pests that are most likely to harm your plants, there are six you want to be aware of: spider mites, mealybugs, whiteflies, aphids, thrips, and scale insects. These pests have one agenda when they sink their little straws, more accurately called "stylets," into plant tissue: They want to suck up the sugar or the cell matter the plant has worked so hard to create. I've often thought "stylets" is too nice a word for the destructive nature of this appendage and would be better suited to a band or dance team. However, I realize it's hard to argue that nature is negative—it just *is*. Anyway, if these sap suckers go unchecked, they can multiply and extract so much sugar and nutrients from the plant that its growth will be stunted, it will have permanent scarring damage, and, in severe cases, it can even die. Imagine bugs coming up to the walls of your sugar-making factory, sneaking long straws into the building through the windows, and sucking out the sugar as it's being produced. That's what these pests are doing.

My Standard Three-Step Pest Protocol

For most of these common plant pests I'm going to recommend similar if not identical treatments. There are extra tips and tricks for a few of them, based on their unique characteristics, but the basic treatment plan I outline here is what I want you to reference whenever I mention the "protocol." The standard pest protocol is also what I recommend when bringing your houseplants indoors for the winter.

Step One: Quarantine the plant. Pests are generally going to spread by way of contact, meaning if the leaves of an infested plant are touching the leaves of another plant, the pest may eventually find its way to that adjacent plant. In a perfect world, you'd move a pest-infested plant to a room all on its own, but that isn't always possible, especially if you're like me and have plants in every room of the house. Do what you can, and at the very least, make sure the infested plant isn't touching other plants.

Step Two: Spray the plant down with water. The next step is to spray the critters off with a strong stream of water. If the weather is appropriate (most houseplants are tropical and shouldn't be in temperatures below 50°F), you can take the plant outside in full shade and spray the bejesus out of it with your garden hose. Make sure to spray all parts of the plant, including the fronts and backs of the leaves, the stems, and the trunk—anything above the soil should be blasted! You may need to support the leaves with your other hand or ask your closest planty friend to lend some help to make sure the leaves don't get damaged while you administer the pest beatdown.

If you're unable to take the party outside, feel free to use the sprayer at your kitchen sink, in your bathtub, or in your shower. I cannot stress enough the importance of being thorough when treating any houseplant pests. They're great at hiding and can easily be overlooked! As long as you're not watering the soil each time, feel free to spray off your leaves daily until you no longer find pests. I like to keep the infested plant in quarantine for two weeks of clean living before they return to their original location.

Step Three: Treat the plant for pests. This step is optional, but you can also treat the plant with your favorite pest spray, making sure it fights the pest you're trying to eradicate. I like to use cold-pressed, organic neem-oil, which comes from the neem tree and is totally safe to use on houseplants. Plus, it's effective in treating all common houseplant pests. You may be tempted by the bottles of pre-diluted neem-oil products that have been sitting on the shelves or in a warehouse for who knows how long, but they can lose their effectiveness over time. Take the time to get cold-pressed, organic neem-oil and use it as directed for best results. Neem-oil does have a unique smell that some people don't like, so it's often applied outdoors. Some products may not mention this, but neem-oil should always be applied in the shade. This slows evaporation, giving the oil more time to

Bonus Pest Treatment

You may have situations where a plant is so dense or so large that it can be difficult to treat pests before they reproduce, perpetuating the cycle. I once had a client who had spider mites on a twenty-foot tree in the entryway of her home. This tree had a thick canopy of leaves, so instead of climbing a ladder and spending hours wiping the leaves down (taking it outside to the hose wasn't an option), I enlisted the help of nature's spider mite control—beneficial bugs! It's obvious when you think about it, but most people don't realize you can actually purchase predator bugs that naturally hunt other pests. I consulted with an expert to make sure I was getting the right predator for the job, placed my order, and released them at the base of the tree. Within a week the tree was pest-free, and the predator bugs had either moved on or died from starvation since they no longer had a food source. They're a bit pricier than insecticides and miticides, but very effective!

be absorbed by the leaves. It also helps prevent leaf burn. One more thing: Be thorough when applying neem-oil.

These three steps alone (quarantining, spraying with water, and treating with pest spray) will eradicate your pest problem *most of the time*. There are cases in which pests develop a resistance to the very products used to kill them. This doesn't happen often for the average houseplant collector, but it's worth noting. Insecticides and miticides work by attacking either the pests' nervous system or their ability to reproduce. If pests persist after three to five treatments of your preferred product, consider switching to a product that uses a different method.

Now that we've discussed my basic approach to ridding plants of pests—the protocol—let's go a bit deeper on different types of pests.

Spider Mites

These tiny critters come in an array of colors, including brown, green, red, yellow, and orange. In my personal experience, brown, red, and orange are the most common, but spider mites are so tiny, you'll likely need a magnifying device to actually see them. I can't tell you how many times I've been helping a client troubleshoot their plant, and they swear up and down that their plant has zero pests. Even when I explain how small spider mites are and the fact that they're often not seen with the naked eye, they insist that the cause of their plant's decline can't possibly be due to pests. They're shocked when I point out the tiny creatures inhabiting their leaves under the macro setting of my phone camera! Even when using your phone's macro setting, you're more likely to see spider mites' white eggs or webbing before you track down any actual spider mites. That's not because they're any larger but because they're stationary and have a larger footprint due to their numbers. Have you ever noticed a sticky, sap-like liquid forming on your plant's leaves? That's called "honeydew" and can also be a sign of the little buggers. Spider mites are most often found hiding on the undersides of your plant's leaves, but in severe cases, they can be seen on the topsides of the leaves as well.

SYMPTOMS: Plants being attacked by spider mites may slow down their growth because their life-giving sugar is being stolen from them. However, "slow growth" is hard to notice because plants already grow relatively slowly. An easier way to detect spider mites is the presence of honeydew, that sticky substance they leave behind once they've processed what they can from the sugar. There are other reasons for small sticky deposits on your plant's leaves, such as extrafloral nectaries—a clever method plants use to attract pollinators—but most houseplant pests extract sugar, so if you see dew on your leaves, it's a good idea to do a thorough inspection for unwanted guests.

Stippling, or tiny dots, found on the tops of leaves is another early sign of spider mites. They're the points of entry where the spider mite's "straw" is inserted, leaving behind a tiny scar of sorts. Stippling is so tiny that you really only notice it when there's a lot of it, indicating that the infestation is advanced. If you check the underside of a leaf with stippling, you'll almost always find spider mites, their webs, and/or their eggs.

Leaf color changes are also a telltale sign that something is amiss and it's worth a good inspection for pests. As spider mites extract nutrients, they also extract chlorophyll, which is green, so if you notice your leaves turning a more yellow or brown hue, check those leaf undersides for further signs of spider mites!

TREATMENT: The standard pest protocol is my recommended approach for treating spider mites. My only bonus tip for these is to be really thorough. I'll definitely mention that with other pests as well, but because spider mites are so incredibly tiny, I want to really emphasize this tip here.

Mealybugs

These small pests are covered in a white cotton-like substance that sort of resembles a cotton swab. This is actually quite helpful, as it means they contrast starkly against most plants, causing them to stick out like a sore thumb. You rarely see a single mealybug by itself, but if you do, good on ya! You'll usually find them in clumps or nests. While mealybugs are excellent at hiding, making them a particularly tricky pest, you may find them on any part of the plant, including the leaves, stems, trunks, and, in severe cases, the roots. Always

check the nooks and crannies for these guys.

SYMPTOMS: Mealybugs are another one of those pests that steal sugar from your plants. As a result, you may notice a sticky substance on your leaves, as well as a slowdown in their growth, because, again, the mealybugs are stealing your plant's sugar. This can also be accompanied by yellowing leaves, which is a stress response to the bugs taking away that vital sugar.

TREATMENT: I want you to use the standard protocol treatment for mealybugs, but I also have a few tips and tricks I've learned along the way to help get rid of these pests in just a few treatments. After following the protocol, I always follow up with a more thorough inspection. Again, I can't reiterate enough that these devilish cotton balls are great at hiding. Don't be afraid to poke and prod in all the crevices of your plant to try and locate them. They'll often build nests deep in the sheaths of your plant's leaves—the sheath is the layer near the base of the stem that protects a leaf as it emerges. You might overlook them unless you peel the sheath back with your finger, often revealing one of their nests. I like to dip a few cotton swabs in some rubbing alcohol and use them to get in all the hard-to-reach places. Being thorough and diligent is key! Repeat the protocol as often as you like and do thorough cotton swab inspections at least once per week until you're confident the mealybugs are gone, at which time you can return your plant to its regular location.

Whiteflies

These sugar thieves resemble tiny white moths. And as their name suggests, they fly! Whiteflies definitely aren't a common houseplant pest, but they do pop up from time to time, so they warrant a mention. Generally, you're going to find whiteflies congregating on the undersides of your plant's leaves, sticking their grubby straws in the leaves and removing the sugar. If you give your plant a little shake and a plume of white flying bugs appears—you've got whiteflies!

SYMPTOMS: Because whiteflies are attacking your plant to steal the sugar, the symptoms may include stunted growth, leaf yellowing, leaf curl (when the edges of plant leaves curl inward or outward), and that telltale honeydew, a byproduct of the sugar they're consuming.

TREATMENT: Start by following the standard pest treatment protocol for this one. Next, I recommend yellow sticky traps. These traps, which you can purchase online or from most plant supply stores, are made for flying pests and should catch any whiteflies you may have missed during the protocol.

Aphids

Aphids come in a wide range of colors, including green, black, brown, yellow, and even pink. In my experience, yellow and brown are the most common. They like to form clusters and are easy to spot—you'll find them covering small patches on the undersides of your leaves and around your stems.

SYMPTOMS: Aphids will cause the standard symptoms you see with all sugar-sucking pests, including stunted growth, yellowing leaves, curling leaves, and the classic honeydew deposits.

TREATMENT: The standard pest protocol treatment will do the trick to deal with aphids, but you may find they stick on the leaves and stems a bit more strongly than other pests. Follow the water-spraying step by wiping down the leaves with a clean cloth to ensure you get them all! As always, being super thorough is the key to speedy recovery.

Thrips

Thrips are small and slender and will be either black, brown, or yellow in color. Although easy to identify, they can be tricky to treat, as they're one of the more mobile houseplant pests, rapidly moving from plant to plant.

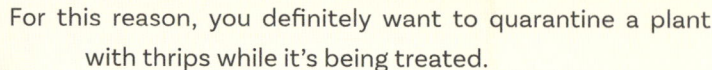

For this reason, you definitely want to quarantine a plant with thrips while it's being treated.

SYMPTOMS: Thrips are going to cause similar damage as other sugar-sucking pests, such as stunted growth, yellowing leaves, and possibly some sticky honeydew. You may also notice your plant's leaves turning bronze in color when thrips are present. This will be most noticeable on the undersides of your plant's leaves, but in developed cases, it can be seen on the tops of the leaves as well. Another unique sign of thrips are tiny black dots, which can appear on any part of the plant but most commonly show up on the leaves. They're the waste thrips leave behind after feasting on the plant's cells. Isn't it nice how these pests leave plenty of signs of their presence? We really appreciate ya, thrips.

TREATMENT: The standard pest protocol is going to make quick work of getting rid of thrips. However, because most thrips have the ability to fly, I also recommend placing a yellow sticky trap in the soil. Thrips are attracted to the yellow, so hopefully any that you missed in the standard treatment will flock to the sticky trap!

Scale Insects

Scale insects come in a couple of different forms and colors. Either they can have a soft body with a waxy coating, or they can be the armored variety that has a hardened shell covering its body. In my experience, armored scale insects are much more common. Scale insects come in white, tan, brown, and black. They're most often found on the stems and branches of your plant but can be on the undersides of the leaves as well. The tricky thing is that scale insects look like small bumps, so they blend in with plant anatomy very easily. Thankfully, once they latch on to a plant, they don't move, which makes treatment quite straightforward!

SYMPTOMS: Both varieties of scale insects can cause the usual signs of plant stress and decline, including stunted growth and yellowing or curling leaves. Soft-body scale insects leave behind the honeydew we've talked about, but armored scale insects do not.

TREATMENT: The type of scale insects you have will determine the treatment plan. For soft-body scale insects, you can use the standard treatment protocol. However, due to their protective shell, armored scale insects require a systemic pesticide. Systemic pesticides are absorbed through a plant's roots in the same way fertilizer and water are absorbed. As the pesticide moves into all parts of the plant, the scale insects will unknowingly extract and consume it, essentially killing themselves from the inside out.

Within a few days of a systemic pesticide treatment, you should be able to simply spray or wipe off the scale insects from your plant. I don't ever wish to have pests, but if I had to choose one pest to have on my plants, it would be scale insects, because systemic pesticide treatments are so easy and effective.

One More Pest: Fungus Gnats

While they're not in the same sugar-sucking category as the six pests we've already discussed, fungus gnats are perhaps the most common pests I am asked about—and for good reason.

They're annoying as all get-out! The good news about fungus gnats is that it's extremely unlikely they'll cause lasting, permanent damage to your houseplants. If you're unsure what a fungus gnat is, think of them like fruit flies. They're technically different bugs, but they look and behave nearly identically to fruit flies. Instead of hovering around your rapidly declining fruit, however, fungus gnats hang around your plant's soil. Their goal is to lay eggs, and they need a consistently damp medium to do that, making frequently watered houseplants the perfect breeding ground.

SYMPTOMS: The only real symptom of fungus gnats is annoyance. These tiny flying bugs love to get up in your face and remind you that they're infesting your plants. Like anything, there are multiple ways to look at the situation. Either you get frustrated and down on yourself that the bugs are there, or you can shake the bugs' hands and thank them for giving you a sign that you may need to let your plant's soil dry out more between waterings. I choose the latter. The only thing is, every time I go to shake their hands, I'm too enthusiastic and wind up clapping them between my hands. Oh well.

Seriously, though, the presence of fungus gnats, as mentioned before, is a very early sign that you might be watering your plants too frequently, and root rot could be right around the corner. There are very few houseplants that don't at least want their topsoil to dry between waterings, which is enough to detract fungus gnats from using your soil as egg-laying material.

TREATMENT: When ridding your plants of fungus gnats, it's important to address them at each stage of their life cycle—adult, larva, pupa, and egg. You'll treat all the stages simultaneously, but each one has its own procedure. The lifespan of a fungus gnat is only about a month, so give yourself that full month to make sure they're completely gone.

Adult fungus gnats are the most annoying, so let's tackle them first. I like to use a fungus gnat trap, and there are several effective options. Yellow sticky traps are one, but there are also small machines specifically designed to attract and kill fungus gnats. For either one, simply follow the instructions on the packaging. If you'd prefer to take the DIY route, fill a small dish with apple cider vinegar and a drop of dish soap. Place the dish near the plant you suspect has fungus gnats and watch the little buggers accumulate in your concoction! Change the solution periodically to keep things fresh.

Fungus gnat larvae and pupae can be addressed at the same time using a product that contains Bti, such as Mosquito Bits. Bti, or *Bacillus thuringiensis* subspecies *israelensis*, is a naturally occurring soil bacterium that kills the larvae and pupae. It comes as a granular product that's used to make a "tea" of sorts that you water your plant with, killing the larvae and pupae in the soil. Be thorough, as there's no good way to know where they're lurking in the soil!

Fungus gnat eggs can be treated two ways. The first is effective, but the second is super effective! The easiest thing to do is to simply let the top inch or so of your soil dry out. Eggs are laid on or near the surface of the soil, and since they need a moist environment to hatch, letting the top inch of soil dry will make them unable to hatch. If you want to further guarantee these winged annoyances are gone for good, let the soil dry out, then sprinkle diatomaceous earth on the topmost layer. Then, even if the eggs do hatch, they will crawl out of the soil and immediately be covered in this abrasive material and die shortly after.

THE "MOST LIKELY" GUIDE TO PLANT PROBLEMS

If you're local to our plant store in Prosper, Texas, then you can take advantage of our repotting service, dropping off your plant to have it repotted by experienced professionals. These repots often come in when a plant is declining and the owner doesn't know what to do but assumes the plant must need a new pot. Because of this service—and because so many fans and followers reach out for help via social media—I've had the opportunity to diagnose, fix, or treat hundreds of declining plants. Through this experience, I've noticed certain issues popping up over and over again, and I've been able to narrow down the cause of these problems to a fairly short list.

I want to be clear that there's nothing absolute about this list, as it's based solely on my personal experiences with houseplants. For each symptom listed, there are, in actuality, a dozen or more possible causes. However, these are the ones I've found to be most common, which is why I call this the "most likely" guide.

Yellowing Leaves

Leaves turning yellow on your plant ultimately means one thing: Your plant is under stress! To determine the cause of that stress, we must ask ourselves some questions to help deduce the most likely culprit. First, where on the plant is the yellow leaf or leaves? If new growth is emerging yellow, or quickly turns yellow and dies off, you probably have a case of root rot and need to intervene as soon as you can.

If the oldest leaves of your plant, the ones located nearest the soil level, are turning yellow, that's most likely a sign of old age. Leaves are made up of cells, and those cells wear out eventually. These old leaves have been working for a longer time than the younger ones, so when you notice them yellowing and dying off, you can confidently chalk that up to it being old growth and understand that it's totally natural for them to expire. I like to think of it as retirement for the leaf. Feel free to have a mini retirement party when this happens. You can prune these leaves, but it's also fine to leave them on the plant and let them expire naturally. In fact, I actually like to keep old, yellowing leaves on my plant as a reminder that I'm dealing with a living creature. Plus, completely yellow leaves can make for a cool Instagram photo.

When leaves that are more centrally located on your plant are turning yellow, this is often a result of pests, disease, or fungal/bacterial issues. As soon as you can, inspect further to identify the problem and treat accordingly. I want to note that leaf yellowing anywhere on the plant can be a sign of pests, depending on what part of the plant a pest chooses to attack, so even if you suspect leaf yellowing to be caused by something else, always do a quick pest check to be sure.

Browning Leaves

As with yellowing leaves, browning leaves mean a plant is under stress, and you have to ask yourself some questions about the plant's environment and care in order to arrive at the most likely source of that stress. When you see leaves browning on a plant, again, you want to focus on location—not only the location of the leaf on the plant but also the location of the browning on the leaf. Where you find a browning leaf on your plant and the likely reason is the same as for yellowing leaves: New-growth leaves turning brown is probably due to root rot, while leaves near the soil turning brown is probably due to old age. The color of an old leaf dying off simply because it's old or a new leaf dying off due to root rot depends on where it is in the dying-off process. The leaf may yellow first, then brown, then fall off, or in some cases simply turn yellow, then fall off.

We can also learn a lot from how a leaf is browning. Is the browning touching the edges of the leaf? In that case, a moisture problem is usually to blame—either underwatering, low humidity, or both. Browning edges are especially common in winter, when most of us in the northern hemisphere kick on the heat as temperatures drop outside. Hot air coming from a furnace or wood-burning fireplace makes the once cool, humid air super dry, causing leaf edges to get crispy. Keeping your plants away from vents blowing air on them will reduce the chances of crispy, brown edges due to low humidity.

If you want to help your plants through an exceptionally dry period, consider investing in a humidifier to combat the dry air. I'm not responsible enough to keep up with a humidifier at this stage of life, so I opt to huddle my plants together during the dry winter months. When plants are kept

close together, the evaporating moisture in each pot of soil gets trapped among the leaves, creating a microclimate that's higher in humidity, thus reducing the chances of any leaf edges browning.

Poor water quality can also cause the edges and tips of your leaves to turn brown and crispy. Keep in mind that plants have different standards of water quality than humans, so water coming from your home tap may be perfectly healthy for you, but it might not be good for your plants. Even though different houseplants originate from different parts of the world, they all have the same water source: rain. For plants, pure rainwater is the gold standard of water and what they have adapted to thrive on. When we give our plants tap water that has been treated according to municipal standards, they can sometimes exhibit browning leaf edges or tips, which is one way that plants show signs of stress.

Watering your plants with tap water won't *usually* cause your plants to croak, but it does mean they might not be as pristine as they could be. Thankfully, there are a few ways to avoid those brown edges that come from poor water quality. First, choose a different water source, such as reverse osmosis (RO) water, distilled water, or collected rainwater. If you use RO water or distilled water, your plants will miss out on some crucial min-

erals they would otherwise get from tap water, but if you're fertilizing your plant with everything it needs to grow, this won't be an issue.

If you're set on using tap water but you want to avoid the browning, you can always purify it or flush it. I use a combination of the two. What we're trying to minimize here is the total dissolved solids (TDS) of your water, which is basically a measurement that shows how many particles of anything but water is in your water. This mostly includes things like salts, minerals, and metals. It's a buildup of these non-water particles (especially salt) that can cause browning on the edges of your leaves.

Using a standard drinking-water filter is a great way to lower the TDS of your water, slowing the rate at which an unfavorable buildup of salts, minerals, and metals will occur. These filters are affordable and can be found at just about any grocery store and certainly online. Lowering the TDS of your water not only helps your plants but is good for humans too. If you want to seem like less of a crazy plant person to friends, family, or a significant other, I suggest justifying your new water filtration system as being for your health—and not the plants!

There's not much to it, but since I admitted to employing both methods of tap-water cleaning, I ought to share the second method, flushing. Whether you're watering with tap water or not, you should be fertilizing. Fertilizers contain salts, minerals, and metals that can build up and cause the edges of leaves to brown. To combat the buildup, which is a natural consequence of confining the plant to a pot, simply water your plants with a generous amount of clean water (RO, distilled, or rainwater). Flush each potted plant a few times, or as much as your water supply allows, to get out as much of the built-up material as possible—I like to imagine all the gunk draining away with each flushing. Ideally, I would be diligent in this arena, but the truth is I flush my soil only as often as distilled water catches my eye at the grocery store, which is roughly once every few months. Another good sign that should expedite the chore is when you discover a white hazing on your topsoil. It will be almost chalk-like in appearance and have no perceivable dimension, unlike mold, which is also white and hazy but extends beyond the soil.

In addition to water quality, you should also consider water quantity. If a plant hasn't been sufficiently watered, it may get stressed to the point of browning on the leaf edges. This sign is frequently coupled with cracks in

Tap Water and Chlorine

City tap water is treated for cleanliness with one of two chemicals: chlorine or chloramine, a mix of chlorine and ammonia. Both chemicals have a reputation for being harmful to plants, but this isn't actually the case. In fact, plants *need* chlorine as a micronutrient. It's true that if the level of chlorine or chloramine in water is too high it can be toxic to plants, but city water legally cannot reach a chlorine or chloramine level high enough to cause harm, which is why they can be ruled out as causing problems for your plants.

your soil, indicating that it has been dry for an extended period. Using your probe, check the moisture level in your soil and water accordingly.

Finally, remember that browning tips and edges can be perfectly natural for a healthy plant! The browning will not return to green upon diagnosing and treating, so feel free to remove the leaf or the brown parts of the leaf. Remember, though, that any time we create open wounds on our plants, we are exposing the plant to diseases that may enter the open wound, and although those chances are small, it's good to keep in mind.

Leaf Spot Disease

Let's start with the good news. As a houseplant parent, you are unlikely to deal with many leaf diseases. This is because most diseases that naturally plague plants—remember that houseplants do actually grow outdoors somewhere in the world—prefer or even require conditions that only an outdoor environment provides. Hooray, another win for houseplant parenthood! There are several leaf diseases that could possibly affect plants kept indoors, but there's one that occurs more often than the rest, and that's leaf spot disease.

Leaf spots look like brown dots on the surface of leaves; they can be dry and crispy or mushy, often with a yellow or reddish ring around the perimeter of the dot. Although leaf spot disease is slow to take over a houseplant and cause its demise, it's unsightly and something you'll want to intervene on. Start by completely removing the affected leaves from the plant and tossing them in the trash. This will instantly restore the beauty of your plant and keep the disease from spreading to other leaves and nearby plants. Next, get a copper-based fungicide and apply it to all the leaves of the plant to further prevent the possibility of spread.

Like all things plant pest and disease related, prevention is key! Leaf spot disease is more likely to occur on leaves that are consistently damp or wet. To mitigate the likelihood of leaf spots popping up on your houseplants, make sure they're getting plenty of airflow to their leaves and avoid splashing them with water if you can. This suggestion may seem like overkill, as it stands to reason that plants in their native environments get rained on all the time and therefore their leaves get wet, so what's the difference? The difference is that plants living outside are subject to more light, heat, and wind than plants kept indoors, and all those factors help dry plant leaves before leaf spot disease can set in.

Leaf Scorch

We've all been guilty of leaving our houseplants in light that's too strong for too long, resulting in leaf scorch, which looks like splotches of white or brown patches that can occur anywhere on the leaf. When I got my very first monstera, I wanted it to grow big as quickly as possible. One weekend in August, I took it outside to give it a thorough soak and what I thought would be better light for the day. I left the plant outside while I grabbed fertilizer, and in the two minutes it took me to get the fertilizer from the garage, several of the leaves on my monstera had gone completely brown and limp. Did I mention I live in Texas? That plant was decimated in no time! Luckily, the larger, taller leaves shielded the smaller, shorter ones from the direct sun and I was able to grow the plant again from those smaller leaves, but it was quite a setback for my big-leaf monstera dreams!

To deal with the leaf scorch, I trimmed off all the brown, unsightly leaves. If the leaf was dead all the way back to the petiole, which is the stem the leaf is attached to, then I removed the entire petiole, as a new leaf wouldn't grow there again. If the leaf was only partially scorched, then I would remove just the affected parts. You can remove a partially brown leaf entirely if you don't like the way it looks, but for the health of the plant, and especially if your plant doesn't have a lot of leaves already, consider keeping as much green as you can so that the plant can photosynthesize more, which will help it recover from the sudden loss of leaves.

When you're doing this kind of plant cleanup, make sure you use clean tools to protect any open wounds on the plant, as well as to avoid bad bacteria getting in and causing more problems. I recommend giving your blades a healthy spritz of isopropyl alcohol before making cuts. I also like to dust open wounds with organic ground cinnamon, because its antibacterial properties protect the plant while it's exposed to the outside environment.

Many of the plants we keep indoors do grow in full, direct sunlight in their native habitat, but the houseplant version of this plant was grown in a greenhouse, so it's no longer acclimated to its native habitat. Greenhouses are designed to protect plants from the harsher conditions of the great outdoors, making the growing conditions easier to manage and creating better rates of success.

Leaf scorch can also happen indoors, and it's quite common for houseplant advice to dictate that certain plants can't be kept in windows facing certain directions because the light is too strong. If you're talking about large windows that face south or west, this may be true, but there's no definitive way to know if a plant is going to get scorched sitting in front of a certain window, because everyone's exposures are different. As I mentioned, I live in Texas, one of the hottest states in the country. I've kept dozens of houseplants—including fiddle-leaf fig, *Monstera deliciosa*, *Ficus elastica*, euphorbia, tiger fern, and golden pothos, along with succulents, philodendrons, anthuriums, and alocasia—in my hottest, biggest, most unobstructed south-facing window, and none of them have ever had leaf scorch. But your large, unobstructed south-facing window could have slightly different exposure, and it only takes a tiny degree of difference to cause leaf scorch.

If you're concerned that your plant might get scorched in a certain window, take it slow. Keep your plant a few feet away from the window, maintaining a view of the sky but avoiding that really strong light. You may find your plant doesn't need as strong of light as you thought, indicated by new, healthy growth. Keep it there if you like, but also feel free to gradually nudge the plant closer to the window each week until you've reached the place where you'd like the plant to stay. Continue to monitor the plant along the way for scorch and back it away from the light if needed. This slower acclimating approach may help avoid some sad, scorched leaves.

Etiolation

When a plant isn't getting enough light, it gets leggy, stretched out, or, to use fancy terminology, etiolated. This sparse-looking appearance may also be coupled with the plant leaning toward a light source, usually the nearest window. This is the plant's way of communicating that it needs more light to reach its full potential. Plant parents are often surprised to discover just how bright true low light is to their eyes, or to learn that a room they consider bright actually has medium light when measured with a light meter. I've had a fair share of plant parents tell me their plant doesn't need bright light and is thriving in low light, only to find that although their plant is tall, it's also stretched out with leaves spaced farther apart on the stem than they should be. In other words, the plant is etiolated. Remember, just because a plant is tall, that doesn't mean it's healthy.

If a plant is etiolated, you don't have to move it to brighter light, but it is an indication that the plant isn't getting as much light as it needs to stay healthy. Lower light exposures may result in a weaker plant with slower growth. It also gives the plant owner less room for error when it comes to watering, because the plant simply won't have the same capacity to process water efficiently. Still, etiolated plants are some of the most charming plants I've ever seen. As they stretch out in search of more light, they can take on new shapes, sometimes unique from their standard form, and the results can be quite whimsical.

GENERAL HOUSEPLANT TROUBLESHOOTING GUIDE

Over the years, I've helped hundreds of clients deduce what's going wrong with their plants and provided plans of action for remedying the issues. And in that time, I've constructed a step-by-step method for accurately weeding out the actual problem, which is super valuable because a single symptom can mean one or potentially multiple different issues. For example, a yellow leaf can be caused by overwatering, underwatering, underfertilizing, overfertilizing, pests, low humidity, high humidity, or even sudden environmental changes. Oh, and it can also be totally natural, as in the case of old leaves simply wearing out and dying off.

This is one of the reasons plant care can be seen as confusing and difficult! Throw in the very real possibility that when you ask friends or professionals for help, they give you a remedy that solved their own specific problem, because they assume you're having the same specific problem, even though it could be something completely different.

I see this type of scenario most often in the case of repotting. I used to participate in tons of houseplant forums and online groups, and I would constantly see repotting as a cure-all for any and all plant ailments. Plant is slow growing? Sounds like it needs a new pot! My plant grew four feet after I gave it room to grow. Yellow leaves on your plant? Definitely needs a bigger pot—it's stressed because the roots have nowhere to go!

Like I've said before, repotting your plant as a default remedy to plant stress is like having brain surgery because you have a headache. It might help the situation, but maybe you just needed to drink some water. The repot may have helped the situation, because now there's more moisture-retaining soil around the roots that prevents the plant from drying out so quickly and the leaves turning yellow, but you could have avoided the stress of a repot simply by watering more frequently or perhaps more thoroughly. Looking at your plant's conditions and analyzing its care will help narrow down the most likely cause of a problem, and that will go a long way in reducing frustration and increasing joy in keeping houseplants.

Now that I've hopefully got you on board with my approach, here's my step-by-step method:

Step One: Consider your plant's lighting. If I haven't stressed the importance of lighting enough in this book, let this serve as one more reminder. Proper lighting is the biggest key to a thriving houseplant, while improper lighting can contribute to every possible problem faced by a plant. Even if your plant has been growing happily in its current light situation, make sure it's receiving enough light before taking any further steps. Keep the following in mind: Outdoor trees grow and can obstruct light coming in through the window, the position of the sun in the sky changes throughout the year, diminishing or increasing the light your plant receives, and plants grow to the point where most of their leaves are no longer "seeing" the sky. Even grow lights lose their effectiveness over time! For more on light, revisit chapter 3 (page 53).

Step Two: Consider your watering habits. Plants and their conditions are constantly changing, and even though these changes are usually small, they can have big impacts over time. For example, proper care will help your plant's roots grow. The more roots there are, the faster they take up water. Having more roots also increases how quickly your soil drains. Anyone who's ever watered a root-bound plant and had the experience of the water barely touching the soil surface before it drained out the bottom can attest to this. Root growth is a relatively slow process, so you might find yourself successfully watering on a schedule. But at some point, the increased drainage and water consumption are going to cause the plant to dry out faster, and, as a result, your plant might need water before your "watering day."

Or maybe you recently repotted your plant and increased the pot size—you may have even changed the pot material. Perhaps you looked up a certain soil recipe for your plant before repotting, making the soil composition different from what you've grown used to while caring for this particular plant. As we learned in the repotting chapter (page 102), soil ingredients and pot material can drastically reduce or increase the amount of water that's held on to, which can cause your plant to dry out faster or slower. It's always important to consider all changes that may have occurred with your plant and adjust your watering habits accordingly. This is why I always recommend checking the moisture level of your soil before watering—you never know when small changes can reach a tipping point! For more on watering, revisit chapter 4 (page 80).

Step Three: Check for pests! This one is obvious but can be a challenge if you don't know what to look for. Heck, even if you do know what to look for, pests can be easily missed due to their small size. Most pests are going to hide on the undersides of leaves, so that's where you want to check. I encourage you to first look with the naked eye for obvious signs of pests, such as sticky deposits and webbing. If you find anything that's not plant material on your leaves, spray or wipe it off, then go about a full pest treatment, according to the pest you've identified.

Step Four: Consider whether your plant has been through any recent changes. Remember that plants haven't evolved to grow indoors in a pot— we're just lucky they can survive such conditions. They're meant to live outside, and the further away a plant gets from receiving the conditions it would in its natural environment, the more stress it experiences. Have you recently moved to a new apartment or home? Has the weather turned cold and the window your plants sit near gone a bit drafty? Did you have to treat the plant for root rot or pests? Even if it was a standard repot, in which everything went off without a hitch, let's not forget that repotting a plant is totally unnatural to this stationary creature.

Perhaps the most common of all houseplant stressors comes from the plant-buying process itself. Our brick-and-mortar plant store, Famous In Oregon, does about 80 percent of its business online and ships plants all over the country. We constantly have to remind our customers that plants may exhibit some "travel fatigue," a term we use to convey how stressful it can be for a plant to be shipped in a dark box. We follow this up by asking how the customer felt the last time they traveled. "How long did it take your body and mind to recover after your last flying experience?" Remember, plants are living, and living things often exhibit signs of stress when put in unfamiliar conditions!

PART TWO

THE PLANTS

There are a host of ways to be successful with your houseplants, and truth be told, everyone sort of finds their own groove with their personal plant collection over time—that's part of the learning curve that I hope was at least somewhat flattened in part one. My goal is that by learning a few basic principles you will be able to decipher plant care and understand it in a way that makes sense for you, that is applicable to you, that serves you, and that helps you to experience all of the tangible, magical, and exciting rewards that having plants in your spaces offers. This is a hobby of a lifetime, for a lifetime!

Part one was about understanding how plants work and the common ideas and concepts you need to grasp to have full confidence in your plant-caring capabilities. Part two is where you're going to apply what you've learned to some of the most popular houseplants of all time. As you go through each plant profile, I hope you notice how the different plant anatomies affect how far down a plant's soil needs to dry between waterings, and why the soil recipes change from plant to plant. This foundation will help you develop a keen understanding of how to take care of houseplants without needing to reference a guide. And that will come in handy, because once you realize how simple plants are to grow, it'll be increasingly difficult to turn them down as they enter your life by way of gifted cuttings, an irresistible photo on a plant website, that cute brick-and-mortar plant shop in your town, a live selling event, or even the produce section at your local grocery store. If you haven't already noticed, plants are everywhere! The excitement and infinite joy you feel around plants will only increase as you build your confidence, and you should have a large supply of that as you enter part two!

BEFORE WE BEGIN...
Homemade Soil Mixtures

Except in special cases, such as carnivorous plants and orchids, you need only three soil recipes for houseplants. For most of the plants profiled in this section, you'll see I've recommended one of these three soils. Of course, you know after reading chapter 5 (page 102) that the type of soil you use isn't going to make or break your houseplant success, and that by not using these soil recipes you absolutely will not be sending your plants to their doom. Feel free to substitute these ingredients with ones of your own choosing. My only caveat is recommending that you follow the guidelines of moisture-retaining and moisture-draining ratios, also discussed in chapter 5.

    Mixing your own soil is a great way to save money! However, if you'd like to purchase premixed soil, that's great too! You can substitute my general-purpose mix with any general-purpose potting mix, and it should have similar moisture-retaining properties. The same goes for the succulent soil—just double-check that the succulent soil you choose is for potted plants and not in-ground use. The aroid soil mixture is the only one you can't purchase, so if that sounds like the one most appropriate for your plant or plants, you'll need to mix that one up yourself.

When mixing your own soil, I recommend doing so outside or in a well-ventilated area, as the fine particles from peat moss and perlite are no good to breathe in! On that note, if you're using peat moss, wet it down before mixing it with other ingredients. It's much easier to work with and less dusty when it's wet.

Aroid Soil: This mixture is light and airy, providing a bit of moisture retention as well as airflow. Aroid soil is the most versatile mixture and can be used successfully on most houseplants, provided the rest of the plant's needs are being met.
Ingredients: Equal parts peat moss, perlite, and orchid bark
* Perlite and orchid bark may be available in different diameter sizes. Smaller diameters will retain more moisture, and larger diameters will drain faster.

General-Purpose Potting Soil: This mixture is great for plants that like to retain a bit more moisture than the average houseplant, such as ferns and peace lilies. It focuses more on moisture retention, but it also contains amendments to help oxygen return to the roots quickly to prevent root rot.
Ingredients: Two parts peat moss, one part perlite, and one part sand
* Always use sand that has been washed, making it a suitable soil amendment.

Succulent Soil: This mixture is perfect for plants that want to dry out quickly—think desert plants. It's a fast-draining mix that allows for minimal water retention and maximum airflow, just what the succulent doctor ordered.
Ingredients: One part peat moss, one part perlite, and two parts sand
* Remember that only washed sand should be used for soil amendments.

I prefer to store my unused dry soil in a plastic storage bin with a lid. This helps keep unwanted bugs out, saves money, and means you always have soil on hand!

Watering

Each plant profile includes my recommendation for when to water. There are a few exceptions, but most direct you to water either when the topsoil is dry or when the soil is dry up to a certain percentage—25 percent, 50 percent, 75 percent, or 100 percent—from the top down. I recommend using a blunt object, such as a chopstick or knitting needle, to test levels of soil dryness by using the "baking method," which I outline in chapter 4 (page 80). For plants that just need their topsoil to dry between waterings, I simply touch the soil with my finger and forgo the chopstick.

Plant Toxicity

We all want to do the best for our pets, so make sure to research plant toxicity or consult your veterinarian before bringing plants where your pets live. That being said, I do want to share a bit of insight on plant toxicity that may offer some comfort when you're deciding whether to bring your plants and pets together.

Most houseplants are toxic to most common pets, that's true. But they're toxic in a similar way that alcohol is toxic to humans. If we drink too much alcohol, we throw it up. If they eat too much of a plant, they throw it up. Of course, we never want our pets to suffer, but hopefully that will help ease your mind a bit. Keep in mind that there are common houseplants that can be deadly to your pets, such as dieffenbachia and some lily varieties, so absolutely consult your veterinarian for questions regarding your pet(s) and plant(s) if you have concerns.

Average Indoor Size

The sizes referenced in the plant profiles represent the average size you can hope to achieve when growing a given plant indoors. Many of these plants will get much larger in their native environment or in a greenhouse setting. Always keep in mind that the size of your plant may differ depending on your conditions.

Propagation

Propagation, which refers to the process of creating new plants from existing ones, is a big topic, and this is not a book about propagation—there are plenty of books on that subject if you want to learn more. However, by including propagation methods as part of each plant profile, my hope is that you'll explore the houseplant hobby further by trying your hand at one of the techniques, allowing you to multiply the plants in your collection.

Propagation exposes you to a beautiful and natural process in the life of plants, an experience you simply cannot get from a store. If you keep up with this hobby, you'll likely find yourself gifting plants you propagated from your personal collection, which makes for a very special present!

Disclaimer: You'll notice the most widely known method for propagation, collecting and planting seeds, isn't included in the list—though it is the method listed for Kentia palm, as this is the only way to propagate this plant. I'm not going to discuss seed propagation, because although it's the most commonly understood method, it's rarely practiced in the houseplant community. I've always assumed it's not popular because most houseplants won't flower indoors, and even if they do, they'd likely need to be hand-pollinated since the bugs that pollinate them are outside. But the truth is that it's much slower to grow plants by seed, and many houseplant seedlings need special conditions you wouldn't find in the average home. The following methods are the most widely used, the most accessible, and the quickest ways to propagate your houseplants.

Cuttings: This method, which is also known as clippings, simulates how a plant might respond to their leaf, stem, or branch being severed in nature. You'll need a pair of clean, sharp pruners or scissors. Keeping them clean avoids the potential spread of disease from one plant to another, and keeping them sharp avoids damaging more of the plant than is needed when taking the cutting. To sterilize my pruners, I keep a spray bottle of isopropyl alcohol on hand and spray the blades between cuts. Although this may be overkill for the average hobbyist, it never hurts to mitigate potential problems, especially when such little effort is involved. There are two methods for propagation via cuttings: leaf cuttings and stem cuttings.

Leaf Cutting: Select a healthy leaf and cut at its base, making sure you have a bit of petiole (stem) still attached at the base of the leaf. Put the cut end in water (there's no need for the waterline to cover more than the cut) and leave it sitting in a warm window until roots form.

Stem Cutting: Locate a node (the spot where leaves or branches grow from the main stem) and cut about one-fourth inch below it. As with leaf cutting, put the cut end in water and wait for roots to form.

Each plant will vary in the amount of time it takes to form roots, but six to eight weeks is the average.

Division: Dividing plants is instant propagation because you're simply dividing a large plant into smaller plants that (ideally) already have root systems and can live on their own. You'll hear the terms "division" and "pup division" used interchangeably when discussing propagation. Division is when you have either multiple plants in a pot that started out as one plant that produced more plants, or multiple plants that were potted together from the beginning and now you're dividing (untangling) their roots from one another so they can be potted on their own. Pup division more specifically refers to the separation of a baby plant from its mother plant. Planting multiple plants in the same pot is a common practice for commercial growers, as it allows them to quickly have a fuller-looking plant to sell—it also means you may be able to divide your plant right when you get it! Keep in mind that not all plants can be divided, as there must be multiple plants in the same pot to have something to divide. You shouldn't need any extra tools for this method, but you may need some extra pots and soil on hand for planting your newly separated plants.

I find division goes more smoothly with wet soil, so plan on trying this method just after a good soak. With wet soil, you can remove the plant from its pot and start massaging the root ball, just like you're going to do a repot except that you want to remove most of the soil. With the soil removed, you should have a better idea of where the plants will separate. Take hold of each plant you're dividing and try to gently wiggle them apart. This requires a bit of patience, but taking your time will avoid unnecessary root loss—although you should expect to find some broken roots by the end of this. If you're finding it difficult to pull the plants apart and feel like you might break something, remove more soil and try again. For really stubborn plants, I swish the roots in a bucket of water or spray them with the sink faucet to loosen the soil. Repeat these steps until you can easily pull the plants apart. Once divided, you can plant your division in its new pot!

Air Layering: This propagation method is like taking a cutting, but we're using the power of the mother plant to grow roots from its stem or branch while still attached! Air layering works best with woody stems and branches, such as those found on the fiddle-leaf fig, or vining plants like *Monstera deliciosa*—although when working with vining plants you skip one step, which I'll explain.

You'll need a knife, pruners, some regular potting soil or long-fiber sphagnum moss, a foot of plastic wrap, some tape or string, and a rag to clean up any drips of sap.

Choose a healthy stem or branch and use a knife to carefully remove a ring of the bark, exposing the flesh of the branch—this is called the "cambium layer." Use your rag to clean up any sap oozing from the wound. Next, use your knife or pruners to carefully scrape the exposed layer to encourage root development; a few passes are plenty. Next, wet down your soil or moss—I've used both mediums with equal success. Squeeze the excess moisture out of your chosen medium and wrap it around the entire wound, making sure to completely cover the cambium layer with it. Hold it in place with one hand while your other hand wraps the plastic wrap around the medium. It should be tight enough that the medium doesn't fall out. Secure each end of the plastic wrap with tape or string. Over the next several weeks the plant will grow roots throughout the moss or soil in the plastic. Check on your plant once per week; you want to keep the medium damp throughout this process. When it has a few inches of roots, you can cut the branch just below your newly formed root ball, remove the plastic, and plant it in its own pot!

If you're air layering a vining plant, then all you'll need to do is secure your damp medium around a node and care for it the same way as described above. New roots will grow from the node when it's exposed to the moisture from your chosen medium, after which you can cut the vine below the roots and plant it in its own pot.

A Few Final Thoughts

Now that you're armed with the truth about houseplants and the methods behind their care, please go and grow! My hope is that you'll use this section as a reference for your plant care. I know the different seasons of life can bring challenges that shift your focus away from tending to your plants, which is why I always include "consistent plant care" in my annual list of New Year's resolutions after often neglecting my collection during the holiday season. I'm a repeat offender, and if plants aren't your living like they are mine, it's easy to forget when plants are supposed to be watered, what fertilizer to use, etc. Thinking about repotting because it's been years since you first bought the plant, and you just realized it's still in the same soil? I hope you crack open that chapter (page 102), get a refresher, and are reminded of how enjoyable it is to get your hands dirty with houseplants.

    I also hope you use part two as a shopping guide, because, as you now know, having happy houseplants doesn't always mean getting the exact plant you want. It starts with getting a plant that can live in the conditions you have available for it! You can even take this book with you to the plant shop and use it as your little cheat sheet.

    And finally, I hope you use this section of the book to discover something new and share it with a friend. While I've never met someone who would hate to have a thriving houseplant in their space, they're often passed up for other decor items, including fake plants, due to a lack of confidence in caring for the real thing. If you find these tips helpful, don't gatekeep! Remember: Plants are for everyone!

THIRTY OF THE MOST POPULAR HOUSEPLANTS— AND HOW TO CARE FOR THEM

COMMON NAME: Ag

Aglaonema
(Aglaonema)

Soil: Aroid soil

Light: Bright (1,000 fc or more), medium (250–999 fc), or low (100–250 fc) light

Watering: When the soil is 25 percent to 50 percent dry from the top down

Fertilizer: General-purpose or organic fertilizer

Toxicity: Toxic to pets and people

Average Indoor Size: 3 feet tall

Native To: Southeast Asia

Propagation: Division and stem cuttings

Pot Selection: A clay pot is best, but any pot with drainage holes will work.

This is one of my top five most beginner-friendly plants (page 49). Aglaonema come in a variety of unique colors and leaf patterns, plus they are easy to care for and versatile for decor. I love Aglaonema because they're one of the few low-light tolerant plants that come in more colors than just green. In fact, some of their most vibrant varieties can get *very* red. I often joke during the holiday season that red Aglaonema needs to replace the poinsettia to become the new Christmas plant. If I could wave a magical influencer wand and make that happen, I would. I mean, which would you rather have, a green plant that requires frequent watering and special lighting conditions to turn red (poinsettia) or a green-and-red plant that requires less frequent watering, lives in a wide range of lighting conditions, and stays red and green year-round (Aglaonema)?

Bonus Tip

Aglaonema are such champions of low-light tolerance that they may even bloom in low light, which is quite uncommon for plants in those conditions. Their bloom, more accurately called an "inflorescence," can get quite sticky during the blooming process. To avoid the mess and possible issues that follow, including bugs looking for the sticky sugar, I recommend removing the inflorescence as soon as it shows up. Blooms are nice confirmations that we're doing all the right things, and I would usually say to keep them on, but if the bloom isn't pretty, and I don't think this one is, you can remove it altogether, saving the energy the plant spends on flowering and directing it to the foliage. With clean, sharp pruners, simply follow the inflorescence stem down to where it emerges from the plant and cut it there.

Bonus Tip

Anthuriums vary greatly in their tolerance to average home conditions, so make sure you research a variety's specific needs before purchasing. Many varieties will do beautifully on your windowsill, while others require conditions more likely found in a greenhouse. That being said, anthuriums are very adaptable to their environment, so give them time to settle into your space before losing hope. I can't tell you how many times I've been asked for help with an anthurium that developed brown, crispy leaves and then lost all or most of their leaves in the weeks following a change of environment, only to have new leaves come in and look absolutely perfect once the plant had time to acclimate to its new space.

Anthurium
(Anthurium)

COMMON VARIETIES: *Crystallinum*, flamingo flower, *forgetii*

Soil: Aroid soil

Light: Bright (1,000 fc or more) light

Watering: When the soil is 25 percent to 50 percent dry from the top down

Fertilizer: General-purpose or organic fertilizer

Toxicity: Toxic to pets and people

Average Indoor Size: 12 to 18 inches tall

Native To: Tropical rainforests of Central and South America

Propagation: Division and stem cuttings

Pot Selection: A clay pot is best, but any pot with drainage holes will work.

There are two types of people who grow anthuriums. The first saw the most common variety, the flamingo flower, at their local grocery store and couldn't resist, or they were gifted that same anthurium by a friend. The second is someone who fell head over heels for plants and then fell further in love when they discovered anthuriums and now have thirty varieties growing on their windowsills and makeshift greenhouses. You've heard of hobbyists obsessed with orchids, begonias, or hoya, but what you may not know is that anthurium people are just as passionate (crazy) about this genus—you just don't hear from them, because they're too busy admiring their plant's stunning leaves, cleaning those stunning leaves, or photographing those stunning leaves. I greatly admire anthurium-obsessed people, because unlike other groups of people who deep dive into one genus, their devotion for the plant almost exclusively comes from the leaves instead of the flowers, which are easy to love. Anthuriums do bloom, but almost none of them produce a flower that's considered pretty, and I think it's special to admire something so small as a leaf with such colossal passion.

All About the Crown

Anthuriums like to be planted with their crowns (where all the stems meet in the middle near the base) above the soil level. You may have noticed this upon purchase. Before repotting, take note of how high your anthurium is planted and replicate that placement when repotting.

Common Problems

Because the most popular variety of anthurium—the flamingo flower—produces a beautiful flower (technically, it's called a "spathe"), the most common problem is it not producing its flower. It takes a lot of energy for anthurium to grow their spathe, and they need adequate light to expend that energy. What's tricky is that this type of anthurium will grow new, happy foliage in lower amounts of light than what's required to grow a flower, and when you see that foliage, you'll think you're doing all the right things, but you're still not getting a flower. If your plant hasn't bloomed in six months to one year, you might consider measuring your light with a light meter to make sure it's getting what it needs.

COMMON NAMES:
BOP, crane flower

Bird-of-Paradise
(Strelitzia)

Soil: Aroid soil

Light: Bright (1,000 fc or more) light

Watering: When the soil is 25 percent to 50 percent dry from the top down

Fertilizer: General-purpose or organic fertilizer

Toxicity: Toxic to pets and people

Average Indoor Size: 3 to 8 feet tall

Native To: South Africa

Propagation: Division

Pot Selection: A clay pot is best, but any pot with drainage holes will work.

This popular plant can be found just about anywhere plants are sold. They're adaptable and fast growing, and they have huge leaves that scream "I'M TROPICAL," which makes them a favorite for decor in places of business as well as in homes. Birds-of-paradise are commonly mistaken for palm trees, due to their large, overarching leaves held up by a relatively narrow stalk. Their symmetrical growth habit is a beautiful balance of what looks like intended symmetry but is still obviously organic, warm, and natural. I can tell you from experience how comforting it is to wake up with the large leaves of a bird-of-paradise creating a natural canopy over your bed, like protective hands making sure you get a good night's rest.

Common Problems

Bird-of-paradise leaves can get *really* big! And as a result, they can get heavy and tear very easily, especially if the plant is kept outside in the wind for any period of time. Leaf tearing is very normal, won't hurt the plant in any way, and should be expected if you want to grow this big beauty in your home. The imperfect leaves are also a not-so-subtle reminder that you're dealing with a living organism and not a fake pile of plastic!

While we're on the subject of giant leaves, as your bird-of-paradise gets larger, you're likely going to need to give it support. When they're grown in the ground, their stems become very thick and strong, allowing them to stay upright even with the weight of the big leaves. But when grown in a pot, birds-of-paradise don't develop that thick stem quite as fast and your plant may lean as a result, which doesn't always look very good. Since the stems fan out near the base of the plant, you can easily hide a sturdy stake on the side of the plant that's not on display. If you're worried about how it looks, I recommend using discreet green tape to tie your stake to the plant.

Bonus Tip

Don't be too concerned if your bird-of-paradise never produces a flower. The truth is, although their flowers are beautiful and responsible for their memorable name, they'll likely never flower if they're primarily kept indoors under average household conditions. If you really want to get a flower, you'll have to replicate its native conditions more closely, keeping your plant either in a greenhouse or outside, if your weather allows it.

Fun Fact

The bird-of-paradise flower, known as a crane flower, is a symbol of freedom and beauty to the people of South Africa, where it grows naturally. But no matter where you are in the world, these striking, vibrant flowers are so unique and long-lasting that they've become a staple in the flower-arrangement industry.

COMMON NAMES:
Nest fern, bird's-nest spleenwort

Soil: General-purpose potting soil

Light: Bright (1,000 fc or more), medium (250–999 fc), or low (100–250 fc) light

Watering: When the topsoil is dry

Fertilizer: General-purpose or organic fertilizer

Toxicity: Nontoxic to pets and people

Average Indoor Size: 1 to 2 feet tall

Native To: Tropical regions of Africa, Asia, and the Pacific Islands

Propagation: Division

Pot Selection: Glazed ceramic or plastic is best, but any pot with drainage holes will work.

Bird's-Nest Fern
(Asplenium nidus)

To all those plant parents who love ferns but haven't been able to keep them alive, start with a bird's-nest fern. Although they don't have the classic fernlike fronds, this variety has beautiful foliage accompanied by more forgiving care than sword ferns typically require. In their own right, they're wonderful plants to grow. I love looking straight down on the crown of a bird's-nest fern to see its new leaves emerging, each one resembling a baby bird reaching its beak up from the nest floor to grab a meal from their mom or dad.

Common Problems

The crown of the bird's-nest fern, where all the leaves meet in the middle, looks like a very inviting place to water, but it's best to keep the center dry to avoid stagnant water rotting the crown. It's true that when these plants grow in nature, their crowns get rained on. However, outdoor conditions provide more light, heat, and airflow than indoor environments, and that allows the crown of the plant to dry before the plant is in danger of developing rot. When it's time to water a bird's-nest fern, it's a good idea to water only the soil.

Bonus Tip

While it's best to water these plants when the topsoil dries, they won't decline even if watered at 25 percent dry, and they do much better than most ferns I've cared for when their soil is allowed to get up to 100 percent dry. I don't recommend letting the soil get that dry, but it's helpful to know that you have more room for error here than with other ferns. You'll know you've let the plant get too dry when its leaves turn a faded green color, similar to mint green. If you observe this, check the soil to confirm its dryness, then give the soil a soak, and within a day the saturated green color should return to the leaves. In extreme cases, you may need to rehydrate the soil, a process we cover in chapter 7 (page 141).

Bromeliad
(Bromeliaceae)

Soil: Cactus potting soil

Light: Bright (1,000 fc or more) light

Watering: Refill "tank" with fresh water when dry

Fertilizer: General-purpose or organic fertilizer

Toxicity: Nontoxic to pets and people

Average Indoor Size: 6 inches to 3 feet tall

Native To: The Caribbean, Central America, South America, and West Africa

Propagation: Division

Pot Selection: A clay pot is best, but any pot with drainage holes will work.

Bromeliads are a family of flowering plants that simply don't get enough attention. While some grow in the ground—we call those "terrestrial bromeliads"—this family is most well-known for its epiphytes—we call these "climbers"—as well as their unique method for collecting water through the use of their "tank," which is the center of the plant where all the leaves converge and form a small cup to collect water and use as needed. The simplicity of care for bromeliads in comparison to the beauty of their vibrant flowers—more accurately called their "inflorescence"—is a gift to humanity and should absolutely be taken advantage of by more aspiring plant parents. I love making bromeliads the focal point of plant arrangements for the long show they put on. It's not uncommon for their blooms to last six to twelve months, even with minimal care.

Common Problems

Be careful to not let the water in your bromeliad tank stagnate, which can harbor unwanted bacteria and fungi that have the potential to harm your plant. If your plant hasn't used up all the water in its tank after a week, dump it out and fill it with fresh water to avoid this issue. Bromeliads can be sensitive to mineral buildup from tap water, so try using room temperature filtered water for best results.

Bonus Tip

When your bromeliad is blooming, feel free to keep it on display for a couple of weeks at a time, even if that means putting it in low light. Short stints like this are fine, as long as you remember to put the plant back in bright light to maintain vigor and help it flower again.

Fun Fact

Bromeliads flower only once in their lifetime, after which the plant will die. This doesn't mean you need to run out and get a new bromeliad, because as the plant is dying off post-bloom, it focuses its energy on producing pups, which are baby plants. It's common to get anywhere from three to five pups (divisions) after each bloom cycle, and each pup can be separated from the mother plant to increase your collection or gift to a friend. Bromeliads can last years with proper care, so don't take its dying after each bloom cycle to mean you'll be in a constant state of propagation!

Digging into Terrestrial Bromeliads

Terrestrial bromeliads aren't as commonly sold as epiphytic bromeliads are, but they make wonderfully easy houseplants. If you pick one up, keep in mind that their care is slightly different. Because they naturally grow in the ground with access to more water, terrestrial bromeliads are much thirstier than their climbing cousins, so water them when the topsoil is dry. Terrestrial bromeliads don't have "tanks" either, so keep their leaves dry and water only the soil.

Fun Fact

In order to retain more water to withstand long periods of drought in their native environment, some cacti developed spines instead of leaves, effectively reducing the amount of water that escapes through their leaves via transpiration. These spines also help them survive the often harsh conditions where they grow by shedding heat and collecting water vapor that can accumulate when there are cool nights.

Cacti
(Cactaceae)

Soil: Cactus potting soil

Light: Bright (1,000 fc or more) light

Watering: When the soil is 100 percent dry

Fertilizer: Succulent or organic fertilizer

Toxicity: Toxicity varies from cactus to cactus, so it's best to check before purchasing.

Average Indoor Size: 6 inches to 6 feet tall

Native To: Cacti are native to many dry and arid parts of the world, most notably in Africa, Australia, Mexico, and the United States.

Propagation: Cuttings and division

Pot Selection: A clay pot is best, but any pot with drainage holes will work.

All cacti are succulents, but not all succulents are cacti. And because cacti are succulents, they, too, have unique water-storing capabilities that help them withstand long periods of drought. Cacti have some of the strangest and most unique structures in the world of plants. I love them for that, as well as for their low-maintenance care requirements. Having a large cactus is one of the easiest ways to bring impactful life into any space, and provided it has enough light, it will be so incredibly low-maintenance that you might even forget it's alive. That is, until your neglect pays off and the cactus blooms, revealing some of the most contrasting, stunning, and mesmerizing flowers on the planet. On a personal note, I've often wondered what it must have been like when humans first started seeing cacti bloom. So many of the areas these plants grow in can be quite dry and dull in color. I have to imagine the deep-red flowers of the claret cup cactus or the massive flowers of the Queen of the Night would stop anyone in their tracks, past or present.

Bonus Tip

I know this is common knowledge, but cacti have a unique ability to withstand long periods of drought. And I mean *long*. I can't emphasize this fact enough, because in nearly every consultation I've had with a customer whose cactus is suffering from overwatering, they've said something to the effect of "I know you're not supposed to water cacti very often, but I just felt so bad for it going a whole week without water!" Although most cacti kept indoors want all of their soil to dry between waterings, they can survive far longer than that. Their growth may slow down if you leave them completely dry for several weeks, but these plants are much more tolerant of infrequent watering than they are of frequent watering. When it comes to watering cacti, if in doubt, wait!

COMMON NAMES:
Baran, bar-room plant, iron plant

Cast-Iron Plant
(Aspidistra elatior)

Soil: Aroid soil

Light: Bright (1,000 fc or more), medium (250-999 fc), or low (100-250 fc) light

Watering: When the soil is 25 percent to 50 percent dry from the top down

Fertilizer: General-purpose or organic fertilizer

Toxicity: Nontoxic to pets and people

Average Indoor Size: 1 to 3 feet tall

Native To: Southeast Asia

Propagation: Division

Pot Selection: A clay pot is best, but any pot with drainage holes will work.

Elegant, regal, and, as their name suggests, *tough*, cast-iron plants have been a houseplant staple since the Victorian era. This is largely because they have such an incredible ability to withstand harsh conditions, especially in the lighting department. This gives you, the plant parent, tons of flexibility when it comes to where a cast-iron plant can be displayed inside your home. The cast-iron plant is also a bit unique in that it can grow outdoors in much colder weather than typical houseplants. While most houseplants are actually tropical plants and can't handle temperatures below 50°F, cast-iron plants can handle temperatures down to about 20°F when planted in a pot and into the single digits when planted in the ground. I love cast-iron plants because they're simple in every way—standard, really—but there is also something about the clean, smooth look of their leaves that delicately balance atop thin stems that I find a bit magical. Coupled with their incredible hardiness, the beauty and uncomplicated nature of cast-iron plants make them an easy choice for those of us who want something simple to take care of and can appreciate a plant that provides ample joy but with minimal effort.

Bonus Tip
Cast-iron plants are slow growers, so don't expect to see new leaves popping up all the time. I recommend taking a photo of the plant when you first purchase it so that you can more accurately monitor its progress. If you tend to worry about your plants, this will help you sleep at night!

Fun Fact
In feng shui, the cast-iron plant is known as a grounding plant, creating a sense of stability and tranquility.

COMMON NAME:
Madagascar tree

Dragon Tree
(Dracaena marginata)

Soil: Aroid soil

Light: Bright (1,000 fc or more), medium (250–999 fc), or low (100–250 fc) light

Watering: When the soil is 25 percent to 50 percent dry from the top down

Fertilizer: General-purpose or organic fertilizer

Toxicity: Toxic to pets; nontoxic to people

Average Indoor Size: 1 to 8 feet tall

Native To: Madagascar and Mauritius

Propagation: Stem cutting

Pot Selection: A clay pot is best, but any pot with drainage holes will work.

There are several popular varieties of "corn plants," but perhaps none is more popular than the *Dracaena marginata*—also called dragon tree. This is one of those plants I refer to as "heirloom plants," because they are often handed down from one generation to the next. This speaks not only to the longevity of the plant but also to the fact that they are hardy, very easy to care for, and tolerant of so many varying household conditions. I believe heirloom plants are some of the most resilient because they have withstood the test of time. After all, what better confirmation that a plant is easy to grow than the fact that they've been hugely popular in the United States (and beyond) for a hundred years?

Common Problems

Because they're so commonly kept for decor, people tend to put *Dracaena marginata* wherever they're going to look best. I get it, but often that means the plant is in such low light that it's not able to use the amount of water given. These conditions are ripe for root rot, which will eventually cause the trunks to wrinkle and the leaves to perpetually droop. Low light is fine, but make sure it's *true* low light, and not your interpretation of it.

Bonus Tip

If you're more of a decor-inspired plant person, meaning you choose plants based on how they fit the aesthetics of your home, *Dracaena marginata* is a STAPLE! I'd be willing to bet your first exposure to this plant was on display as a focal point or accent piece in a place of business, such as a mall or restaurant. The organic, funky shape they take on when grown indoors brings a one-of-a-kind look that's a perfect example of living art and beauty.

Elephant Ear
(Alocasia)

COMMON NAMES:
Taro plant

Soil: Aroid soil

Light: Bright (1,000 fc or more) light

Watering: When the soil is 25 percent to 50 percent dry from the top down

Fertilizer: General-purpose or organic fertilizer

Toxicity: Toxic to pets and people

Average Indoor Size: 1 to 4 feet tall

Native To: Tropical and subtropical areas of Asia and Australia

Propagation: Division

Pot Selection: A clay pot is best, but any pot with drainage holes will work.

Elephant ear, which is also frequently called by its genus name, *Alocasia*, is one of those plants that have a cultlike following among their fans and admirers. They all grow with a similar structure but boast a wide range of sizes, leaf shapes, colors, and textures. Alocasias are most well-known for their large foliage that can be used to create an interesting and impactful look whether they're being placed indoors or out. While huge leaves are the draw for alocasias kept outdoors, we're talking about the varieties most typically kept as houseplants. I implore you to take a deep dive into what I feel is their true beauty—the vastness in their interesting foliage, which can rival even the prettiest flowers, not to mention the prettiest of leaves.

Common Problems

Like many houseplants, it's easy to tell when this plant is truly thirsty and in need of water by letting the soil dry until the leaves wilt. I never recommend this approach and especially not for alocasias, as it can have more detrimental consequences than with other plants. Usually, when a plant wilts from dry soil, you can simply give it a good soak, and within a few hours the leaves will be hydrated and perky again. However, the leaves of alocasias are disproportionately large compared with the stems, so when the plant wilts, those long, slender stems can collapse and get pinched, which cuts off the water supply and can kill the leaf. Think of it like a kinked hose. Sometimes you can fix the kink by straightening the stem and taping a bamboo stake to it as a sort of splint. This will restore the flow of water and nutrients to the leaf above, but sometimes the kink is too severe for this trick to work, which means it's better to avoid the issue in the first place!

Bonus Tip

Don't be alarmed if your new alocasia drops leaves at first, as long as the dying leaves are coming nearer the base of the plant rather than from the top, where new leaves grow. This really could apply to all houseplants, but I've found the anxiety over dying leaves to be especially common with alocasia owners, because it's so obvious and impactful when one of their large leaves dies. Alocasias are rapidly growing plants, and part of that growth is shedding older leaves. It's super common to have a new leaf grow from the top while one drops from the bottom simultaneously. I always tell people that alocasias will grow one leaf and lose two or grow two leaves and lose one, etc. They stabilize with maturity and proper care, so hold on through the roller coaster of leaves coming and going—these plants are worth it!

Fun Fact

Some alocasias have traditionally been used as a food crop. You may have even noticed one of the common names, taro, as an option at your local ice cream or frozen yogurt shop. But keep in mind that taro must be specially prepared to eliminate toxins before it can be consumed.

Fiddle-Leaf Fig
(Ficus lyrata)

COMMON NAMES: Fiddle fig, fig, fig tree

Soil: Aroid soil

Light: Bright (1,000 fc or more) light

Watering: When the soil is 25 percent to 50 percent dry from the top down

Fertilizer: General-purpose or organic fertilizer

Toxicity: Toxic to pets and people

Average Indoor Size: 1 to 10 feet tall

Native To: Western Africa

Propagation: Air layering and stem cutting

Pot Selection: A clay pot is best, but any pot with drainage holes will work.

Fun Fact

These trees can grow up to one hundred feet tall in their native habitat, and they do actually produce fruit, though that's unlikely when they're kept only indoors. And don't get too excited: Their fruit has little flavor and an unpleasant mouth-drying effect!

The fiddle-leaf fig must be the most popular houseplant tree in the world! They have wonderful canopies and sturdy wooden trunks that lend a lot of natural warmth to a room. If you've struggled with this plant before, I hope after reading this book you'll try again with a renewed sense of confidence in your plant-parenting abilities. And if you're trying it for the first time, don't be nervous! The Internet has given fiddle-leaf figs a bad name, but they're actually very simple plants to care for, provided you give them the nonnegotiables detailed below.

Common Problems

Fiddle-leaf figs tend to get edema very easily, and it can be alarming if you don't know what it is—on these trees, edema tends to show up as small red dots, most visible on new leaves. If your plant has these red spots, don't be alarmed. They won't harm your plant, but it's a reliable sign from your plant to stop watering as often as you have been.

Bonus Tip

Don't fall into the trap of believing you need specific fiddle-leaf-fig products to be successful with this plant. Due to its incredible popularity, many companies see an opportunity to label fertilizers, soils, and sprays as fiddle-leaf-fig fertilizer, soil, etc. Although these products can bring peace of mind, I want you to know that using fiddle-leaf-fig-specific products is not going to make or break your plant-caring experience.

Fittonia
(Fittonia albivenis)

COMMON NAMES:
Mosaic plant, nerve plant

Soil: General-purpose soil

Light: Bright (1,000 fc or more), medium (250–999 fc), or low (100–250 fc) light

Watering: When the topsoil is dry

Fertilizer: General-purpose or organic soil

Toxicity: Nontoxic to pets and people

Average Indoor Size: 3 to 6 inches tall

Native To: Tropical regions of South America

Propagation: Stem cutting

Pot Selection: Glazed ceramic or plastic is best, but any pot with drainage holes will work.

Houseplant hobbyists often refer to Fittonia as "drama queens," due to the fainting (wilting) act they perform when their soil gets too dry. I believe their theatrics actually make them very simple to care for, as it's very obvious when they need to be watered—a welcome reminder that few other houseplants provide. I love Fittonia for their size, versatility, and cheery appearance. They're particularly popular for beginners, always attracting new eyes with their distinctive leaf patterns that challenge the idea of what houseplant leaves should look like.

Bonus Tip

Although they can easily be grown as a regular houseplant, because of their petite size, Fittonia grow especially well in terrariums. However, they also grow very quickly and may require regular trimming if you want to maintain a compact look. Growing Fittonia in a terrarium is also ideal if you're the type of person that tends to underwater their plant. These guys are thirsty, and keeping them in a terrarium, which has high humidity, will reduce how often they need to be watered compared with growing them on a windowsill.

Fun Fact

Fittonia constantly move their leaves throughout the day to give themselves optimal exposure to light. But they change even more drastically when their soil has been too dry for too long, resulting in leaves and stems that resemble deflated balloons draped over a fence. You never want them to wilt to this degree, but it's great fun to soak a dry *Fittonia* and use the time-lapse function on your camera phone to capture the resurrection of the leaves, which readily perk up to their full rigidity within hours of receiving water.

Golden Pothos
(Epipremnum aureum)

COMMON NAMES: Devil's ivy, ivy, pothos

Soil: General-purpose potting soil

Light: Bright (1,000 fc or more), medium (250–999 fc), or low (100–250 fc) light

Watering: When the soil is 25 percent dry from the top down

Fertilizer: General-purpose or organic fertilizer

Toxicity: Toxic to pets and people

Average Indoor Size: 6 inches to 8 feet long

Native To: French Polynesia

Propagation: Stem cuttings and division

Pot Selection: A clay pot is best, but any pot with drainage holes will work.

Behold, the houseplant of all houseplants! If you're into plants of any kind, you likely have one of these absolute classics. This character checks all the boxes and takes a spot in my top five beginner-friendly plants (page 49). They're tolerant to a wide range of conditions, and they propagate very easily—and quickly, which is likely why you have one. Tons of people attribute their start in plants to a cutting a friend or relative gave them of their thriving golden pothos. Even though they're not the trendiest plant on earth, they're prized for their ease of care, as well as their habit of growing lush and vibrant.

Bonus Tip

As a golden pothos ages, it will lose leaves near the soil. To keep your plant looking full, you can take a long vine, coil it up, and pin it to the soil with a bobby pin or paper clip at the nodes—those bumps along the vine where leaves come out—or where the leaves once were. Once the nodes come in contact with the soil, they'll begin sending out new roots. After a couple of months, you'll have new leaves growing in multiple directions, keeping your plant looking its best.

Fun Fact

It's most common to grow golden pothos trailing out of a basket, but it's actually a climber. Wrap your vines around a moss poll, trellis, or stake of your choosing and watch the leaves grow larger. In fact, when golden pothos climb structures in nature (mainly trees and other plants), their leaves can grow to be more than two feet long and develop fenestrations, which are holes or splits in the leaves.

COMMON VARIETIES:
Christmas cactus (*Schlumbergera × buckleyi*), Easter/spring cactus (*Rhipsalidopsis gaertneri*), Thanksgiving cactus (*Schlumbergera truncata*)

Soil: Cactus potting soil

Light: Bright (1,000 fc or more) light

Watering: When the soil is 50 percent to 75 percent dry from the top down

Fertilizer: General-purpose or organic fertilizer

Toxicity: Nontoxic to pets and people

Average Indoor Size: 6 inches to 2 feet long

Native To: Tropical regions of southeast Brazil

Propagation: Leaf or stem cuttings and division

Pot Selection: A clay pot is best, but any pot with drainage holes will work.

Holiday Cacti

There are three varieties of holiday cacti, and their names coincide with the season in which they typically flower. Thanksgiving cacti flower in fall, while Christmas cacti flower in winter, and Easter cacti, also known as spring cacti, flower in spring. Thanksgiving cacti are far and away the most popular variety and are often confused with the other two due to their similar leaf shapes and flowers. Over the years, as I've consulted with many folks about their Christmas cacti, the plants have often turned out to be Thanksgiving cacti! All three varieties are very easy to grow and beginner friendly. In fact, they are so low-maintenance that they top the list of plants most commonly handed down from one generation to the next, making them heirloom plants. It's easy to fall in love with any of the holiday cacti. Their blooms are something to look forward to and offer a sense of tradition and nostalgia around the holidays.

Common Problems

Winter blooms are actually made in the summer! If your holiday cactus isn't flowering each year, or if you're unsatisfied with the number of flowers, the most likely cause is the plant not receiving enough light during the spring and summer months.

Bonus Tip

If temperatures are above 50°F, put your holiday cactus outside in full shade. Avoiding direct afternoon sun will prevent the leaves from getting scorched, but keeping your plant in full shade as long as the weather allows will provide the plant with the light it needs to *explode* with flowers when its respective blooming period arrives.

Fun Fact

There's an old wives' tale that says in order for a holiday cactus to bloom, it must be placed in a closet. This is, of course, completely false. But it is rooted in truth. These plants are photoperiodic, meaning they can actually recognize a change in the length of the day, which triggers their bloom cycle to begin. For best results, I recommend putting the plant in 100 percent darkness for thirteen hours, then returning it to its regular bright light for eleven hours. However, as long as your cactus is in bright-enough light, it will flower with natural daylight fluctuations—the flowers just might not be as plentiful.

COMMON NAMES:
Wax plant, porcelain flower

Hoya Rope
(Hoya carnosa compacta)

Soil: Aroid soil

Light: Bright (1,000 fc or more) light

Watering: When the soil is 75 percent dry from the top down

Fertilizer: General-purpose or organic fertilizer

Toxicity: Nontoxic to pets and people

Average Indoor Size: 6 inches to 3 feet long

Native To: Australia and East Asia

Propagation: Stem cutting

Pot Selection: A clay pot is best, but any pot with drainage holes will work.

Hoya and Pot Size

Hoya rope is just one of the many types of hoya. The biggest hoya I ever had was twenty-five feet long and was growing in a seven-inch pot!

"If you have hoya light, get a hoya!" This is what Erika says any time a customer or friend is interested in growing a hoya. I tend to agree, as there's hardly a more visually grabbing cluster of flowers found anywhere in the houseplant world. It's not just the blooms, though; this plant is equally admired for its interesting curly leaves that resemble a twisted rope. Our kids call hoya the tortellini plant, due to its resemblance to the famous pasta, and I think that's spot-on.

Common Problems

The most interesting part of this type of hoya, its curly leaves, is also what causes the most problems with this plant. This is because all of the nooks and rigid, tight curls of the leaves provide perfect hiding spots for pests like mealybugs. The best way to treat any pest is to catch them when their numbers are few, which is more of a challenge when they're even harder to find than normal. Be intentional with your checks so you don't find yourself with an advanced infestation.

Bonus Tip

Hoya tend to grow much better and bloom wonderfully when grown in tighter pots. In fact, among hoya-growing enthusiasts, it's common to keep the plants in the same size pot for several years, and when they do increase pot size, it's only by small increments. Growing hoya in tighter pots doesn't guarantee blooming, but don't be too anxious to repot this plant at the same intervals as some of your other houseplants.

Fun Fact

Not only are the prized flowers of the hoya rope plant beautiful in appearance but they smell lovely too. The blooms are especially fragrant at night, releasing their chocolaty scent for their naturally nocturnal pollinators. Don't worry: Your blooming hoya are more likely to attract gawking plant friends into your house than pollinator bugs!

Kentia Palm
(Howea forsteriana)

COMMON NAMES:
Palm court palm, thatch palm

Soil: Aroid soil

Light: Bright (1,000 fc or more), medium (250–999 fc), or low (100–250 fc) light

Watering: When the soil is 25 percent to 50 percent dry from the top down

Fertilizer: Palm-specific or organic fertilizer

Toxicity: Nontoxic to pets and people

Average Indoor Size: 3 to 12 feet tall

Native To: Australia's Lord Howe Island

Propagation: Seed

Pot Selection: A clay pot is best, but any pot with drainage holes will work.

In the world of indoor palms, the kentia is royalty! They're about as elegant as you could hope for, with huge, deep-green, arching fronds—aesthetically speaking, they pair perfectly with the cast-iron plant. Kentia palms are known to be slow growing, which is due in part to the fact that they can tolerate low light and therefore often find themselves in such conditions, but even in perfect conditions, they seem to be in no hurry to grow up. It may be difficult to find this collector's palm local to you, as it's mostly sold in boutique-style plant shops or smaller, family-owned operations. I assume its low availability and high price tag keep the kentia palm out of big-box stores. Speaking of, yes, they will cost you significantly more money than more common varieties, such as the majesty palm, and you may be tempted to purchase a more affordable variety for all your palm needs. However, if there's ever been a clearer case for "you get what you pay for" in plants, it's here.

Bonus Tip

Kentia palms are susceptible to spider mites (page 156), so be on the lookout for tiny webbing on the backs of the fronds. Regular checks during watering and dusting will help keep this issue at bay.

Fun Fact

Due to their indoor hardiness—they tolerate low light, dry air, and drafts better than most palms—and cost, kentia palms as potted plants are largely used in high-end installations, such as luxury hotels, casinos, and restaurants. In fact, for the first few decades that they were available as a potted plant, only royalty or aristocrats could afford to buy them, giving them a reputation as a sort of status symbol from the late 1800s into the early 1900s. Be on the lookout for this beauty in the next period film or drama you watch!

COMMON NAMES:
Mexican breadfruit, split-leaf philodendron, Swiss cheese plant

Soil: Aroid soil

Light: Bright (1,000 fc or more) light

Watering: When the soil is 25 percent to 50 percent dry from the top down

Fertilizer: General-purpose or organic fertilizer

Toxicity: Toxic to pets and people

Average Indoor Size: 1 to 6 feet tall

Native To: Central America and southern Mexico

Propagation: Air layering, division, and stem cuttings

Pot Selection: A clay pot is best, but any pot with drainage holes will work.

Monstera
(Monstera deliciosa)

These might as well be the mascot of houseplants! Monstera are super easy to care for and instantly add jungle vibes to your space. I love how their peculiar, torso-size leaves deliver massive visual impact in a space while requiring very little effort. This plant will make you feel like a certified plant person faster than anything else. In fact, this was the plant I used to test out most of my early ideas and curiosities about watering, and it lived to tell the tale, despite frequent repots and several cases of root rot. This is more of a nod to monstera's hardy nature than to my early skill with plant care.

Bonus Tip

Giving your monstera something to climb, such as a trellis or moss pole, will contain its unruly nature and help the leaves grow larger when proper care is provided. Improper conditions, such as light that's too low, may result in the leaves losing their unique splits and holes, and reverting back to completely solid leaves if left unchecked.

Fun Fact

Although it's not likely to happen indoors without intense grow lights, this plant does have the ability to bloom, and it will actually produce fruit! This is where monstera gets one of its common names, Mexican breadfruit. People have differing opinions on exactly what this fruit tastes like, but to me, the dominant flavor and texture is similar to banana. Be careful, though, as the unripe fruit is toxic!

COMMON NAMES:
Funeral plant, spathe flower, white sails

Peace Lily
(Spathiphyllum)

Soil: General-purpose potting soil

Light: Bright (1,000 fc or more), medium (250–999 fc), or low (100–250 fc) light

Watering: When the soil is 25 percent dry from the top down

Fertilizer: General-purpose or organic fertilizer

Toxicity: Toxic to pets and people

Average Indoor Size: 1 to 3 feet tall

Native To: Tropical areas of Central and South America

Propagation: Division

Pot Selection: Glazed ceramic or plastic is best, but any pot with drainage holes will work.

This houseplant, like so many others, has the unfortunate reputation of being "finicky," or being labeled a "drama queen." While peace lilies are not actually difficult to care for, they are traditionally given in solemn remembrance of a beloved person or pet, which means many people end up owning them even though they didn't sign up to care for this particular plant, and at a time when they are in the midst of grieving. None of this is a recipe for plant-parenting success. But if you take a step back and forget all associations you've learned about peace lilies, they're actually very remarkable and beautiful plants with deep-green, arching leaves and "flowers" that pop up so cheerfully above them. With proper care, peace lilies can even flower multiple times per year, which, in my mind, completes their image of elegance and elevates their status in the plant world. After all, how many plants can you grow indoors and be rewarded with such beauty? That list, my friends, is short.

Bonus Tip

If your plant isn't producing flowers—peace lily flowers are called "spathe" and are not true flowers—at least once per year, then it most likely isn't getting enough light. Peace lilies' reputation for being low-light plants only means that they can survive low light, and although they may produce new leaves under these conditions, that doesn't necessarily mean they're getting enough light to produce flowers.

Fun Fact

Although the most popular name for this plant is peace lily, it's not actually a lily! This is especially helpful for pet owners, because although peace lilies are considered toxic to pets, they're not as toxic as true lilies, which can be fatal when ingested.

Keiki

"Keiki" is the Hawaiian word for "child" and is also used in reference to baby orchids.

Do You Need an Orchid Pot?

Orchid pots, which provide extra airflow via increased slits and holes, more closely mimic the type of airflow orchid roots get in nature. Although they can be helpful, they are not a requirement for growing a thriving orchid.

Phalaenopsis Orchid
(Phalaenopsis)

COMMON NAMES: Moth orchid, moon orchid

Soil: Orchid bark

Light: Bright (1,000 fc or more) light

Watering: When the soil is 100 percent dry

Fertilizer: Orchid-specific or organic fertilizer

Toxicity: Nontoxic to pets and people

Average Indoor Size: 10 to 20 inches tall

Native To: China, India, and Southeast Asia

Propagation: Pup division (keiki)

Pot Selection: A clay pot is best, but any pot with drainage holes will work.

I love orchids because they are such a vast family of plants that produce an equally vast array of interesting flowers that can delight all the senses. Phalaenopsis, which we'll explore here, is one of the most popular kinds, but orchids are the largest flowering plant family in the world, with nearly thirty thousand different species. Some grow in the ground, while others grow attached to trees and rocks. Some can weigh up to two tons, but others weigh in at just a few grams. Some are happy to be alive when temperatures drop to -40°F, while others deem 40°F too cold and die off. Regardless of the type, there's no plant that will reward you with so much beauty for such little work as an orchid! These plants have a bad reputation because most folks think they're dead when their flowers die, but that's not the case. All living things require a bit of rest, and such is the case with orchids when they drop their flowers. But with proper care, an orchid's flowers will come back in droves.

Bonus Tips

If you plant an orchid in a clear plastic pot—it must have adequate drainage—it's easy to tell when it's ready for water simply by looking at the roots. When the roots are wet, they turn a green color, very similar to the color of the leaves. When the roots are dry and need water, they turn a silver-gray color. There's no need to water on a schedule—just look at the roots! Also note that it's best to limit fertilizing orchids to when there are no flowers on the plant.

Fun Fact

It can take up to a year in proper conditions for a phalaenopsis orchid to produce flowers, at which point the blooms will typically last a couple of months. Once the flowers are spent, the plant focuses on growing leaves until it's ready to flower again.

COMMON VARIETIES:
Birkin philodendron, heartleaf philodendron, pink princess philodendron

Soil: Aroid soil

Light: Although some philodendron varieties can survive low (100–250 fc) light, they grow best in bright (1,000 fc or more) light.

Watering: When the soil is 25 percent to 50 percent dry from the top down

Fertilizer: General-purpose or organic fertilizer

Toxicity: Toxic to pets and people

Average Indoor Size: 1 to 5 feet tall

Native To: Tropical rainforests of Central and South America

Propagation: Stem cuttings or air layering

Pot Selection: A clay pot is best, but any pot with drainage holes will work.

A Low-Light Option

Heartleaf philodendrons grow much better in bright light, but they are as tolerant of low light as other more well-known plants like golden pothos. Because the list of plants that can grow in that environment is so short, I always like to highlight that heartleaf philodendrons fare exceptionally better than most!

Philodendron
(Philodendron)

Is there anyone who doesn't like philodendrons? I've heard some of the most widely adored plants receive hate for one reason or another, but I've never in my life heard someone say they just don't like philodendrons. How could you? They're easy to grow and tolerant of a really wide range of conditions. Their leaves are interesting, diverse, and often huge. Some philodendrons trail (heartleaf), some of them climb (pink princess), and some of them just get bushy (birkin), so if you decorate with plants, I can all but guarantee there's a philodendron out there to suit your needs.

Common Problem

One day you might look at your philodendron and notice a clear, sticky, sap-like substance on its leaves or stems. This can be alarming, especially if you already know that pests often leave behind similar-looking deposits. I can't say for sure that the sticky deposits aren't a sign of pests, but philodendrons excrete a nectar of their own, largely as a defense mechanism. It's called "extrafloral nectaries," and it attracts beneficial bugs that ward off the pests that would cause harm to the plant. If you notice this type of substance, I still recommend looking for pests, but know that it's also likely to be extrafloral nectaries, and just a sign that your plant is healthy.

Bonus Tip

Many philodendron varieties are climbers and may produce mature, larger leaves when given something to climb, such as a moss pole or trellis. In some cases, the difference between a juvenile philodendron that's trailing and the same plant that has access to a climbing support is so drastic that you'd never guess they're the same plant! Allowing them to climb is not only natural for many philodendron varieties and necessary for producing big leaves but also practical. When you realize how quickly these plants can grow and sprawl out over a room, securing their vines to a structure is a welcome idea.

Fun Fact

The word "philodendron" comes from Greek. "Philo" means "love" or "affection," and "dendron" means "tree." I think this makes them the undisputed original "tree huggers."

Prayer Plant
(Calathea)

COMMON NAMES: Cathedral plant, peacock plant, rattlesnake plant

Soil: General-purpose potting soil

Light: Bright (1,000 fc or more) or medium (250–999 fc) light

Watering: When the topsoil is dry

Fertilizer: General-purpose or organic fertilizer

Toxicity: Nontoxic to pets and people

Average Indoor Size: 1 to 3 feet tall

Native To: Tropical regions of Central and South America

Propagation: Division and corm propagation

Pot Selection: Glazed ceramic or plastic is best, but any pot with drainage holes will work.

The question I always ask myself when I see a prayer plant—also commonly called calathea—is simply "Why?" Why are the leaves so intricately detailed? They're gorgeous. If other plants around the world can get by on just being green, what's the explanation for the fine art that is every calathea leaf? I suppose their beauty is for defense, reproduction, or any number of reasons that contribute to their survival. Whatever the purpose, I'm happy calatheas exist, and what a special treat it is that we can grow these plants inside our homes no matter where we live in the world. Believe it or not, these plants get a lot of hate for being finicky drama queens. And though it's true that they require a bit more effort on your part to keep them happy, calatheas are really no more difficult to care for than most houseplants. In fact, I'd posit that these plants don't pass away just because they don't like their owners but because their care needs are misunderstood.

Common Problems

Spider mites can be your worst enemy when growing calatheas, but I don't entirely believe what others suggest is true—that spider mites are simply more attracted to calatheas than other plants. Even if there is truth to that idea, the issue is compounded by improper care, specifically when it comes to watering. When plants are stressed, it can make them more susceptible to pests like spider mites. Wilting is a sign of stress in a calathea, but a commonly taught method is to wait until they wilt before watering. I believe this constant cycle of wilting between each watering is what really brings the spider mites around. Instead, I recommend watering as soon as the topsoil is dry, which will prevent calatheas from wilting from dehydration and avoid attracting pests. I also think it helps to regularly wipe your calathea's leaves, front and back, with a damp cloth to further prevent pest attacks.

What Is Corm Propagation?

Corms are small bulblike structures that grow beneath the soil of mature calatheas. I can't tell you exactly how mature they need to be to grow corms, but the smallest calathea I've seen produce corms was in a four-inch pot, and since they're not often sold in pots smaller than four inches, you can likely assume your calathea has the ability to grow them.

To propagate your corms, you'll have to remove the plant from its pot and shake off the soil to find them. To avoid the extra stress of taking a calathea out of its pot, this project is best done when you're already planning on repotting. Your propagation success rate will go up if you choose corms that have roots and/or leaves growing from them, but corms without either can be propagated too. How you tackle the next part is up to you, but the basic idea is to put the corms in something to increase their humidity and light while they grow into a new plant. I've had favorable outcomes by simply dropping the corms in a resealable plastic bag full of damp sphagnum moss, then keeping the bag partially open for airflow to prevent mold and setting it in a bright window. I've also made it as complicated as building full-on terrariums for my corms and using grow lights instead of the sun. Both ways can work and both are equally enjoyable.

Bonus Tip

This is a perfect plant for someone who likes to water frequently. In my experience, the most common reason folks don't do well with calatheas is because they let the soil dry too much between waterings, which can cause stress to the plant, inviting a host of potential anxiety-inducing problems, such as wilting and browning leaf edges. It's for these reasons that I often suggest removing all the soil from the calathea's roots and keeping it dangling in a vessel of water full-time—a setup also known as "water culture." There is a ton of information about keeping your houseplants in water, and I recommend researching the subject before diving in, but I've seen dozens of clients who have struggled with calatheas in soil be far more successful when keeping them in water. Whichever method you choose, make sure the water you're using is of higher quality, as calatheas can develop brown, crispy edges on their leaves quite easily from poor-quality water high in salt and dissolved minerals. I recommend rainwater or filtered water. Tap water can be fine, but the quality varies from city to city, so if you know the water from your tap isn't great, and you notice those crispy leaf edges, consider changing water sources.

Fun Fact

The leaves of calathea plants move *a lot* throughout the day as they orient themselves to capture the most amount of light—one of their special adaptations for growing in their native habitat, which is often deeply shaded. On the next clear day you have, try setting up a time-lapse camera and watch your calathea dance to the sunlight.

Radiator Plant
(Peperomia)

COMMON VARIETIES: *Peperomia obtusifolia*, watermelon peperomia, hope peperomia

Soil: Cactus potting soil

Light: Bright (1,000 fc or more) or medium (250–999 fc) light

Watering: When the soil is 50 percent to 75 percent dry from the top down

Fertilizer: General-purpose or organic fertilizer

Toxicity: Nontoxic to pets and people

Average Indoor Size: 5 to 15 inches tall

Native To: Tropical and subtropical areas, including parts of Central and South America, Australia, Africa, and Southeast Asia

Propagation: Division, leaf cutting, and stem cutting

Pot Selection: A clay pot is best, but any pot with drainage holes will work.

Having a peperomia (sometimes called a radiator plant) is a lot like having a fake plant, but with all the benefits of a real plant! They're low-maintenance, generally slow growing, and aren't known for having many problems. Peperomia don't have a cult following like some other plants do, but they are the sneaky favorite for many people due to their simple care requirements. They're a lot like that friend you can call at any time to help with something and you know they'll show up. They're not the flashiest friend, and you definitely wouldn't choose them for a wingman, but they're reliable and won't let you down!

Common Problems

Peperomia dying from root rot, or too-frequent watering, is super common. This is because many of them have quite shallow root systems, which means they may process water more slowly than plants with extensive, robust root systems. What's difficult is that peperomia are such an anatomically diverse group of plants with drastically different water-storing capabilities that putting a general rule of thumb for care means any advice won't apply to all varieties. However, most of the peperomia that we keep and that are known as houseplants prefer a faster-draining soil such as the cactus soil I suggest here. So, when it comes to peperomia, my suggestion is to err on the side of letting your plant's soil be dry rather than wet.

Fun Fact

Peperomia are in the Piperaceae family and the Piper genus, which also includes *Piper nigrum*, the plant we get black pepper from. The name "peperomia" comes from Greek and means pepper (*peperi*) resembling (*homoios*).

Bonus Tip

All peperomia have the ability to bloom, but none are known to have particularly beautiful ones. In fact, you may even hear them referred to as rattails! If you're like most people and don't find them attractive, feel free to remove them. I usually pinch them off with my fingernails right where they come out of the plant, but you can use pruners if you want a cleaner cut. Removing the blooms will tell the plant to refocus on growing leaves instead of spending a bunch of energy on something that doesn't help it grow and isn't that pretty.

COMMON NAME:
Rubber fig

Rubber Tree
(Ficus elastica)

Soil: Aroid soil

Light: Bright (1,000 fc or more) light

Watering: When the soil is 25 percent to 50 percent dry from the top down

Fertilizer: General-purpose or organic fertilizer

Toxicity: Toxic to pets and people

Average Indoor Size: 1 to 8 feet tall

Native To: Southern Asia

Propagation: Air layering and stem cutting

Pot Selection: A clay pot is best, but any pot with drainage holes will work.

This ficus is very popular in home decor due to its large, dark leaves. I love this plant because it doesn't drop leaves as readily as some other ficus varieties, and yeah, those dark, moody leaves, paired with a matching or contrasting colored pot, are "chef's kiss." The rubber tree is one of two ficus I most often see passed down through generations as an heirloom. This could mean the tree has been so popular for so long that enough of them survived to be passed down, or it could mean they're actually one of the easier plants to grow. Based on my own experience owning rubber trees, I lean toward the latter, although I suspect it's a bit of both.

Common Problems

Rubber trees can get quite tall indoors, but when they are grown in pots, their trunks don't always mature to a thickness that can keep the tall branches upright. To provide a bit of extra support for the branches and maintain the size your rubber tree grows to, I recommend putting inconspicuous bamboo stakes in the soil and securing them to the branches.

Bonus Tip

Dust the leaves of your rubber tree regularly. They're quite large and therefore collect a lot of dust, which is more noticeable on their dark leaves. This not only keeps rubber trees looking their best but also helps keep pests at bay.

Fun Fact

When you cut into the trunk or branches of a rubber tree, a white latex sap will ooze from the wound. Before synthetic rubber was created, this latex sap was used in the production of natural rubber.

COMMON NAMES:
Satin pothos, silver pothos, silver vine

Scindapsus
(Scindapsus)

Soil: General-purpose potting soil

Light: Bright (1,000 fc or more), medium (250-999 fc), or low (100-250 fc) light

Watering: When the soil is 25 percent dry from the top down

Fertilizer: General-purpose or organic fertilizer

Toxicity: Toxic to pets and people

Average Indoor Size: 6 inches to 3 feet long

Native To: Southeast Asia

Propagation: Stem cuttings and division

Pot Selection: A clay pot is best, but any pot with drainage holes will work.

Scindapsus are what you buy when you've figured out the other common trailing plants, like pothos, but want something more unique looking, without unique care. They're every bit as hardy and easy to grow as other beginner-friendly trailing plants, but most varieties have added flair thanks to silvery flecks that make the leaves sparkle when light hits them. There are nearly forty species of Scindapsus, which is quite small for a genus of plants. Still, with Scindapsus you get plenty of variety in leaf shapes, colors, textures, and interesting details like the silver variegation. As the plant grows, you'll find yourself falling in love with the matte-finished, satin-feeling leaves. If you're like me and touch the leaves of your plants on a daily basis, this will become one of what I like to call your "high touch" plants. Running my fingers along the leaves reminds me of the first time I tasted chocolate after receiving the advice to savor it and let it melt in my mouth. The silky sensation I enjoyed as a child is now satisfied by touching Scindapsus leaves, which has got to be the most plant-person thing I've ever said.

Common Problems

The leaves of Scindapsus are very quick to curl up when things aren't going well. A leaf that was flat one day may suddenly roll up on itself the next, which isn't uncommon in plants—it's just that Scindapsus seem to do it better (or worse, depending on how you look at it) than others. Leaf curling usually means the plant has either been overwatered or not watered enough. If your leaves are curled and your soil is wet, your plant likely has root rot. If your leaves are curled and your soil is dry, your plant likely needs a thorough soak to rehydrate and lose its curl.

Fun Fact

Despite its common name, these aren't actually pothos at all! This fact isn't important to the care of the plant, especially considering that pothos and Scindapsus thrive under identical conditions, but if you're trying to collect all the pothos (yes, that's a very common thing), then just know you can steer clear of Scindapsus. However, I wouldn't—they're rewarding, beautiful plants!

Bonus Tip

Not only do Scindapsus love to climb but they also have a special way of going about it. I'm talking about shingling, which is where the plant plasters its leaves against the surface it's growing on, as if they were wet pieces of paper carefully pressed into the details of their host. In the wild, they're found growing up trees, but indoors we provide a plank of wood or trellis for them to climb. Shingling isn't unique to Scindapsus, but it is a hallmark characteristic of the genus. That being said, there's no obvious reason for shingling plants to shingle. Unlike other observed adaptations in nature, there doesn't seem to be an advantage to them climbing this way. In fact, some shingling leaves will shingle right over existing healthy leaves, which could easily be argued is a negative adaptation. Still, these wonderful plants thrive!

COMMON NAME:
Mother-in-law's tongue

Snake Plant
(Dracaena trifasciata)

Soil: Cactus potting soil

Light: Bright (1,000 fc or more), medium (250–999 fc), or low (100–250 fc) light

Watering: When the soil is 100 percent dry

Fertilizer: General-purpose or organic fertilizer

Toxicity: Toxic to pets and people

Average Indoor Size: 6 inches to 4 feet tall

Native To: Western Africa

Propagation: Leaf cuttings and division

Pot Selection: A clay pot is best, but any pot with drainage holes will work.

Always on my list for beginner-friendly plants (page 49), you can't go wrong with a snake plant! They are tolerant to the widest range of indoor conditions and come in many different shapes and sizes, and even have a considerable color palette. I call them utility plants because, from a decorating perspective, they're one of the few plants you can put just about anywhere in the house and they're going to live. In our house, any awkward spaces, nooks, or corners get a little touch of living greenery in the form of a snake plant.

Common Problems

Many varieties of snake plants have "crowns," which is where their leaves come together at a single point, near the base of the plant. The crown looks like a natural place to water the plant, but that can actually lead to crown rot, a common snake plant killer. When watering snake plants, it's best to water only the soil and avoid getting the leaves wet to prevent other problems associated with stagnant water on foliage. In nature, these plants do get their leaves and crowns wet, but when they are outdoors, they are subject to more heat, airflow (wind), and light than we have indoors, and those conditions usually help the plant dry before problems set in.

Bonus Tip

Although snake plants are well-known for their ability to survive in low light, they actually do best when grown in bright light. In fact, in their native habitat, you'll often find them growing in full sun! If the idea of faster growth isn't enough to entice you, snake plants also bloom a sweetly scented flower when put in bright light.

COMMON NAMES:
Vegan deer mount, elkhorn fern

Staghorn Fern
(Platycerium)

Soil: General-purpose potting soil

Light: Bright (1,000 fc or more) light

Watering: When the topsoil is dry if potted, or when the moss is dry to the touch if mounted. In either case you can soak the entire plant, including the leaves!

Fertilizer: General-purpose or organic fertilizer

Toxicity: Nontoxic to pets and people

Average Indoor Size: 1 to 3 feet long

Native To: Tropical regions of Africa, Australia, and Southeast Asia

Propagation: Division

Pot Selection: When potted, glazed ceramic or plastic is best, but any pot with drainage holes will work.

This is one of the first plants that stopped my Instagram scrolling in its tracks. That is a very millennial way to communicate how much I love this fern, but can you blame me? It's not often you see a plant growing vertically on a plank of wood, and that is exactly how a staghorn fern grows. Well, technically, they grow on tree trunks and branches in nature, but you get the idea. Don't worry, they're not parasites—they just use the trees for anchoring. Staghorn ferns can also be grown in regular houseplant pots, but you'll usually only find them grown this way when they're small. It's far more common to see them attached to a piece of wood. Not only are these very easy-to-grow houseplants but they also add a ton of visual interest to homes, which is what first caught my eye. There are many varieties of staghorn ferns, all with their own unique shapes, sizes, and interesting growth habits. I find myself wanting to collect them all, and I have grown several kinds over the years. Other than personal satisfaction, this next tidbit offers no value, but I appreciate how perfectly this plant was named for its resemblance to stags' horns.

Bonus Tips

Staghorn ferns naturally grow as climbing plants, clinging to trees, branches, and rocks for support. A popular way to grow these plants indoors is on a wooden plank, replicating their natural growth habit. You can hang the plank and display it as a sort of living piece of art! If you choose to grow using this method, choose rot-resistant wood, such as cedar, and cover the root ball in long-fiber sphagnum moss. It's also important to remember that staghorn ferns need bright light in order to thrive, so keep that in mind when hanging your plant, as "bright light" can be difficult to achieve on a wall.

COMMON NAMES:
Bead plant, rosary plant, string of beads, string of peas

String of Pearls
(Senecio rowleyanus)

Soil: Cactus potting soil

Light: Bright (1,000 fc or more) light

Watering: When the soil is 100 percent dry

Fertilizer: Succulent or organic fertilizer

Toxicity: Toxic to pets and people

Average Indoor Size: 4 inches to 3 feet

Native To: Southwest Africa

Propagation: Stem cuttings and division

Pot Selection: A clay pot is best, but any pot with drainage holes will work.

The rounded, pearl-like leaves of this trailing succulent capture everyone's attention. After all, a spherical object resembling a gemstone from a mollusk isn't the first thing a person typically thinks of when imagining a plant, but here we are. These quirky plants have charmed and befuddled hobbyist houseplant growers for as long as they've been available. I suspect they, too, are victims of the reputation of being finicky that most wildly popular houseplants get due to the sheer number of people that have tried to grow them. The more people who attempt to grow something, the higher number of failures there will naturally be.

Common Problems

When positioning your string of pearls plant, make sure to hang or place it low enough so that the top of the pot is getting bright light. One of the biggest mistakes I see with this plant is hanging it so high in a window that most of the leaves don't even get low light, resulting in the plant slowly declining. Making sure bright light is hitting the top of the pot will also help the soil dry faster, which is critical for your string of pearls to thrive.

Bonus Tip

As your vines grow longer, the leaves nearest the soil level will eventually die from old age, leaving a plant that looks bald on top. To avoid this, you can select a long vine, coil it up, and set it on the topsoil, making sure as much of the vine comes in contact with the soil as possible. Pinning the vine to the soil will help keep them in contact. Over the next several weeks, that coiled-up vine will grow roots from its nodes, and with proper care, those new roots will begin growing more vines, keeping the plant looking full!

Succulents

Soil: Cactus potting soil

Light: Bright (1,000 fc or more) light

Watering: When the soil is 100 percent dry

Fertilizer: Succulent or organic fertilizer

Toxicity: Toxicity varies from succulent to succulent, so it's best to check before bringing them around pets and people.

Average Indoor Size: 2 inches to 3 feet tall

Native To: Succulents come from many dry and arid parts of the world, but Africa, Australia, and the Americas, including Mexico, are well-known for their native succulent populations.

Propagation: Leaf pullings and stem cuttings

Pot Selection: A clay pot is best, but any pot with drainage holes will work.

I lovingly call succulents "gateway plants" because so many of us crazy plant people started our obsession with them. They're readily available just about anywhere you go, including garden centers, plant shops, supermarkets, and furniture stores. Succulents have achieved the unique position of being simultaneously easy and difficult to maintain. In fact, one of the most frequent lines we hear in our plant shop is "Oh, I'm so bad with plants—I killed a succulent!" The fact that this or a similar statement is used on an often daily but definitely weekly basis tells me that folks believe succulents should be easy to care for, but my unique experience in owning a plant shop tells me that succulents rarely live up to this reputation. As with any popular plant, the more people that try to take care of one, the more people that fail. This is exacerbated by the fact that in media—whether home-decor TV shows, magazines, or online—succulents often show up, looking beautiful on coffee tables, kitchen islands, and even bathroom sinks, all areas unlikely to even come close to providing enough light for your average succulent. This is why we never shy away when a customer conveys their inability to grow plants by way of succulent demise. Chances are, they had an inaccurate understanding of what these plants actually need, probably because pop culture gave them some very misguided ideas.

What Is Leaf Pulling?

Leaf pulling is a common way to propagate succulents, but not much else. It's similar to leaf cuttings, except that many succulents don't have petioles—the little stem that connects the leaf to the main stem—which means there's no place to make the traditional cut. Therefore, we pull! This works because succulents store water and energy in their leaves, so all you need to do is firmly grasp a leaf between your thumb and index finger and gently twist right and left until you feel a small "pop," signaling a successful removal. Let your leaf pulling rest in place, either on the soil or directly on the windowsill—a sunny windowsill or other warm location is ideal. Over time, the fleshy part where the leaf was disconnected from the main plant will callous over. Wait a bit longer and the leaf will begin to wrinkle, then grow roots, and wrinkle some more. After a few months' time, your leaf pulling will be shriveled and brown, but there will also be a new, identical succulent now ready for planting! Leaf pulling is most commonly practiced with Echeveria and Graptopetalum succulents, so make sure you research your plant type and its propagation methods before trying this approach.

Bonus Tip

This rings true for all plants but is especially important for succulents: If you've severely underwatered a succulent, the leaves will wilt and wrinkle, and if you've overwatered a succulent, the leaves will also wilt and wrinkle. However, the cures are different. Keep in mind that if your succulent's leaves are wrinkled and the soil is wet, you likely have root rot and will need to intervene. If the leaves are wrinkled and the soil is super dry, then you likely haven't watered it enough, in which case a thorough soaking of the soil should eventually make the leaves plump again.

COMMON NAMES:
Air plant

Tillandsia
(Tillandsia)

Soil: Doesn't apply here!

Light: Bright (1,000 fc or more) light

Watering: Use a spray bottle to mist the leaves every three to five days.

Fertilizer: Tillandsia-specific fertilizer

Toxicity: Nontoxic to pets and people

Average Indoor Size: 3 to 12 inches wide

Native To: Tropical and subtropical regions of the Americas, including the Caribbean

Propagation: Division

Pot Selection: It's clear by now that air plants don't live in pots. However, keep in mind that whatever you choose to display your plant on will be getting wet from frequent misting. Choose something that doesn't mold or rot easily to avoid complications.

Tillandsia, or air plants, are plants that grow entirely out of soil! They don't technically grow in the air as their name suggests. Instead, they use their roots to grab on to other structures such as trees or rocks and use them as anchors. Air plants are part of the bromeliad family, which we covered earlier in this section (page 194), but keep in mind that while all air plants are bromeliads, not all bromeliads are air plants. The beautiful thing about air plants is the diversity in how they can be displayed because they don't need soil! Unleash yourself from potted plants and get those creative juices flowing. What would your air plant setup look like? I'm partial to keeping them in terrariums or tucked into the nooks and crannies of driftwood or rocks. By the way, air plants are especially perfect for those who love routines because this is one of the few plants I recommend watering on a schedule. I usually warn folks not to water their plants on a schedule, and to instead water when the soil has reached a certain level of dryness. But when there's no soil to measure, there's no risk of overwatering it, so setting a schedule in this case is advantageous to help avoid underwatering, which is very easy when a plant doesn't have wet soil to grab water from.

Common Problems

Crown rot can happen when water is allowed to rest in the leaf crevices. Always prop your air plant upside down immediately following a watering and allow the crevices to dry before putting it back on display. This usually takes an hour or so and will help prevent the dreaded crown rot!

Fun Fact

Because tillandsia are bromeliads, each adult plant will flower just once in its lifetime. After flowering, they leave behind "pups," a.k.a. baby plants, to be separated into individual plants that can be gifted to friends or used to expand your own collection.

COMMON NAMES:
VFT, flytrap

Venus Flytrap
(Dionaea muscipula)

Soil: One part peat moss to one part perlite

Light: Full sun is best, but bright (1,000 fc or more) light will work

Watering: Venus flytraps grow in bogs, so when we bring them home, it's best to re-create those conditions by keeping them in a pot of soil resting in a tray of water.

Fertilizer: No fertilizer needed!

Toxicity: Nontoxic to pets and people

Average Indoor Size: 1 to 5 inches tall

Native To: North and South Carolina

Propagation: Division

Pot Selection: Glazed ceramic or plastic is best, but any pot with drainage holes will work.

Watch out—these plants bite! The Venus flytrap is hands down the most well-known carnivorous plant and performs a unique "biting" motion that allows it to trap small insects that fly into its "mouth," which is made of modified leaves. These plants have fallen victim to a common price of popularity—being labeled "finicky"—but that reputation has more to do with folks assuming flytraps need to be fed bugs or ground beef and less with them being difficult to grow. Despite what many people think, light is still the most important aspect of growing a Venus flytrap and should be your first consideration (for this reason, they are often kept outdoors), followed by watering. In fact, in many cases you won't need to feed your Venus flytrap at all. I often have customers ask, "What if I don't have any bugs in my house?" Trust me, everyone has bugs in their house, but Venus flytraps still live primarily off photosynthesis. Their habit of "eating" bugs is simply an adaptation to their native boggy growing conditions, which aren't rich in nutrients. This quirky plant decided that if the soil wasn't going to provide nutrients, it would figure out how to eat bugs, which seems like a totally reasonable alternative.

Common Problems

Keeping a flytrap in too low of light is the most pervasive problem, because unlike most plants we keep indoors, these grow in full sun in their native habitat, and that is a far cry from the brightness of the light found anywhere we would keep them inside. They'll live their best life outside, in full sun. I only recommend you avoid direct afternoon sun, which is the harshest of the day, and frost, which can damage your flytrap. Don't take this to mean the plant must live outside, just that the lighting outside will absolutely be enough, while keeping them indoors is more of a guessing game if you aren't using a light meter.

Bonus Tip

Venus flytraps are sensitive to the minerals and dissolved solids found in tap water and may develop brown edges on the tips of their leaves if tap water is used over a prolonged period of time. To avoid this, consider using rainwater, distilled water, or reverse osmosis (RO) water. The latter two can be found at your local grocery store—just make sure the only ingredients are water, as many companies like to add minerals for taste, which is exactly what your Venus flytrap doesn't want! This is a good rule of thumb to follow with all carnivorous plants in your charge.

Fun Fact

Everyone who learns the famous Venus flytrap trick wants to see it in action, so they'll trigger the traps to close using the nearest probe, to the great delight of any observers. It's wonderful to share your excitement for the plant, but keep in mind that triggering their traps needlessly is a significant waste of energy and causes more harm than good. Nothing bad will immediately happen, but if the traps are going to spend their energy closing, they should at least have the opportunity to gain some energy back by way of an insect or other food source. Speaking of food sources, it's best if they're living. Still, it's unlikely you'll need to feed your flytrap, even if keeping it indoors. Because they live primarily off sunlight, you can think of feeding your plant insects more like giving it fertilizer than providing an energy source.

Bonus Tip

This is based absolutely on personal experience—not science—but I have owned hundreds of varieties of houseplants over the years, and my ZZ plants always respond to fertilizer tremendously well. They may not be the fastest-growing plant in the world, but the difference in their growth between when they get fertilizer and when they do not is one of the most obvious I've ever witnessed. Find a way to be consistent in that department—it will serve you well!

COMMON NAMES:
Emerald palm, Zanzibar gem

ZZ Plant
(Zamioculcas zamiifolia)

Soil: Cactus potting soil

Light: Bright (1,000 fc or more), medium (250-999 fc), or low (100-250 fc) light

Watering: When the soil is 100 percent dry

Fertilizer: General-purpose or organic fertilizer

Toxicity: Toxic to pets and people

Average Indoor Size: 1 to 3 feet tall

Native To: East Africa

Propagation: Division, leaf cutting, and stem cutting

Pot Selection: A clay pot is best, but any pot with drainage holes will work.

"ZZ is EASY!" That's what I always say when it comes to these forgiving beauties. ZZ plants never cause trouble for me, and they adapt to just about any conditions I put them in, which is why they are one of my top-five beginner-friendly plants (page 49). If you're familiar with the term "utility player," that's the ZZ. Due to the ease of their care and their attractive symmetrical growth pattern, ZZ plants are frequently used as decor in office buildings, businesses, and the like. And that is not a coincidence. Many of these professional buildings hire experts to provide, style, and maintain their indoor plants—just as someone would hire a gardener for their outside plants. If the pros are using a plant for this kind of client, you can bet your bottom dollar that they're hardy and can withstand the abuse that often comes with living in a high-traffic, public setting.

Common Problems

You may notice horizontal black markings on your ZZ plant stems. They may resemble striping or can also be a bit splotchy in appearance, but they should be smooth and flush with the stem rather than protruding from the stem like a bump or blemish. As long as these markings aren't mushy, it's perfectly fine and simply a natural attribute of the plant. But if the black markings are mushy, then the plant has likely sustained some physical damage, such as stem breakage or being exposed to cold temperatures. Mushy stems can also come from root rot, in which case intervention is recommended—see chapter 7 (page 141).

ACKNOWLEDGMENTS

Thank you to my wife, whom I love and to whom I owe the words of this book! Your commitment, exemplification of work and play, support, and encouragement made this book a reality. We did it, baby! Kids, thank you for being positive and interested throughout this process—I hope watching me achieve a dream inspires you to do the same one day.

To my staff at Famous In Oregon, your commitment to this passion of ours made it possible to dream about turning these pages into a book, and I'm grateful to each of you for allowing us that capacity.

Before Lauren, I only knew *that* this book was possible. You showed me *how* this book was possible and made it something I'm proud of. Thank you!

Ashleigh, I'll always be grateful for the experience and comfort your immense skill and energy brought to this book. Your photographs make me *feel*. Thank you.

Nancy, the quality and detail of your illustrations are the cherry on top of this book. Thank you for being an artist and for giving this project exactly what it needed.

A huge thank-you to my agent, Leigh—your thoughtful guidance and advice gave my mind the capacity to focus on my magic.

Thank you to my editor, Justin—your belief in me changed my self-perception and gave me the opportunity to realize a dream. And to each person at Simon Element who has put their efforts into this book, I want you to know that I'm grateful for each minute and thought you devoted.

Finally, to our late cat. You spent so much time with me while I was writing, it feels like this book is a bit of yours. Rest easy, Tina!

INDEX

A

aglaonema, 49, 186
airflow, soil dryness and, 95
air layering, 181–82
air plants (tillandsia), 48, 245
air purification benefits, 21
alocasia (elephant ear), 202–3
aloe vera plant, 53–54, 58, 59, 80–81, 97, 112
ambient humidity, 95
ancient Egypt, 21
anthurium, 144, 170, 188–89
aphids, 154, 159
aroid soil, 178, 186, 222, 231
Aspidistra elatior (cast-iron plant), 198
Asplenium nidus (bird's-nest fern), 193
autumn season, 63, 78, 94, 106, 130–31

B

banana-peel tea, fertilizing with, 139
baran plant. *See* cast-iron plant
bar-room plant. *See* cast-iron plant
bead plant (string of pearls), 239
big-box stores, care of plants at, 38–40
bird-of-paradise, 190
bird's-nest fern, 193
black dots, thrips and, 160
black markings, on ZZ plant stems, 249
blinds, 69
bottom, watering plants from the, 85–86
bright light, 55–57, 58–59, 64, 73. *See also* specific plants
bromeliad(s), 194–95, 245
brown dots, leaf spot disease and, 168
browning leaves, 95, 97, 104, 164–68. *See also* crispy edges
Bti (*Bacillus thuringiensis* subspecies *israelensis*), 162

C

cache pots, 85, 111, 112, 149
cacti
    about, 196–97
    fertilizer and, 124, 128
    holiday cacti, 210
    type of pot for, 111
cactus potting soil, 113, 114, 194, 197, 210, 228, 235, 239, 240, 249
calathea (prayer plant), 91, 93, 225–26
calcined clay, 113, 114

calcium, 122, 138
care of plants. *See* houseplant care
carnivorous plants, 123, 177. *See also* Venus flytrap
cast-iron plant, 77, 198
cathedral plant. *See* prayer plant (calathea)
ceramic pots, 110–11
chemical elements, for healthy plants, 122. *See also* fertilizer(s)
chlorine, 167
chopstick
    breaking up compacted soil with, 149
    repotting a plant using, 108, 109, 119
    testing watering needs using, 91, 92
Christmas cactus, 210
coconut chips, 113
coco peat, 106, 113, 115
coffee grounds, fertilizing with, 138
compacted soil, 148, 149
compost(ing), 113, 132–33
corms and corm propagation, 225, 226
cover pot system, 111, 112
COVID-19 pandemic, 14, 44
crane flower. *See* bird-of-paradise
crispy edges. *See also* browning leaves
    low humidity and, 164
    overfertilizing and, 131
    on prayer plant, 226
    underwatering and, 148, 149
    water quality and, 166
    during the winter, 164
crown rot
    of snake plant, 235
    tillandsia (air plant) and, 245
crystallinum. *See* anthurium
curtains, 68–69
cuttings. *See* stem cuttings

D

daily light integral, 57, 63
desert cacti, 48, 111, 128
devil's ivy. *See* golden pothos
Dionaea muscipula. *See* Venus flytrap
direct light, 66–67, 70–71
distilled water, 87–88, 97, 131, 166, 167, 247
division, propagating plants by, 181, 186, 189, 190, 193, 194, 197, 198, 202, 209, 210, 217, 218, 221, 225, 228, 232, 235, 236, 239, 245, 246, 249

DIY fertilizers, 137–39
dormancy, of houseplants, 129
Dracaena marginata (Dragon tree), 201
dracaenas, 150
Dracaena trifasciata (snake plant). *See* snake plants
dragon tree, 201
drainage holes, pot, 111, 112
drop pots, 111

E

Easter/spring cactus, 210
east-facing windows, 64, 65
Echeveria, 242
edema, 146–48, 205
eggshells, fertilizing with, 138
Egypt, ancient, 21
elephant ear, 202–3
emerald palm. *See* ZZ plant
emergency repot, 106
epiphytes, 194
Epipremnum aureum. *See* golden pothos
etiolation, 76–77, 170–71
extrafloral nectaries, 157, 222

F

fall season. *See* autumn season
Famous In Oregon (store), 14
"fast draining" materials, 113
ferns, 48
    bird's-nest fern, 193
    maidenhair fern, 111, 114–15
    root rot and, 144
    staghorn fern (platycerium), 236
    testing watering needs of, 91
    type of pot for, 111
    underwatering and, 148
    water storage in, 93
fertilizer(s), 46, 121–32
    for aglaonema, 186
    author's recommendations on, 139–40
    during autumn and winter months, 130–31
    bottom watering and, 87
    DIY, 137–38
    frequency of using, 128–31
    giving all your plants the same, 125
    importance of, 122–23
    NPK in, 124–25

organic, 127–28
root-bound plants and, 51
shopping for, 128
signs of not using enough, 132
signs of using too much, 131–32
storing, 128
synthetic, 125–27
ZZ plant and, 248
Ficus elastica (rubber tree), 231
Ficus lyrata. See fiddle-leaf fig plant
fiddle-leaf fig plant
   about, 205
   air layering and, 181
   light requirements, 56–57
   put in the wrong location, 38
"finger test" for watering, 88
fittonia, 206
flamingo flower. *See* anthurium
flowering plants
   anthurium, 188–89
   bird-of-paradise, 190
   Bromeliad, 194–95
   fertilizing, 129
   holiday cacti, 210–11
   light and lack of flowers on, 77
   peace lily, 218
   phalaenopsis orchid, 221
flushing, 87–88, 126, 131–32, 167
foliar feeding, 135–36
foot-candles, 58, 59–60, 62, 64
forgetii. *See* anthurium
full sun plants, 54, 57, 246. *See also* bright light
funeral plant (peace lily). *See* peace lilies
fungi, 134–35
fungus gnats, 133, 142–43, 152–53, 161–62

G

general-purpose potting soil, 178, 186, 189, 190, 193, 194, 198, 201, 202, 205, 206, 209, 210, 213, 217, 218, 222, 225, 228, 231, 232, 235, 236, 249
golden pothos, 49, 77, 124, 209
Graptopetalum, 242
greenhouse soil, 105–6
"green thumb" myth, 24, 25–26
grow lights, 72–76, 77, 78
Guess-the Foot-Candles game, 64

H

Hale, Mandy, 22
heartleaf philodendron, 49, 222
holiday cacti, 210–11
honeydew, 156–57, 159, 160

hope peperomia (radiator plant), 228
horticultural charcoal, 113
horticultural sand, 113
horticultural therapy, 21
houseplant care. *See also* fertilizer(s); light(ing); water(ing)
   becoming consumed with "must dos" for, 43–44
   being at the right stage in your life for, 26–28
   at big-box stores versus boutique plant stores, 38–40
   confronting challenges with, 31–33
   deriving joy from, 30–31
   "green thumb" myth and, 25–26
   intuition versus logic for, 24–25
   learning about, 42
   for small plants, 41
   social media influence and, 37–38
"houseplant hysteria," 42–46
houseplants. *See also specific plants*
   author selling, 121, 142
   average indoor size of, 179
   benefits of, 21
   draw to, 23
   as for everyone, 11
   having opinions about where they live, 33–34
   "magic" in watching growth of, 11–12
   matching to the environment, 47–48
   natural habitat of, 9–10
   personifying, 33
   plant owners taking responsibility for killing, 40–41
   plant parent's attitude toward failure of, 10–11
   plants returning to the earth after dying, 34
   propagating, 179–82
   purchasing. *See* purchasing houseplants
   relaxing and enjoying your, 100–101
   setting goals for, 28–30
   shifting your mindset about, 22, 24
   signs of a healthy, 49–50
houseplant soil, 44, 51, 112, 113. *See also* general-purpose potting soil
Howea forsteriana (kentia palm), 180, 214
hoya rope, 213
humidifier, 46, 48, 96, 164
humidity
   browning and crispy leaves, 164
   considering, when purchasing a houseplant, 48

   edema and, 147–48
   on light meters, 62
   soil dryness and, 95
hydrogen peroxide, 108, 144, 145
hydrophobic plant, 149–50
hydrophobic soil, 149
hydroponics, 98
hyphae, 134

I

inflorescence, 186, 194
intuition, 24–25
iron plant. *See* cast-iron plant
isopropyl alcohol, 108, 116, 169, 180

K

kentia palm, 180, 214
knitting needles
   checking soil moisture with, 90
   repotting a plant using, 108, 109

L

lava rock, 117
leaf cuttings, 180, 228, 235, 249
leaf pulling, 240, 242
leaf scorch, 64, 129, 131, 169–70
leaf spot disease, 82, 168
leaves, plant. *See also* wilting
   bronze color, 160
   browning on tips/edges of. *See* browning leaves
   curling, 232
   dusting rubber tree, 231
   dying, on elephant ear, 203
   getting water on, 86
   getting wet when top watering, 86
   yellowing. *See* yellow(ing) leaves
LECA (lightweight expanded clay aggregate), 43, 117
"leggy" plants, 76–77, 170–71
lifestyle
   choosing plants suited for your, 27–28
   considering, when purchasing a houseplant, 48
light(ing), 53–78
   for aglaonema, 186
   for anthurium, 189
   bird-of-paradise, 190
   bird's-nest fern, 193
   bright light, 55–57, 58–59, 64, 73
   bromeliad, 194
   cacti, 197
   cast-iron plant, 198
   common misconceptions about, 70–72

light(ing) (*cont.*)
    considering, when purchasing a houseplant, 47-48
    daily light integral for plants, 57-58
    direction of your, 65
    direct light, 66-67, 70-71
    dragon tree, 201
    edema and, 147
    elephant ear, 202
    etiolation and, 170-71
    fiddle-leaf fig, 205
    foot-candle unit of measurement for, 59-60
    grow lights, 72-76
    holiday cacti, 210, 211
    leaf scorch and, 169
    "leggy" plants (etiolation) and, 76-77
    a less science-y approach to measuring, 65-66
    low light, 55, 57, 63, 64, 73, 77
    measured with light meters, 59-62
    medium light, 55, 63, 64
    plant owner expectations and, 46
    plants adapting to household, 71
    plants getting "enough," 66-68
    role of, 55
    rotating location of plants for appropriate, 77-78
    slow plant growth and lack of, 76
    soil dryness and, 94
    subjective interpretation of brightness of, 58-59
    three signs a plant needs more, 76-77
    throughout the seasons, 63-64
    types of light diets, 55-58
    for Venus flytrap, 246
    where you live and, 64-65
    window exposure and, 71-72
    window treatments and, 68-69
light meters, 60-62, 64, 88, 91, 189
liquid-soluble fertilizer, 126, 127
long-fiber sphagnum moss, 113, 182, 236
low light, 55, 57, 63, 64, 73, 77. *See also* specific plants

M

macronutrients, 122
Madagascar tree (dragon tree), 201
magnesium, 122
maidenhair fern, 111, 114-15
mealybugs, 152, 154, 157-58
medium light, 55, 63, 64. *See also* specific plants
Mexican breadfruit. *See* monstera plant

mindfulness, plants increasing, 21
minerals and mineral buildup
    bromeliad and, 194
    on pots, 87-88, 131, 194
    from tap water, 131
    TDS (total dissolved solids) of water and, 167
    Venus flytrap and, 247
    watering method and, 87-88
moisture-draining potting materials, 113
moisture meter, 88
moisture-retaining potting materials, 112-13, 115
monstera plant
    about, 217
    air layering, 181
    confronting problems with growing, 31-33
    root rot and, 144
    soil for, 114
    testing watering needs of, 93
moon orchid (phalaenopsis orchid), 221
mother-in-law's tongue (snake plant). *See* snake plants
moth orchid (phalaenopsis orchid), 221
municipal water, 95, 101. *See also* tap water
musical chairs for plants, 77-78
mycorrhizae, 108, 134-35

N

NASA study, 21
neem-oil, 153-54, 155-56
nest fern. *See* bird's-nest fern
nitrogen (N), 122, 124, 134, 135, 138
northern hemisphere/north-facing windows, 64, 65, 130, 164
NPK (nitrogen, phosphorus, potassium), 124-25, 127, 129, 138, 139

O

orchid bark, 113, 114, 118, 178, 221
orchids
    phalaenopsis orchids, 129, 221
    setting a goal for growing, 29-30
organic fertilizer, 127-28, 137-38
overfertilizing, 126, 131-32
overwatering, 54, 81, 146, 162, 228. *See also* root rot
oxygen, 98

P

palm court (kentia palm), 180, 214
PAR (photosynthetically active radiation), 74

peace lilies, 144, 178, 218
peacock plant. *See* prayer plant (calathea)
peat moss, 106, 113, 114, 115, 246
peperomia (radiator plant), 228-29
Peperomia obtusifolio (radiator plant), 228
perlite, 43, 113, 114, 115, 117, 246
pesticides, 161
pests
    aphids, 159
    checking for, when purchasing plants, 49-50
    common harmful houseplant, 154
    fungus gnats, 161-62
    mealybugs, 157-58
    overview, 151-54
    predator bugs for, 156
    scale insects, 160-61
    spider mites, 156-57
    standard three-step protocol for, 154-56
    thrips, 159-60
    whiteflies, 158-59
pest spray, treating with, 155-56
petioles, 242
phalaenopsis orchids, 129, 221
philodendron, 222-23
phone apps, for measuring light, 60
phosphorus (P), 122, 124, 134, 138
photosynthesis, 55
"plant blind," 20
plant owners
    believing they cannot grow plants, 67
    emotions related to death of a plant, 34
    "green thumb" myth and, 25-26
    modeling a healthy relationship with plants for future generations, 35
    personifying plants, 33
    plant's failure and, 10-11
    releasing expectations about plants, 10, 22, 24
    shifting mindset about houseplants, 22, 24
    unrealistic expectations of plants, 46-47
plant parent. *See* plant owners
plants. *See also* houseplants
    early ancestors' use of, 23
    feeding, 132-36. *See also* fertilizer(s)
    photosynthesis and, 55
    role of light for, 55
    slow growth of, 76
plant toxicity, 179
plastic pots/containers, 110, 111

platycerium (staghorn fern), 236
pon, 43–44, 117
ponytail palms, 149
porcelain flower (hoya rope), 213
potassium (K), 122, 124, 138
pot-bound plants, 50
pothos. *See* golden pothos
pots
    choosing size of, 110
    increasing size of, when repotting a plant, 107
    mineral buildup on terra-cotta, 87
    selecting a type of when repotting a plant, 110–12
    slapping, when repotting, 118–19
    soil dryness and material of, 95
    soil dryness and size of, 94
    types of materials, 110–11
pot size, soil dryness and, 94
potting mix, store-bought, 152
PPF (photosynthetic photon flux), 74–75
PPFD (photosynthetic photon flux density), 75
prayer plant (calathea), 225–26
propagation
    about, 179–80
    of golden pothos, 209
    methods, 180–82
    of prayer plant (calathea), 226
    of succulents, 240, 242
pruners, 107
pumice, 112, 117
pup division(s), 181, 195, 221, 245
purchasing houseplants
    beginner-friendly plants when, 49
    factors to consider when, 47–48
    finding a healthy plant when, 48–50
    quality of plants at different locations and, 38–40
    root-bound, 50–52

Q
quarantining a plant, 152, 153, 155, 159

R
radiator plant (peperomia), 228–29
rainwater, watering plants with, 95, 97, 166, 226, 247
rattlesnake plant (prayer plant). *See* prayer plant (calathea)
repotting plants, 102–20
    as a default remedy for plant problems, 171–72
    pot selection and, 110–12
    problem with monstera plant, 31–32
    reasons for, 104–6
    to slow down the growth of a plant, 104
    soil selection and, 112–15
    step-by-step instructions for, 106–20
    supplies for, 107–8
    when plant health is declining, 103–4
    when treating root rot, 145–46
    when you want the plant to grow larger, 104
reverse osmosis (RO) water, 97, 166, 167, 247
rice hulls, 113
root ball, cutting away, 116
root-bound plants, 50–52
root pruning, 116
root rot, 40, 41, 54, 78, 106. *See also* overwatering
    about, 132
    author's approach to, 145–46
    bottom watering and, 87
    browning leaves and, 164
    compost and, 133
    hydrogen peroxide and, 108
    mycorrhizae and, 108
    repotting plants and, 106, 110, 111
    scindapsus and, 232
    succulents and, 242
    symptoms of, 142–43
    treatment, 144–45
    water storage and, 94
    yellowing leaves and, 163
    ZZ plant and, 249
roots
    checking for healthy, 50
    checking when repotting plants, 116
    drying out, 144
    kept in water, 98
    of monstera plant, 114
    pruning, 145
    repotting plants and growth of, 104–5
    sitting in water, 100
    watering and, 82
rosary plant (string of pearls), 239
rubber tree (*Ficus elastica*), 231

S
satin pothos (scindapsus), 232
scale insects, 154, 160–61
scindapsus, 232–33
Senecio rowleyanus (string of pearls), 239
sheer curtains, 68–69
shingling, 233
shutters, 69
silver pothos (scindapsus), 232
silver vine (scindapsus), 232
slip pots, 111
slow-release fertilizers, 126
small houseplants, 41
snake experiment, 35
snake plants, 27, 48, 49, 57, 77–78, 235
social media
    inaccurate information about plants on, 37–38
    keeping houseplants portrayed in, 81
    negative impact on houseplant care, 46
    plant-related videos on TikTok, 14–15
    selling plants through, 12, 14
soil
    air gaps providing oxygen to, 98
    checking the moisture level in, 89–93
    compact, 148
    compacted, 148, 149
    drying at different rates, 94–95
    edema and, 147
    mixing your own, 177–78
    moisture-draining ingredients for, 113
    moisture-retaining ingredients for, 112–13
    oxygen for, 98
    pests in store-bought, 152–53
    removing around the roots, when repotting a plant, 109–10
    for repotting plants, 105–6
    saturating with water, 83–84
    that is overfertilized, 131
    white haze on, 87
soil amendments, 117
soil moisture, measuring, 89–91
solar screens, 69
southern hemisphere/south-facing windows, 64–65
spathe flower (peace lily). *See* peace lilies
spider mites, 31, 152, 154, 156, 214, 225
split-leaf philodendron. *See* monstera plant
spring season, 63, 64, 104, 106
staghorn fern (platycerium), 236
stem cuttings, 180–81, 186, 189, 201, 205, 206, 209, 210, 213, 217, 222, 228, 231, 232, 239, 240, 249
stippling, 157
stomata, 82
storage, fertilizer, 128
store, houseplant, 14
strelitzia (bird-of-paradise), 190
stress reduction, plants helping with, 21
string of pearls (*Senecio rowleyanus*), 239

succulents
  about, 240–41
  fertilizer and, 124
  overwatering (root rot) and, 144–45
  soil for, 115
  testing watering needs of, 91, 92
  water stored in, 93, 115
succulent soil, 177–78
sugar-making process analogy, 53, 82, 83, 122–23, 130
sulfur, 122
summer season, 63, 64, 106
SWEN light hierarchy, 65
Swiss cheese plant. *See* monstera plant
synthetic fertilizers, 125–27, 128
systemic pesticides, 161

T

tap water
  browning leaves and, 166–67, 247
  chlorine and, 167
  Venus flytrap and, 247
  water quality and, 95
  white haze and, 131
Taro plant (elephant ear), 202–3
TDS (total dissolved solids) of water, 167
temperature, soil dryness and, 94
terra-cotta pots, 87, 95, 111, 112
terrariums, plants for
  edema and, 147–48
  fittonia, 206
  tillandsia (air plant), 245
terrestrial bromeliads, 194–95
Thanksgiving cactus, 210
thatch palm (kentia palm), 180, 214
thrips, 154, 159–60
TikTok, 14–15
tillandsia (air plant), 48, 245
top watering, 84–85, 86
toxicity, plant, 179, 218
transpiration, 82, 98, 146, 196
troubleshooting, 142–73
  browning leaves, 164–68
  edema, 146–48
  etiolation, 170–71
  general guide to, 171–73
  leaf scorch, 169–70
  leaf spot disease, 168
  overwatering (root rot), 142–46
  pests, 150–62
  underwatering, 148–50
  yellowing leaves, 163–64

U

underfertilizing, 132
underwatering, 98, 148–50, 242

V

Venus flytrap, 83, 123, 246–47
vermiculite, 113

W

water(ing), 80–101
  aloe plant, 54
  anxiety about, 100
  bird's-nest fern, 193
  bromeliad, 194
  browning leaves and, 166–67
  cacti, 197
  edema and, 147
  elephant ear, 202
  frequency of, 88–89
  goal of saturating the soil when, 83–84
  how plants store, 93–94
  measuring soil moisture for, 89–91
  overwatering, 81, 97–100, 142–46
  phalaenopsis orchid, 221
  plants storing, 112, 113–14
  prayer plant (calathea), 225, 226
  quality of, 95, 97
  radiator plant, 228
  recommendations, 179
  repotted plants, 120
  repotting plants and, 103–4
  role of, 82
  root-bound plants and, 51
  rotating location of plants and, 77–78
  snake plant, 235
  soil selection and, 112–15
  succulents, 242
  TDL (total dissolved solids) of, 167
  techniques, 82–84
  tillandsia (air plant), 245
  from the top versus the bottom, 84–88
  using the cover pot system, 111, 112
  water quality and, 95, 97
water culture, 98, 226
water filters, 167
watermelon peperomia, 228
water quality, 95, 97, 166
water storage, soil selection and, 114–15
wattage, grow light, 73
wax plant (hoya rope), 213
west-facing windows, 64
whiteflies, 154, 158–59
white hazing, on topsoil, 87, 131, 167
white sails (peace lily). *See* peace lilies
wilting
  in elephant ear, 202
  overwatering and, 143
  in prayer plant, 225
  succulents and, 242
  troubleshooting, 91–93
  underwatering and, 148
window exposures, 64–65, 71–72
window treatments, 68–69
winter
  bringing plants inside for the, 153–54
  browning of leaves during, 164
  fertilizing and, 130
  light during, 63, 64
wood, staghorn ferns growing on, 236
wood-burning fireplaces, 48, 164
World Wars I and II, horticultural therapy used in, 21
worm castings, 108, 133–34, 140

Y

yellow(ing) leaves
  finding cause of, 163–64
  mealybugs and, 158
  overwatering and, 143
  repotting and, 104
  scale insects and, 160
  thrips and, 160
  troubleshooting, 163–64
yellow sticky traps, 159, 160, 162

Z

Zanzibar gem. *See* ZZ plant
zeolites, 117
ZZ plant
  about, 248–49
  as beginner-friendly plant, 49
  lifestyle considerations and, 27, 48
  rotating location with another plant, 77–78